RESOLVING INDIA'S MAOIST CHALLENGE

LOOKING BEYOND SECURITY AND DEVELOPMENT

RESOLVING INDIA'S MAOIST CHALLENGE

LOOKING BEYOND SECURITY AND DEVELOPMENT

Col Shashank Ranjan

KNOWLEDGE WORLD
KW Publishers Pvt Ltd
New Delhi

Centre for Land Warfare Studies
Delhi Cantt
New Delhi

The Centre for Land Warfare Studies (CLAWS), New Delhi, is an autonomous think tank dealing with contemporary issues of national security and conceptual aspects of land warfare, including conventional and sub-conventional conflicts and terrorism. CLAWS conducts research that is futuristic in outlook and policy-oriented in approach.

Centre for Land Warfare Studies
RPSO Complex, Parade Road, Delhi Cantt, New Delhi 110010
Tel: +91.11.25691308 **Fax:** +91.11.25692347
Email: landwarfare@gmail.com **Website:** www.claws.in
CLAWS Army No. 33098

ISBN 978-93-86288-26-4
e-book ISBN 978-93-86288-27-1

KNOWLEDGE WORLD

KW Publishers Pvt Ltd
4676/21, First Floor, Ansari Road
Daryaganj, New Delhi 110002
Phone: +91 11 23263498/43528107
Marketing: knowledgeworld@kwpub.com
Editorial: jose@kwpub.com
Website: www.kwpub.com

2011 FIP BMA BEST PUBLISHERS AWARD (ENGLISH)

Printed and bound by Bhavish Graphics.

CONTENTS

Foreword

Lt Gen Vijay Oberoi, PVSM, AVSM, VSM
Former Vice Chief of the Army Staff (VCOAS)
Former Founder Director
Centre for Land Warfare Studies (CLAWS)

Left Wing Extremism (LWE) has emerged as one of the major security challenges in India. It is also known by other names, like Maoist insurgency. It is a manifestation of a number of problems, which have combined over a period of time to make it an intractable problem in more ways than one.

It would be incorrect to perceive LWE only as another aspect of the many state-building processes within the country that have been witnessed since independence. The movement can be better interpreted as an effort towards dismantling the prevailing unequal socio-economic and political structures that have been espoused by some radical left wing groups, who feel that it serves the dual purposes of propagating the Communist/ultra socialist ideology and, at the same time, serves the interests of the exploited Adivasis (Tribals) of the huge tribal belt of central India.

In our country, the geographical spread and growing militarisation of some of the left extremist groups– mainly the Communist Party of India (Maoist) – CPI (M) – has been a cause for concern since independence. The main issue being propagated is the feeling of massive exploitation of the Adivasis, who have been living for ages in the tribal areas of a number of states of India, but are being exploited by outsiders. Most of their habitat is forested and is full of natural resources – not just timber, but also a variety of minerals. Their exploitation is not of recent origin, but dates back to centuries. It was the kings, princes and other rulers who first exploited them, but that exploitation was at a much lower scale because the princely states were ignorant of the natural potential of the entire area, except the wild life and timber.

It was only during the British colonisation period, with the insatiable desire for natural resources that the British needed for feeding their growing industries in Britain and elsewhere, that real exploitation started in the tribal areas. There were many protests, both peaceful and violent, by the indigenous people inhabiting the area, but these were brushed aside, including by force. The British faced the strongest challenge in the form of resistance from the people, when they commenced making inroads in tribal areas. Against severe opposition, they were forced to retreat initially. In the Rampa region of east Godavari district, for example, more than a dozen tribal revolts occurred between 1770 and 1924.

Thereafter, by massive deployment of troops, the British quelled the Adivasi uprisings across the regions. Of these, the Birsa Munda movements of the tribals were the most important in the late18th century struggles against British rule and their local agents.

During the early years of the 20th century, the Communists commenced espousing the cause of the tribals. However, there was a number of splits in the original party, both on account of ideological differences and on how the anger of the tribals could best be exploited. There were also differences between individual leaders of the Communist Party. These led to a number of splits in the original party. Consequently, the challenge of the tribals' waned and waxed.

At one time, the then Prime Minister Manmohan Singh had characterised Maoist insurgency as *"India's greatest internal security threat."* Although there is still some confusion regarding the nature and quantum of the threat that various LWE groups pose to the country, it is abundantly clear that in the years to come, LWE would have the potential of seriously challenging India's integrity as a nation.

The LWE movement is being carried forward by various operationally and organisationally exclusive, but ideologically-linked groups. Though they have different structures; strategies and goals; and areas of influence and operation, there have been some efforts recently to integrate such movements. The relative success that these groups have been able to achieve varies from place to place and group to group.

The entire area where LWE groups are operating is now called the 'Red Corridor', as it has experienced considerable Naxalite-Maoist militant activity and violence. The Naxalite group mainly consists of the armed cadres of the CPI (M). These are also areas that suffer from the greatest illiteracy, poverty and overpopulation, as compared to the rest of the country. They span parts of the states if Andhra Pradesh, Bihar, Chhattisgarh, Jharkand, Madhya Pradesh, Maharashtra, Odisha, Telengana, Uttar Pradesh and West Bengal.

A key characteristic of this region are the non-diversified economies that are solely primary sector-based. Agriculture, sometimes supplemented with mining or forestry, is the mainstay of the economy, which is often unable to support the rapid increases in population. The region has significant natural resources, including mineral, forestry and potential hydroelectric generation capacity. Odisha, for example, has 60 percent of India's bauxite reserves; 25 percent of its coal; 28 percent of its iron ore; 92 percent of its nickel; and 28 percent its of manganese. reserves.

The area encompassed by the Red Corridor tends to have stratified societies, with caste and feudal divisions. Much of the area has large indigenous tribal populations (Adivasis), including the Santhal and Gond tribes. Bihar and Jharkhand have both caste and tribal divisions and violence associated with friction between these social groups. The Telangana region, similarly, has deep caste divides with a strict social hierarchical arrangement. Both Chhattisgarh and Odisha have significant impoverished tribal populations.

The Red Corridor is almost contiguous from India's border with Nepal to the northern fringes of Tamil Nadu. There is, however, a significant gap consisting of coastal and some central areas in Odisha state, where Naxalite activity is low and indices of literacy and economic diversification are higher. However, the non-coastal districts of Odisha, which fall in the *'Red Corridor'*, have significantly lower indicators, and literacy throughout the region is well below the national average.

Maoists are known to have their presence in 21 States. Estimation of Maoist cadre strength varies from 10,000 – 15,000 to as much as 25,000. Similarly, the geographical spread of Maoist activities is estimated over 190 districts. Maoist violence has been reported in 90 districts out of 627 districts in the country. These figures may be somewhat exaggerated, but they do highlight the extent of the problem.

This grave challenge needs to be met by a combination of welfare oriented policies; vast and early improvement of infrastructure; close coordination of all affected states; firm but humane police action; sustained improvements in both education and health; and above all fairness to the tribal population, including retention by them of parts of their traditional lands and maximum compensation for lands acquired by the government for mining, industrial or other purposes.

The above is exactly what the author of this fine book has recommended. The author, Col Shashank Ranjan has carried out deep research, going back nearly two centuries and has covered all facets of the problem, from the human to strong implementation of the laws by the many governments involved, including the Central Government. He has illustrated his book with citations from many authors backed by a plethora of notes. These indicate that a vast variety of sources has been consulted, thus, making it as authentic as possible.

For ease of understanding as well as chronological narration, the author has divided his book into four comprehensive sections. The narrative is crisp; to the point; and without any verbosity.

I am of the view that this book is a seminal work on the important subject of Left Wing Extremism. It will appeal to both the serious academician, as well as to the lay reader who wants to know about the various nuances of LWE or Maoist insurgency.

I congratulate Col Shashank Ranjan on producing a highly readable and comprehensive book on a subject that is both current and where this major national problem needs to be settled quickly, ensuring that no party to the problem remains dissatisfied. The book is a valuable addition to the existing literature on the subject.

I also hope that Col Shashank Ranjan continues his pursuit of knowledge in a similar vein. I convey my best wishes to this young and intrepid Army officer for success in all his future endeavours.

August 17, 2016 Lt Gen **Vijay Oberoi**

Introduction

1. GENESIS AND EVOLUTION OF LEFT RADICALISM IN INDIA

India's Naxalite movement was sparked on May 25, 1967, in a village called Prasadujot in the Naxalbari bloc in West Bengal. A group of peasants led by two left-wing activists Kanu Sanyal (1929-2010) and Jangal Santhal (?-1981) who were supported by a Communist ideologue, Charu Mazumdar (1918-72), tried to forcibly seize land from some landlords who controlled the land, to which the peasants had the legal entitlement. This resulted in a violent confrontation between the agitating peasants and police, with the police supporting the landlords. This seemingly isolated revolt in a far-flung village eventually gave birth to a movement that attracted the attention of the world, and some Anglicised journalist/commentator gave it the name 'Naxalite'. The terms,'Naxalism' or 'Maoism' or 'Left Wing Extremism (LWE)' have interchangeably been used in this work and while doing so, the intent has not been to convey different connotations.

The fallout for Indian politics after nearly 50 years from that seemingly isolated revolt may be judged by an astute remark made in 2006 by Dr. Manmohan Singh while he was the Prime Minister. He said that the Naxalite movement was the single biggest internal security threat to India. This chapter attempts at giving an overview of LWE in India, to include the ideological and organisational evolution that the movement has undergone over last 50 years or so.

The movement's first phase came to an end in 1972 but it resurfaced in a different form, quite powerfully in the last decade. It had a close relationship with the overall political culture of India and the world during post World War II in general and during the late 1960s, in particular.

Genesis: An Ideological Background

The roots of the Naxalite movement lie in India's Communist movement. India's Communist movement was born shortly after the Bolshevik Revolution. After the degeneration of the Bolshevik Revolution and the rise of Stalinism in Russia, a very small section of the Indian left was sympathetic to the opposition led by Trotsky. The bulk of India's Communist Party went with Stalin not because of any specific admiration for Stalin or his policies but out of loyalty to the Soviet Union, considered then as the mother country of Communism. The Soviet Union's role in defeating Nazi Germany did endear Stalin not only to the Communist Party members and sympathisers but also to the broader sections of Indian society that viewed Hitler and the Nazi ideology unfavourably. This broader societal attitude towards Stalin's role in the defeat of Nazi Germany reinforced India's Communist movement's admiration for Stalin and allegiance to the Soviet Union under him.

The Communist Party of India (CPI) did participate in the anti-colonial struggle against British rule in India; however, it also directed its criticism at the 'bourgeois' leadership of the Indian National Congress (INC), led by Gandhi and Nehru. There were several other currents in the Indian people's struggle against British colonial rule which were influenced in varying degrees by the ideals of Communism. The most well-known was the group led by Indian revolutionary Bhagat Singh who played a leading role in organising terrorist attacks on the symbols of the colonial establishment in India.

If the Gandhi-led movement adopted a path of non-violent resistance and struggle against the colonial rule, Bhagat Singh epitomised the goal of its violent overthrow. This competition between peaceful and armed struggle paths to India's independence was to leave a permanent legacy in India's Communist movement too. Soon after India became independent in 1947, India's

Communist Party was ridden with factional conflict between two tendencies; one advocating participation in India's parliamentary democratic institutions set up under the framework of the Constitution of the new republic, and the other advocating a path of armed insurrection.

This conflict became accentuated by the success of the Chinese revolution under Mao's leadership. The faction deriving inspiration from the Chinese success and advocating the path of armed insurrection gained leadership temporarily and launched an armed uprising in the Telangana region. This uprising was crushed by the Indian government. The armed insurrection attempt having failed, the constitutionalist tendency gained the upper hand in the leadership of the CPI. As a result, the CPI started participating actively in central parliamentary and state assembly elections. The CPI became the main opposition party in the Parliament and remained so for almost the entire decade of the 1950s. The most glorious success of the CPI was to win a majority in the elections to the state assembly of Kerala in 1957 and the formation of the democratically elected Communist government there for the first time in India and the second time in the world after the tiny republic of San Marino which had the world's first democratically elected Communist government from 1945 to 1957.[1]

The success of the democratic constitutional path did not end the ideological contestation between the two tendencies in the CPI. The Sino-Soviet conflict sharpened this ideological contestation between the peaceful path supported by the Soviet Union and the armed struggle path supported by China. The Sino-Indian border conflict in 1962 brought the two contradicting lines into sharp and polarised opposite positions. The CPI formally supported the Indian national government of Nehru and accused China of launching an armed attack on India. This decision of the CPI was opposed by a substantial, though not majority, section of the top party leadership which included some leading lights of India's Communist movement. This section expressed solidarity with China and criticised the Nehru government for military aggression against the socialist China. This pro-China section characterised and denounced the political position of the pro-Indian nationalist leadership of the CPI as 'revisionist'.

The word 'revisionist' was meant to suggest that the pro-Indian nationalism leadership of the CPI had abandoned the revolutionary path and had become collaborationist with the Indian state. The opposing tendencies in the party became so acutely polarised that the pro-China section eventually left the CPI in 1964 and formed a new Communist Party that was named Communist Party of India (Marxist) (CPI (M)), written more generally as CPM. The CPM, while emerging out of the constitutionalist and 'revisionist' CPI had projected itself as a militant Communist Party, keeping open the option of the armed struggle path. However, later, the CPM jumped at the opportunity of using constitutionally guaranteed power through elections with the intention partly of "wrecking the Constitution from within" as a leading CPM leader and strategist EMS Namboodiripad had once put it. However, this strategy of using the parliamentary path disillusioned the more militant cadre who had left the CPI and had joined the CPM in the hope of launching militant class struggles and, if necessary, through armed actions against the class enemies.

This conflict between the parliamentary path and the armed struggle path manifested on the fateful day in May 1967 when the peasants led by Kanu Sanyal and Jangal Santhal forcibly occupied the land of the landlords and forced them to flee. The West Bengal United Front government in which the CPM was a major partner sent the state police to repress the rebellious peasants. The police firing led to the death of 11 peasants who included eight women and two children[2].The Naxalite movement was born that day and the killed peasants, became the first martyrs of the movement.

The CPM was further split—one section in support of the 'revolutionary peasants' and the dominant section supporting the party against the 'left-wing adventurism' of the Naxalbari activists. Beijing Radio and the *People's Daily* from China hailed the Naxalbari rebellion by calling it "a spring thunder in India".

The formation of the Communist Party of India (Marxist-Leninist) (CPI (ML)) was formally declared at a rally in Calcutta on April 22, 1969 (Lenin's birthday). The CPI (ML) declared open allegiance to China (and Mao) and announced that its aim was the overthrow of the Indian state through an armed uprising of the Indian peasantry that would liberate the rural areas from the class enemies. The liberated zones were to be used to create a Red Army that would eventually surround the cities and overtake them, leading to the overthrow of the Indian state. The CPI (ML), proclaiming itself as the revolutionary party, would lead the revolutionary march of the Red Army from the rural to the urban areas. It denounced the CPM as "neo-revisionist" implying that the CPM merely spoke about the revolution but in practice was following a reformist parliamentary path which it had once denounced while splitting away from the "revisionist" CPI.

The significance of the 1967 revolt may be seen in the context of the political culture prevalent at that time—locally, nationally and globally. At the local or state level in West Bengal, it represented a tension in the growing militancy and strength of the Communist movement in the state and the restraint being imposed on that militancy by the pressure of governance in the state where the Communist Parties were part of the governance. At a national level, it represented the declining importance of the Congress Party in some regions of India and the emergence of tensions in Centre-state relations as a result of that; and equally important was the unresolved agrarian question of land ownership and control. Overall, it represented that the dreams and hopes that might have been raised by India becoming independent of direct colonial control, could no longer be sustained after about two decades of India's independence. At a global level, it represented the contestation between the Chinese Communist Party (CCP) and the Communist Party of the Soviet Union (CPSU), for control of the global Communist movement.

This contestation took various forms but the form it was taking most prominently in India was the split between the parliamentary path and the armed struggle path. What was most interesting was that this split was not on a generational basis as might have been expected, namely, the younger members opting for armed struggle and the older ones opting for the parliamentary path. For example, the most prominent Naxalite leader in Punjab, Baba Bujha Singh who supported the armed path, was in his 80s and was not the only one in the mature age group[3]. Concerning the challenging theoretical issues for Marxist theory raised by the revolt, the most demanding was the importance of the peasantry in the struggle for overthrowing capitalism (or feudalism or semi-feudalism) in the less developed capitalist economies in the Third World.

Immediate Implications of 1967 Revolt for the Left and Bourgeois Politics in India

There were three armed Communist rebellions in India, all revolving around control over land ownership and produce from the land, before the rise of the Naxalite movement. One was in the Telangana region which coincided with India's independence from British colonial rule in 1947[4]; the second one was in the Tebhaga region in West Bengal in 1948[5]; and the third one was a Lal Communist Party (Red Communist Party)-led revolt in the erstwhile Patiala and East Punjab States Union (PEPSU) region of the present state of Punjab in 1948[6]. The Naxalite movement in 1967 represented a reconnection with that armed struggle heritage.

Apart from the similarity of the Naxalite movement with the 1940s/1950s struggles in terms of primacy to armed struggle, there was one critical difference too. All the three 1940s/1950s struggles were localised in nature and not linked with movements in other parts of India, although these localised struggles were influenced by external ideological directions from the Soviet Union. The Naxalite movement, in contrast, started as a spontaneous local conflict, but became very quickly an all-India phenomenon spreading to Andhra Pradesh, Kerala, Bihar, UP, Punjab, Himachal Pradesh and, to some extent, Delhi[7].

The movement that erupted from Naxalbari came to be compared with other Maoist and Communist guerrilla organisations such as the Huks of Philippines, the Tupamaros of Uruguay, and the Shining Path of Peru. Some even dreamt of the liberated zones in Indian turning into little Vietnams. These dreams were to be shattered. The government came down with a heavy hand and the leaders of the movement were arrested or defeated in engagements with the police. The initial phase of the movement appeared to peter out. The flame was doused, but the embers remained—and there was a resurgence of the movement in the states of Andhra Pradesh and Bihar in the 1980s.

The history of the Naxal movement post-Charu Mazumdar, is characterised by a number of splits, brought about by personalised and narrow perceptions of the revolutionaries about the revolutionary line and attempts at course-correction by some of the major groups. Even Kanu Sanyal, one of the founders of the movement, could not escape this. He gave up the path of "dedicated armed struggle" by 1977 and accepted parliamentary practice as a form of revolutionary activity.

It was during 1974 that an influential group of the CPI (ML), led by Jauhar (Subrata Dutt), Nagbhushan Pattnaik and Vinod Mishra, launched a major initiative, which they termed 'course-correction'. This group renamed itself the CPI (M-L) Liberation in 1974, and in 1976, during the Emergency, adopted a new line that called for the continuation of armed guerrilla struggles along with efforts to form a broad anti-Congress democratic front, consisting of even non-Communist Parties. The group also suggested that pure military armed struggle should be limited and there should be greater emphasis on mass peasant struggles, in an attempt to provide an Indianised version of Marxism-Leninism- Maoism.

However, during the next three years, the movement suffered further splits with leaders such as K Seetharamaiah (Andhra Pradesh) and N Prasad (Bihar) dissociating themselves from the activities of the party. This led to Prasad forming the CPI (M-L) (Unity Organisation) and Seetharamaiah starting the People's

War Group (PWG) in 1980. While Seetharamaiah's line sought to restrict the "annihilation of class enemies", the PWG's emphasis was on building mass organisations, not developing a broad democratic front.

Since then, the principal division within the Naxalite movement has been between the two lines of thought and action, as advanced by the CPI (ML) Liberation and the PWG. While Liberation branded PWG a group of "left adventurists", the PWG castigated the Liberation group as one of the "revisionists" imitating the CPI (M). Also, on the other hand, the growth of the Maoist Communist Centre (MCC) as a major armed group in the same areas, created the scope for multifarious organisational conflicts among the Naxal groups. Liberation took a theoretical stand of correcting the past mistake of "completely rejecting parliamentary politics". On the other hand, PWG and MCC completely rejected the parliamentary democratic system of governance and vowed to wage "people's war for people's government".

The following years witnessed certain distinct phenomena in the history of the Naxal movement. First, the intra-organisational conflict and rivalry among the different groups touched several high points, resulting in the loss of a considerable number of cadres of rival groups. Secondly, despite the large-scale inner conflicts, there were always ongoing efforts at various levels to strive for unity. Thirdly, 1990 onwards, the affected state registered a considerable increase in the number of violent incidents and, at the same time, a considerable change in the policy approach of the government was also witnessed. While the Naxal movement has mostly been characterised by fragmented groups and innumerable splits; successive governments at the national and state levels were never able to follow a uniform approach to deal with the problem of Naxalism, thus, leading to a marked impact in its growth.

The following are the main issues on which there appear to be considerable differences among the Naxal groups and which are the primary causes of conflict between them.

- The analysis of the first phase (1967-71) of the Naxalite movement and the line of annihilation that was followed.
- The position that armed struggle is the principal form of struggle and the armed guerrilla squad, the primary unit of struggle.
- Since the principal form of struggle is armed struggle, the entire activity of the agrarian struggle should be underground.
- Whether the contradiction between feudalism and the Indian masses is the principal contradiction in Indian society or whether India has emerged as a capitalist state and, hence, the contradiction between capitalism and the general public is the principal contradiction. The Naxalites have never been able to read the prevalent Indian scenario accurately—that is one of their falsified foundational premises.
- Whether it would be prudent to form a united front with various forces and movements like the Dalits, farmers, ethnic and regional, and ecological movements, etc[8].

A brief description of major Naxal outfits is given below with an aim to understand the overall context of the movement, given its current tenor.

Communist Party of India (Marxist-Leninist) Liberation

Historically, the origin of CPI (ML) Liberation dates back to 1974. However, the post-emergency phase of 1977, when most leaders of the Communist movement were released from jail, was the time when the activities of Liberation first came to notice. The Party Central Committee (PCC), in a move to unite the splinter groups which owed their origin to the CPI (ML), called a meeting during January 30-February 02, 1981. However, the meet did not deliver the expected results. “From this point onwards whereas the PCC group goes on to become irrelevant and splits up into various factions, the M-L movement begins to polarize between the Marxist-Leninist line of CPI (ML) (Liberation) and the anarchist line of the CPI (ML) (People’s War)”.[9]

In 1982, the Indian People's Front (IPF) was launched in New Delhi at a national conference and, in due course, became the party's open political platform, actively intervening in national politics. The same year, the Third Party Congress finalised the issue of participation in elections. This shift in the outlook of the CPI (ML) Liberation proved to be vital in designing the subsequent course of activity of the Naxal movement. The Liberation group considered itself the true inheritor of the CPI (ML) legacy, although its political line changed dramatically from that of the original CPI (ML)[10].

The CPI (ML) Liberation recorded its first electoral victory under the banner of the IPF in 1989 and Arrah (a Lok Sabha constituency in central Bihar) sent the first Naxalite member to Parliament[11]. In 1994, the IPF was disbanded. The Election Commission recognised the party in 1995, and since then the CPI (ML) has been contesting successive elections at both national and state levels.

The CPI (ML) Liberation, though functioning overground within the parliamentary democratic set-up, has not completely disbanded the path of armed rebellion. "The Party does not rule out the possibility that under a set of exceptional national and international circumstances, the balance of social and political forces may even permit a relatively peaceful transfer of central power to revolutionary forces. But in a country where democratic institutions are based on essentially fragile and narrow foundations and where even small victories and partial reforms can only be achieved and maintained on the strength of mass militancy, the party of the proletariat must prepare itself for winning the ultimate decisive victory in an armed revolution. A people's democratic front and a people's army, therefore, remain the two most fundamental weapons of revolution in the arsenal of the Party"[12]. This again points to the dilemmas within the ultra left movement, which is very often reflected in the unpredictable character of the Naxal movement.

People's War Group (PWG)

The PWG is the most important among all the splinter groups representing the Naxal movement because the dominant line within the Maoist politics today is the PWG line of thought. If today, Naxalism is considered as the greatest internal security problem and Naxals claim to be running a parallel government in different parts of the country, the credit mostly goes to the PWG. "The CPI (ML) (People's War) was formed on Lenin's birth anniversary on April 22, 1980"[13]. Kondapalli Seetharamaiah, one of the most influential Naxalite leaders from Andhra Pradesh and a member of the erstwhile Central Organising Committee of the CPI (ML), was the founding father of the PWG; who later, was, ironically, expelled from the group.

As per the party document, "The programme of our Party has declared that India is a vast 'semi-colonial and semi- feudal country', with about 80 per cent of our population residing in our villages. It is ruled by the big-bourgeois, big landlord classes, subservient to imperialism. The contradiction between the alliance of imperialism, feudalism and comprador-bureaucrat-capitalism, on the one hand, and the broad masses of the people, on the other, is the principal contradiction in our country. Only a successful People's Democratic Revolution i.e. New Democratic Revolution (NDR) and the establishment of People's Democratic Dictatorship under the leadership of the working class can lead to the liberation of our people from all exploitation and the dictatorship of the reactionary ruling classes and pave the way for building Socialism and Communism in our country, the ultimate aim of our Party. People's War based on armed agrarian revolution is the only path for achieving people's democracy i.e. new democracy, in our country"[14].

From the above quote, it is clear that there were organisational, strategic and tactical conflicts going on within the CPI (ML), which paved the way for the split and creation of a more radical party. Broadly speaking, the party programmes of the CPI (ML) Liberation were mostly focussed on the cause of peasants, while the group led by K. Seetharamaih wanted the party to be a platform for peasants, workers, tribals and other weaker sections of society. It was the prime agenda of Liberation to build up a political front focussing on peasant struggles, whereas the PWG was more interested in the formation of an all encompassing, mass organisation, instead of any democratic front; suiting the prevalent circumstances in the regions where the group was active[15].

For a considerable period after its birth, the PWG's activities were chiefly limited to Andhra Pradesh, while the CPI (ML) Liberation continued to hold its turf in Bihar. It was during this period that another organisation came into existence on January 01, 1982. It was named the Communist Party of India (ML) Party Unity, which came into existence due to a merger between the CPI (ML) Unity Organisations and Central Organising Committee CPI (ML). Hereafter, LWE in India witnessed some of the worst-ever conflicts which again forced many organisations to take a position and adopt new tactics. Clashes between the CPI (ML) Party Unity and CPI (ML) Liberation, were very frequent, especially in Bihar[16].

When these conflicts were taking a toll on the cadres on both sides, another development was simultaneously taking place. In August 1998, the Party Unity (PU) merged with the CPI (ML) People's War Group and the group came to be known as People's War (PW). "The merger of the two parties is the culmination of the unity process which began in March '93 and continued for over five years during which differences on several political, ideological and organizational questions were resolved through threadbare discussion"[17].

With this merger, the PWG became a force to reckon with in Bihar and in other areas where PU had a presence. Further developments suggest that with the merger, the element of armed rebellion of the Naxal movement became stronger, while, on the other hand, with its parliamentary practices, Liberation was losing its turf to the PWG. Not only in Bihar, but elsewhere also, Liberation was systematically shrinking on the map of Naxalite politics. By advocating electoral methods and not being able to make an impressive mark, the Liberation's movement became weak and the PWG's armed operations started gaining momentum[18].So while the Liberation, with its changed *modus operandi*, was being reduced to a small political party, the PWG in the same period, managed to register its presence outside Andhra Pradesh and gradually gained strongholds in different areas of Bihar, Odisha, Madhya Pradesh, Jharkhand, Chattisgarh, and Maharashtra.

The formation of the PWG also resulted in tactical changes in several aspects of the Naxal movement in general. "In our agenda for a new democratic revolution, there are two aspects -- the agrarian revolution and fight for nationality".[19] This statement shows the amount of organisational change witnessed by the Naxal movement in all those years. In 1967, it started in the name of 'agrarian revolution', which gradually took the stance of replacing the parliamentary form of government; but the question of nationality was never raised. This reflects the pattern of conflict between the PWG and Liberation. By questioning 'nationality', the PWG wanted to make it clear that it wanted a broad revolutionary pattern and while 'land to tillers' could be a programme, it could not become the sole agenda of the revolution. The CPI (Maoist) has often supported separatism and sub-national agendas of various parties at conflict, in other regions of India[20]. As recently as in July 2016, a CPI (Maoist) press release appealed for support for the Kashmiri separatism, demonstrating their stand on issues related to sub-nationalism and secession[21].

The PWG, on the basis of its assessment of the people's level of preparedness for an armed struggle, discarded 'annihilation of class enemies' as the only form of struggle and stressed instead, on floating mass organisations. It established several front organisations. During the 1980s, the Radical Students' Union and Rayatu Kuli Sangham emerged as organisations with an impressive mass following and most of the PWG's present base and political cadres developed through that practice. However, during the 1990s, the growth of militarisation became the characteristic feature of the PWG. The formation of the People's Guerrilla Army (PGA), special guerrilla squads, Permanent Action Team (PAT) and Special Action Team (SAT) were the distinctive features of PWG activities for quite some time, before it merged with the MCC to form the CPI (Maoist)[22].

Maoist Communist Centre (MCC)

The next important group within the broad spectrum of the Naxal movement is the MCC. It stands apart from a number of organisations, since, conventionally speaking, it was never a part of the CPI (ML), the mother of all Naxal organisations. "The MCC, while supporting the Naxalbari struggle, did not join the CPI (ML) because of some tactical differences and on the question of Party formation"[23]. The MCC was formed on October 20, 1969, around the same time that the CPI (ML) was formed, although during those days it was known as Dakshin Desh. It was in 1975 that the group renamed itself the MCC. In 2003, the MCC merged with the Revolutionary Communist Centre of India-Maoists (RCCI-M) to form the Maoist Communist Centre-India (MCC-I).

Right from its inception, the MCC stood for taking up armed struggle as the main form of resistance and waging a protracted people's war as the central task of the party. This position of the MCC has been repeatedly expressed and emphasised in a great deal of Maoist literature. As per a party document, "This armed revolutionary war is the war of the armed people themselves; it is 'Protracted People's War' as shown by Mao – the very path of the Protracted People's War is the only path of liberation of the people of India, the path of victory of the New Democratic Revolution"[24].

Communist Party of India (Maoist)

The Naxal movement in India entered yet another phase of organisational transformation with the merger of two of the principal armed organisations, viz. PWG and MCC-I, which resulted in the formation of the CPI(Maoist). "The formation of the unified CPI(Maoist) is a new milestone in the history of the revolutionary Communist movement of India. A unified Maoist party based on Marxism-Leninism-Maoism is a long delayed and highly cherished need of the revolutionary minded and oppressed people of the country, including all our ranks, and also all the Maoist forces of South Asia, and internationally. Now, this long-aspired desire and dream has been transformed into a reality".[25] This statement, made by the first Secretary of the CPI (Maoist) Ganapathy, assumes a great deal of importance as it reflects the organisational politics that was going on all these years between these two organisations representing the Naxal movement.

The improvised aim of the CPI (Maoist) as announced on the occasion of its formation was to establish a Compact Revolutionary Zone (CRZ), stretching from Nepal to Bihar to Andhra Pradesh and beyond. While continuing their pursuit of a people's democracy, the ultimate aim of the CPI (Maoist) was to seize power through a protracted armed struggle.

It is important to examine the significance of the merger, particularly when earlier attempts had been unsuccessful. In fact, the merger was largely being seen as a result of the gradual convergence of views of these two groups on areas such as the role of the party, approaches to revolution, and adoption of strategies and tactics. In the formative years, Charu Mazumdar and Kanhai Chatterjee represented two irreconcilably different lines and approaches to 'revolution'. At the time of the formation of the Communist Party of India (Marxist- Leninist) CPI-ML in 1969, the Dakshin Desh (the earlier form of the MCC), remained opposed to the process due to sharp differences with the CPI-ML over issues such as the formation of a Communist Party, existence of a revolutionary mass struggle and preparedness of the people to participate in it[26].

However, this is not to suggest that the formation of the CPI (Maoist) was the final stage of the Naxal movement. As one official Maoist document mentions, "Revolutions never proceed in a straight line. The history of all successful revolutions shows this. The path is zig-zag, there are ups and downs, there is victory and defeat repeated a number of times.....before final victory. Of course, there is no final victory until the stage of Communism is reached".

The abovementioned analysis makes the forceful plea that since the Naxal movement is essentially a political problem, it needs to be examined from the perspective of organisational politics. The history of the Naxal movement, right from its first phase of 1967, demonstrates that even if there has been a continuous evolution in terms of its understanding of the Indian situation, the focus of the movement, its character, and the fighting capabilities and financial resources of these groups; they have remained more or less consistent as far as their core ideology is concerned. Barring the Liberation, they all reject the parliamentary system of governance and want to bring about a fundamental change in the nature of the Indian state. For this, they have adopted the strategy of protracted armed struggle, which entails building bases in rural and remote areas and transforming them first into guerrilla zones and then liberated zones, besides area-wise seizures and encirclement of cities and, finally, the seizure of political power. The history of the movement so far, has been the history of conflicts and splits. However, one cannot deny that its history is also that of 'mergers'.

The movement has acquired a pan-India presence and has since spread to 20 states of the Indian Union. It continues to spread in ever-widening circles not so much because its ideology is appreciated or even understood by the large majority of its followers but more because of the inefficiency, corruption, and callousness of the government machinery. There is, unfortunately, no long-term policy to deal with the Maoist threat to the Indian state. Different states under different political dispensations have their own approach to tackle it. As police and public order are state level responsibilities under the Indian Constitution, the federal government feels hamstrung beyond a point. The government's approach is to deal with LWE in a holistic manner, in the areas of security, development, ensuring the rights and entitlements of local communities, improvement in governance and public perception management[27].

The success of this approach depends essentially on the ability of the government to implement the development projects at the ground level and improve governance in geographically distant areas, particularly those inhabited by the tribal communities. And since insurgencies are about people, the challenge in its current *avataar* is better contextualised through the perspectives of the 'tribal narrative', vis-à-vis exploring a way ahead towards conflict resolution.

Notes

1. Alan James Mayne, *From Politics Past to Politics Future: An Integrated Analysis of Current and Emergent Paradigms* (Greenwood Publishing Group, 1999).
2. On the piece of land where the conflict led to the deaths, the CPI (ML) has put up busts of Lenin, Stalin, Mao and Charu Majumder, and a memorial column erected there has the names of the people who died during the police firing. The names are 1. Dhaneswari Devi (F), 2. Simaswari Mullick (F), 3. Nayaneswari Mullick (F), 4. Surubala Burman (F), 5. Sonamati Singh (F), 6. Fulmati Devi (F), 7. Samsari Saibani (F), 8. Gaudrau Saibani (M), 9. Kharsingh Mullick (M) and "two children". See https://en.wikipedia.org/wiki/Naxalbari
3. Pritam Singh, *Economy, Culture and Human Rights: Turbulence in Punjab, India and Beyond* (New Delhi: Three Essays Collective, 2010).
4. Shantha Sinha, *Maoists in Andhra Pradesh* (Delhi: Gian Publishing House, 1989).
5. Rabindra Nath Mandal, *The Tebhaga Movement In Kakdwip* (Kolkata: Ratna Prakashan, 2001).
6. Bhagwan Josh, *Communist Movement in Punjab 1926–1947* (Delhi: Anupama Publications, 1979) and Gurharpal Singh, *Communism in Punjab: A Study of .he Movement up to 1967* (Delhi: Ajanta, 1994).
7. Ibid.
8. Louis Prakash, *People's Power: The Naxalite Movement in Central Bihar* (New Delhi: Wordsmiths, 2002), p. 277.
9. "Thirty Years of Naxalbari", an undated publication of the CPI (ML) Liberation.
10. Bela Bhatia, "Naxalite Movement in Central Bihar", *Economic and Political Weekly*, April 09, 2005.
11. "History of Naxalism", Hindustantimes.com
12. A party document of CPI (ML) Liberation titled "The General Programme".
13. "30 Years of Naxalbari", undated Maoist literature (Vanguard Publication), p. 30. Vanguard was the organ of the PWG.

14. "Path of People's War in India – Our Tasks!", a comprehensive PWG party document highlighting its aims, objectives and strategies. The document was adopted by the All-India Party Congress, 1992.
15. Rajat Kujur, "Naxal Movement in India : A Profile", IPCS Research Paper, September 2008.
16. Ibid.
17. People's War literature titled "Joint Declaration by Communist Party of India (ML) People's War and CPI (ML) (Party Unity)", August 1998.
18. Ibid.
19. Interview of Muppalla Lakshmana Rao alias Ganapathy, the then head of the Communist Party of India-Marxist-Leninist People's War, http://www.rediff.com/news/1998/oct/07gana.htm
20. http://archive.tehelka.com/story_main47.asp?filename=Ne061110 incoldblood.asp
21. "Indians Must Support Kashmiris:Maoists", *The Indian Express*, July 22, 2016, ENS
22. http://www.satp.org/satporgtp/countries/india/terror istoutfits/peoples_guerrilla_arms_left_wing_extre mists.htm
23. n. 13, p.36.
24. *Red Star*, Special Issue, p. 20. *Red Star* is the English language organ of the MCC, as quoted by Aloke Banerjee in a pamphlet titled "Inside MCC Country", dated June 2003. Also quoted in "MCC India Three Decades Leading Battalions of the Poor", http://www.awtw.org/back_issues/mcc_india.htm.
25. Ganapathy, in an interview given on the occasion of the formation of the CPI (Maoist), *People's March*, Vol. 5, No.11-12, November- December 2004.
26. Kujur, n. 15.
27. http://mha.nic.in/naxal_new

Section One
The Tribal Narrative

2. INHERITENCE OF DISCONTENT AND ALIENATION: THE HISTORY AND ANTHROPOLOGY

The tribal people are at a critical point in their history...'. They are 'losing command over resources at a very fast rate and are also facing social disorganisation, which is unprecedented in history'. And yet the 'tales of woes from tribal areas are hardly heard outside, and when they come, they are not taken seriously.' What was worse, 'the state itself sometimes tends to adopt a partisan role and become a privy even for actions not quite legal simply because the matter concerns voiceless small communities. (28th Report of National Commission on SC and ST)

— BD Sharma, former Chairman,
National Commission for SC and ST

LWE that began in 1967 in a corner of the country (Naxalbari, West Bengal), and which effectively ceased to be a force to reckon with by the mid-1970s, has gathered momentum since the late 1990s, and continues to fester. At present, 106 districts in 10 states have been identified by the Ministry of Home Affairs (MHA) as LWE affected,[1] with 35 districts identified as most affected. A state-wise breakdown is as under:

Table 2.1

State	Number Of Districts	Worst Affected (taken up for focussed development)
Andhra Pradesh	08	01
Telangana	08	01
Bihar	15	05
Chhattisgarh	09	07
Jharkhand	18	11
Odisha	15	05
Maharashtra	03	02
Madhya Pradesh	01	01
Uttar Pradesh	03	01
West Bengal	03	01

The government and its agencies, on the one hand, and the Maoists, on the other, are locked in a bitter, long-drawn out, violent, military engagement, with the former determined to crush the insurgency, and the latter's goal being to capture state power by armed insurrection.

Central to arriving at an understanding of the challenge of LWE–affected districts is the following set of facts. Although the problem is confined to only 9 states, the fact is that these states constitute two-thirds of what are called the major states (which number 15).Also, 90 percent of the affected districts are accounted for by five states – Andhra Pradesh, Bihar, Chhattisgarh, Jharkhand and Odisha. And a fact of enormous importance is that these states have a high concentration of Scheduled Castes (SCs) and Scheduled Tribes (STs) (referred to as tribals or Adivasis; interchangeably hereafter), much higher than found in any other state. It is this section of the population with a very low Human Development Index (HDI), which constitutes the backbone of LWE in the country and is led in the movement by a minority non-tribal leadership.

The tribals who constitute 8 to 10 percent of India's population, usually live in highly forested, relatively hilly, rugged terrain. They have traditionally held rights over forest produce, which they have used to sustain themselves. However, this often brought them into conflict with government officials of the Forest Department (FD). The Maoists found favour with the tribals because the former usually supported the latter in the struggles of tribals v/s the FD and, thus, the government.

In the past two decades or so, an increase in investments, especially to mine these tracts, has brought about major upheavals. By customary law, the land and forests were seen as belonging to the tribals. They had *usufructuary* rights over the resources on the land occupied. Mining by private and public enterprises in these areas became another source of conflict with the tribals. Herein lay the roots of a conflict that has continued to simmer across a large swath of territory of India, which is the theme of this section.

The intent being to open our minds to the fact that consequences have causes and these causes need to be addressed in a holistic manner by the government. As various aspects related to 'the tribal narrative' are dealt with, an opening for conflict resolution is hoped for. There is ambivalence amongst the tribal population in the LWE affected states towards the Maoists, which suggests that these rural poor are hungry for peace as also for justice, and no blind-faith for the Maoists prevails.

Scholars have shown that there are references to forest dwellers in ancient and medieval literature, to their volatile nature, and the mode of production of some of them as consisting of hunting and gathering are also noted. The state, by and large, left them with considerable autonomy in the management of their affairs and control of their resources. In the later periods, several processes appear to have been at work, affecting the organisation of tribal communities. To begin with, they were small peasants on the fringe of society, sharing features with the mainstream. What distinguished them was the aspect that they were in no manner, surplus producing peasants, with their affairs not depending on the markets or on the law and order institutions of the larger society. Tribal society had a degree of self-sufficiency and, therefore, had a simpler structure vis-à-vis class and society of the mainstream.[2] One may add that these communities did not have a notion of private property, and had a distinct culture.

Verier Elwin[3] has been invoked here, to delve into the 'psyche' of tribals as it has evolved over the past few centuries; so as to connect to the current manifestations.

The Tribal Identity and History of Alienation: Extracts from the Writings of Verrier Elwin[4,5◊]

Gonds, a great tribe, over three million in number, are distributed all over central India, with a history of prosperity. There was very little knowledge of how they lived until the 14th century, when they were found established as Rajas in different parts of central India, which at that time was known as Gondwana. Their government seemed to have been tolerant and kindly, the country prospered, forts were well built, palaces were filled with wealth. The kings built royal tombs, lakes and palaces and surrounded their cities with great walls. Herds and flocks increased and even peasants were known to pay tributes in elephants and gold mohurs. But the Gonds had no organisation, no ability for wars, and faced with the invasions of Maratha chieftains in the 18th century, their kingdoms collapsed almost without any resistance, and they were driven into the recesses of the forests.

By the beginning of the 19th century, they had split up into a number of wild and war-like groups, making a living by plundering caravans and raiding smaller towns from their mountain strongholds. Under the British rule, they grew pacific, settled on their land and took to the present occupation of farming. But (now) they suffered oppression and exploitation, for soon there came merchants and liquor venders, cajoling, swindling, tricking them in their ignorance and simplicity until bit by bit, their broad acres dwindled and they sank into the poverty in which most of them still live today.

This poverty was not only material, and in tandem, there came a poverty of culture, to an extent. However, for the culture that depends mainly on character, Gonds were a highly cultured people. They had royal blood in their veins, and even the poorest and simplest of them had strength of purpose, a dignity, a redeeming sense of humour, and courage in the face of the disasters of life that anyone may envy. The honest peasant in his field, the devotee of Mother Earth, drawing his strength from the elemental forces of nature—in this sense as truly cultured as the most sophisticated intellectual.

At this time, as experienced and realised by Elwin—the requirement was to work for the health of the community; to see that there was enough food; to help people get and save more money and, finally, to give them sufficient knowledge to enable them to resist their exploiters as also to widen their vision of the world. Above all, the need was to arouse the people from their apathy (the prevailing attitude was that 'God has made us poor: it is no good trying to be anything else').

As time went by, the people did become more alive to the possibility of gathering strength and gradually a completely new spirit came to them. Elvin goes on to say:

> One day, a Gond lady walked into the dreaded police station, on being ordered out by the sub-inspector, she said, "But this is our police station, not yours, it belongs to the people". And another day when a Brahmin revenue official told one of the Gonds that it was useless to send his son to school, the Gond replied, "Naturally you would think so, because you know that he would then get your job".

As far as the aspects related to the forests were concerned, Elwin, during his stay with the Adivasis in the forests, has written extensively, giving us an insight into their forest related issues. The centrality of forests in the lives of the tribals can be gauged by what Elwin writes:

> They love the forests with a passionate devotion, it is to them, 'the forest of joy', 'the forest of sweet desire', it is 'the scene of their early romances of childhood, the arena in which they engage upon their most heroic struggles with nature.

The Baigas regarded themselves as true *Pashupatis*, the lords of all wild animals; the magical protection of forests was their charge; they had derived material sustenance from the forests for hundreds of years. The reservation of vast tracts of forests, inevitable as it was, therefore, a very serious blow to the tribesman. He was forbidden to practise his traditional methods of cultivation, was ordered to remain in one village and not to wander from place to place. When he had cattle, he was kept in a state of continual anxiety for fear they should stray over the boundary and render him liable to what were for him heavy fines. If he was a forest villager, he became liable at any moment to be called to work for the FD. If he lived elsewhere, he was forced to obtain a licence for almost every kind of forest produce. At every turn, the forest laws cut across his life, limiting, frustrating and destroying his self-confidence.

During the years 1933-34, there were 27,000 forest offences registered in the central provinces and Berar[6*]. It is obvious that such a great number of offences would not occur unless the forest regulations ran counter to the fundamental needs and sentiments of the tribesman, who became timid and obsequious, and it was almost impossible to develop in his mind a sense of citizenship, for he no longer felt at home in his own country.

There was a great deal of burden which police and court investigations placed upon the tribals, as well as the physical distress and nervous exhaustion of the long journeys to distant courts, the demoralising contact with the lawyers, their touts, petition writers, and the bewilderment of dealing with laws they did not understand and which often ran counter to their traditions. "On one occasion, in a fairly simple registration case, the applicant and four witnesses had to travel an aggregate of 3,700 miles before their business was over". Also, there were cases of intimidation by the more sophisticated villagers, some of whom impersonated police or revenue officials and took money from the simpler ones. *(It has been this class of sophisticated villagers that has evolved into the present day 'rural elites', as termed by Alpa Shah[7], signifying an internal class structure within the tribal society).*

The tradition and pride of the Baigas brought them into conflict with the government in two ways. The first was that since they were born from the womb of Mother Earth, they believed that it was very wrong for them to lacerate her breasts with ploughs i.e. when they were forced into settled farming by the British. The second was that since they were the true *Pashupatis*, they considered that they should have the freedom of the forests for their hunting. Nothing shows more clearly the evils of an administration ignorant of tribal mythology and indifferent to its customs than the way the government dealt with the Baigas on these two points. From 1867 to the end of the century, the unfortunate Baigas were pursued by zealous FD officials, determined to make them stop their axe and hoe cultivation and take to the plough.

Elwin, in support of protecting their ways of livelihood vis-à-vis harm to forests, writes:

> Shifting cultivation is a bad thing; unfortunately, it is often the only possible thing. The Baigas used to cut down a track of forest, set fire to the wood when dry, and sow their seeds in the ashes. After repeating this for three years, they would move to another patch. Obviously, even where a tribe had a religious passion for this type of cultivation, it could not be permitted on a large scale and forever. But where only a few tribesmen practised it – and the Baigas were a very small tribe – and where a regular rotation of at least twenty years was observed, the harm it did to the forests was greatly exaggerated.
>
> At the same time, much of their hunting was stopped and some of them were even forced to make heaps of their precious arrows and burn them. Having been forced to plough, many were reduced to penury, for they hated the taboo-ed implement, and all suffered psychological disturbance deep in their souls. They have today sunk into the position of impoverished and inferior cultivators. They have lost much of what used to make life so rich and enjoyable.

British economic policies, favouring individual titles to property and creating a market for land, dispossessed thousands of tribal families and placed many others in a position of bondage to moneylenders. Forest and game laws reduced the access of aboriginals to the fruits of nature, and, in some instances, for example, where shifting cultivation was banned, deprived them of their livelihoods altogether. The suppression of the home distillery, forcing the tribal to buy liquor only from licensed government outlets brought him into contact with a most 'degraded type of alien', the liquor contractor. The Indian Penal Code and the Indian Forest Act formed two pillars of a massive, alien system of jurisprudence which ran counter to the endless harassment at the hands of lawyers, touts, etc.[8]

A decade after independence, the Home Ministry constituted a committee headed by Elwin to enquire into the functioning of government schemes in the tribal areas. It reported:

> The officials in charge of these schemes 'were lacking in any intimate knowledge of their people [and] had very little idea of general policies for tribal development'. Worse, there was 'a tendency for officials to regard themselves as superior, as heaven-born missionaries of a higher culture. They boss the people about; their chaprasis abuse them; in order to 'get things done,' they do not hesitate to threaten and bully.

After studying twenty blocks spread across the country, the committee concluded:

> Of the many tribal problems the greatest of all is poverty. Much of the poverty and degradation that existed was the fault of 'us', the 'civilised' people. We have driven [the tribals] into the hills because we wanted their land and now we blame them for cultivating it in the only way we left to them. We have robbed them of their arts by sending them the cheap and tawdry products of a commercial economy. We have even taken away their food

by stopping their hunting. We look down on them and rob them of their self-confidence, and take away their freedom by laws which they do not understand.[9]

Evolution of Forestry in India : Background to Rising Discontent

Few tribal groups practise hunting and food gathering as their sole occupation. A majority of them, nearly 51 percent, are cultivators, followed by 28 percent,who are agricultural labourers. The rest are engaged in household industry, construction work, plantation, mining and quarrying, and in other services.[10] Apropos, their dependence on the forests, for a variety of reasons, was substantial.

Agriculture, both shifting and settled, was closely interlinked with the forests. The forests had been a major source of food, timber for house construction and agricultural implements, fuel wood, medicines, and other necessities of everyday life: 50 to 80 percent of the food requirements of the Adivasis was provided by the forests.[11] Sale of Non-Timber Forest Produce (NTFP) was an important source of income. For the tribals, their Gods and spirits reside in the forests, so do trees and animals, which were objects of devotion. In short, the forest was the *leitmotif* of their material and spiritual existence.

Although the governments that preceded the British had appropriated certain parts of the forest for imperial purposes, regulated cutting of certain trees and plants, and taxed certain products of the forest, by and large, the forest communities enjoyed free access to the forests. From the scanty evidence available, it appears that the forest communities enjoyed a degree of freedom in the use and management of the forests they inhabited and they developed their own mechanism, cultural and religious, to regulate the forests. One still finds among the tribals, norms and rules of forest management, although in the face of rampant exploitation and destruction of forests all over, these norms have inevitably broken down.

It is difficult to reconstruct the picture of the economy of the 'forest dwellers' before the British intervention. The crucial watershed in the history of Indian forestry is undoubtedly the building of the railway network. This was created to meet the need for rapid troop communication, felt after the first war of independence (1857) and for enabling the characteristic pattern of the colonial trade; i.e. import of finished goods and export of raw materials into and from the colonies. Lord Dalhousie, in 1853, while visualising a vast market for British manufactures in the most distant parts of India, saw that railway construction represented immense potential for surplus British capital that was seeking outlets abroad.[12]Dominion enabled Britain to build, at Indian cost, a system of road and rail transport which linked the colonial ports to their hinterlands and tilted the terms of trade in favour of its own nationals who dominated India's foreign trade.[13]

The early years of railway expansion saw an unprecedented assault on the accessible forests and no supervision was exercised over the felling operations, while destroying the forests. The continued depredation finally woke the colonial authorities to the fact that India's forests were not inexhaustible. Railway expansion continued unabated and the methods by which private enterprises were working the forests, forced the state to step in 'to safeguard their long-term imperial interests'. The Governor General, in 1862, called for the establishment of a department that could ensure the sustained availability of the enormous requirements.

The FD was started because the government became aware that the magnificent forests of India and Burma were being worked by private enterprises in a wreckless and wasteful manner, and were likely to get exhausted if supervision was not exercised. The FD was formed in 1864, however, the task of checking 'deforestation' and 'consolidation of the forest state' could not be accomplished without the assertion of state monopoly rights over the forests. It was in this dual sense that the railways proved to be the watershed with respect to forest administration in India. Having founded the FD, a need arose to enact a legislation for its effective functioning i.e. to curtail the previously exercised unlimited rights of users. Thus, commenced the progressive curtailment of these rights, and was an especially difficult task since it ran contrary to the traditional practices of the village and particularly the tribal communities.

The first attempt at asserting state monopoly right was through the Indian Forest Act of 1865, which was replaced by a much more comprehensive piece of legislation, 13 years later. The provisions of the 1878 Act ensured that the state could demarcate 'valuable' tracts of forests, needed especially for railway purposes, and retain enough flexibility over the remaining extent of forest land to revise its policy from time to time. Monopoly right was established by a legal sleight of hand, which sought to establish that the customary use of forests by the villagers was based not on a 'right' but on a 'privilege' and this 'privilege' was exercised only by the local rulers. Since the British were now the rulers, the right of absolute ownership was held to be vested in them.

Laws relating to the management of forests and forest produce were subsequently consolidated in the Indian Forest Act of 1927, paving the way for the creation of a large area of 'reserved' forests in India under the control of the state, supervised and managed by the FD. The aforesaid resulted in the restriction of the customary rights of the forest communities, endangering their very survival. These communities suffered great hardships at the hands of forest officials who enforced the restrictions with great severity, so that even a minor breach of the regulations was treated as a crime.[14]

The scientific management of forests introduced by the British also resulted in the enhanced commercial value of the forests, and opened up an important source of revenue for the government. Consequently, the FD showed a consistent rise in surplus. The ever expanding demands from the urban centres, military cantonments, railways, and the rising commercial value of teak, and other so-called Minor Forest Produce (MFP), all added to the economic value of the forests.[15] Due to the severity of the FD, the dwellers (tribals) were treated as enemies of the forests and continue to be treated in this manner. There was no place in this model of forestry for the involvement of local forest communities in matters pertaining to the management and use of forests. Scientific arrogance, economic compulsion and sheer callousness towards the basic needs of the poor have largely guided the working ethos of the FD. Even today, the representative of the government or Sarkar for a tribal is the FD guard, who has policed everyday life, for, at least, the last century and a half.[16]

There were two important processes through which land and forests under tribal control were brought under state control and management. Firstly, under the system of administration introduced during the colonial rule and which continued after independence, village ownership of land was not recognised, resulting in non-recording of Adivasi land during surveys. Secondly, shifting agriculture was not recognised as a legitimate agricultural practice, except in northeast India. The post colonial government continued with the colonial policy, and as a result, the lakhs of shifting cultivators had no legitimate rights over the forests that had been their own for centuries.[17]The cultural shock of switching over from a shifting to a settled version of agriculture and the dissatisfaction bred by it was reflected in Elwin's writings, as brought out earlier.

The traditional rights of the tribals were neither recognised nor recorded. And those who continued to use forest land were deemed 'encroachers'. Also, in spite of the state control, depletion and destruction of forests as a result of the combined activities of the FD and private interests has gone on unchecked. This progressive diminution of 'rights', and the consequent loss of control over their natural resources, evoked a sharp reaction from the forest communities.

From the early days of forest administration, there have been revolts in different tribal areas centred on the question of forests. These revolts, which attempted to restore the 'golden past' where the tribal roamed freely in his forest habitat, were swiftly crushed by the colonial state. Nevertheless, they recurred throughout the period in almost all tribal areas, where "forests have always been the fortress of social movements against successive Governments".[18]

The history of conflict and the Adivasi struggle can be seen essentially as emanating from alternate conceptions of property rights and obligations. There did not exist a developed notion of private property in these tribal communities, where the relationship to the overlord was expressed in terms of mutual obligations that had to be fulfilled. Colonial rule, on the other hand, was based on a notion of private property that ran contrary to the experience of these communities. Moreover, the state dealt with its subjects, individually, in an impersonal fashion via the medium of an abstract rule of law that was, in theory, neutral. As a consequence, the individual was now brought directly under the subjugation of the colonial state, without the benefit of a mutual aid system of the community acting as a cushion, as hithertofore. The tribals were exposed to the vagaries of the colonial market economy that continually eroded their lifestyles – simultaneously, the assertion of state primacy over natural resources deprived them of an important subsidiary means of subsistence.

There has prevailed a marked degree of continuity between the colonial and post colonial forest policy, characterised by an explicit assertion of state monopoly right at the expense of the forest communities. This exclusion is legitimised in the name of the 'national interest', so as to ensure that the "country as a whole is not deprived of a national asset by the mere accident of a village situated close to a forest". However,during both the time-zones cited above, the dominant interests behind the formation and execution of state policy have differed. While before 1947, the forests were strategic raw materials crucial for imperial interests such as railway expansion and the World Wars; in the post-independence period, the commercial and industrial interests have dictated the policy. In both cases, however, the successful implementation of the policy has been achieved only at the expense of the forest communities and their life-support systems. Changes in Acts and legislations during the post-independence era have been more in the nature of modifications and additions, rather than significant departures from established colonial practices.

As per views held by a former administrator who worked for the interests of Adivasis, independent India has been worse for the the Adivasi community.[19]

The communities, thus, deprived have responded through different forms of protests – ranging from relatively spontaneous outbursts and agitations to more organised social movements. The Adivasi revolts predate the advent of the Naxalites by more than a couple of centuries. Displaced from their homes, alienated from their lands and deprived of their resources, the tribal people have often taken to armed revolt in the past.

A Tradition of Rebellion: Preceding the Naxalites

In the Rampa region of east Godavari district more than a dozen tribal revolts occurred between 1770 and 1924. The main causes of these were the general discontent with the local administration, jagirdaars, traders, and exploitation by outsiders. Several revolts between 1879 and 1916 were against the creation of forest reserves and restrictions on tribals' access to the forests.[20]Alluri Sitaramaraju who became a local legend, led the 1922-24 rebellion, against the restrictions on shifting cultivation, and access to forests and the tyranny of petty local officials. In Adilabad district, which has a predominant Gond population, the Bebijhari uprising in 1940 was against exploitation by the non-tribal people and land alienation, and restrictions on shifting cultivation and access to forests.[21]

Elsewhere in India, too, the tribal ferment predates even the freedom movement. As soon as the British took over the eastern part of India, tribal revolts broke out to challenge the foreign rule. In the early years of colonisation, no other community in India offered such heroic resistance to the British rule or faced such tragic consequences, as did the numerous tribal communities of what are now Jharkhand, Chhattisgarh, Odisha and Bengal. In 1772, the Paharia revolt broke out, followed by an uprising led by Tilka Manjhi who was hanged in Bhagalpur in 1785. This was followed by the Tamar and Munda revolts.[22]In the next two decades, revolts took place in Singhbhum, Gumla, Birbhum,

Bankura, Manbhoom and Palamau, followed by the great Kol Risings of 1832 and the Khewar and Bhumij revolts (1832-34). In 1855, the Santhals waged war against the permanent settlement of Lord Cornwallis, and a year later, numerous tribal leaders played key roles in the 1857 war of independence.[23]

The British, through massive deployment of troops, quelled the Adivasi uprisings across the regions. The Birsa Munda movement was the most important of the late18th century struggles against British rule and their local agents. The long struggle led by Birsa Munda was directed at British policies that allowed the zamindars and moneylenders to exploit the Adivasis. In 1914, Jatra Oraon started what is called the Tana movement (which drew the participation of over 25,500 Adivasis). The Tana movement joined the nationwide Satyagraha movement in 1920 and stopped the payment of land taxes to the colonial government. During British rule, several revolts also took place in Odisha that naturally drew participation from the Adivasis. The significant ones included the Paik rebellion of 1817, the Ghumsar uprisings of 1836-56, and the Sambalpur revolt of 1857-64.[24]

In Bastar (then a feudatory state in the Central Provinces) forest reservation began in the early 1900s. Shifting cultivation, hunting, and collection of forest produce was restricted, land taxes were raised. A number of villages were displaced from the reserves. Also, the influx of officials, policemen, foresters, and malguzars that followed, led to a rise in demand for corvee(unpaid labour exacted by a feudal lord). In February 1910, the entire area rebelled, led by their majhis and village headmen. Thereafter, for several decades, till mid 20th century, the administration of the area was kept deliberately light, yet commercial exploitation of the forests continued unabated.[25] The two major projects post independence, the Dandakaranya resettlement project, and the Bailadilla iron ore mines which started exporting to Japan in 1966, provided neither land nor employment to the locals. In the 1960s, under the leadership of the ex Raja, Pravir Chandra Bhanj Deo, people protested, asking for land, access to forests and cheaper rice. Pravir was killed in 1966 and the protests eventually faded out.

The Legacy: 'Loss of Land and Livelihood'

With a view to wean the tribals away from shifting cultivation, which was considered wasteful and destructive and to open up a regular source of revenue, the British government forced sections of the tribals to take up land for cultivation on lower rates of assessment. As brought out, this measure of the British had a deep psychological effect and was a source of resentment amongst the tribals. Switching over to settled agriculture resulted in doom for small farmers who could not get an encouraging yield due to factors like lack of agricultural implements, poor quality of soil, frequent crop failures, and rigid revenue demands; forcing farmers (both tribals and non-tribals) to turn to moneylenders. The moneylender, although not a creation of the British rule, acquired great power over his debtor during this period, since the British judicial system made alienation of land a (dangerously) simple matter. In several parts, the trend of increasing indebtedness and transfer of land from the cultivating to the moneylending classes was to be noticed.[26] Eventually, a powerful class which amassed large amounts of land and wealth through the combined activities of trading, moneylending, etc emerged which reduced the tribals to a position of bonded labourers and tenants.[27] The exploiter known as 'diku' (outsider) became the target of attacks in many tribal revolts during the colonial period.

Thus, from a low subsistence, but a relatively independent existence, the tribals became totally dependent on the network of the landlord–moneylender–trader–shopkeeper (sahukar) for their survival. The exploitation and oppression not only reduced them to penury, but also bruised their self-respect. The necessary pre-condition for the dependence and bondage was the alienation from their means of subsistence, forest and land, which was almost complete by the end of the 19th century. Increase in population only increased the pressure on the natural resources. As brought out, in many parts of the country, tribals, at times joined by non-tribal peasantry, revolted against the local oppressors and administrators, to demand for land, forest rights, lower taxes, lower prices, etc.[28]

Ironically, the decades following independence were the decades of intense development planning in India; as also, these were the times of marginalisation of the tribal communities from mainstream development. The economic agenda of nation-building centred on industrialisation and urbanisation. What accompanied this process was the construction of large industrial complexes, dams, infrastructure, opening of mines and forests for the market and overexploitation of natural resources to satisfy the urban and industrial demands from mineral and resource rich tribal land – with nearly 80 percent of the minerals, 70 percent of the forests and 90 percent of the coal mines located in these areas.

The effect of these processes on the tribal communities was clearly reported by the International Alliance of IndigenousTribal Peoples of the Tropical Forests (IAITPTF). The report mentions:

> The tribal people carried the burden of economic growth of the nation. The land acquisition, a piece of colonial legislation, used to acquire lands for the Crown, became the main tool in the hands of the new state to take over tribal resources in the name of public interests, and, by proxy, hand over the same or divert its benefits to the advanced and advancing sections, who reaped the gains, while the tribals paid the cost. More than 10 million have been displaced and lost all they had, millions others stood by helplessly as the juggernaut of national development pushed their communities to the brink of ethnocide. The economic path chosen by the rulers has effectively marginalized the tribals in their own domain.[29]

That the tribal situation had reached alarming proportions by 1986-87 was noted by BD Sharma, the Commissioner for SCs and STs, in the 28th Report of the Commission for SCs and STs. The report remarks:

> There is simmering discontent in almost the entire middle Indian tribal belt, particularly on the issue of lands and forests. In some cases, a state of near confrontation has been created between the people and the state which is marked by intermittent eruption of violence. The tribal people are continuously losing command over their resources on almost all counts – pressure from advanced people, claims of the state in utter disregard of their traditional rights and virtual forced displacements in favour of a variety of developmental projects. With regard to forests and forests produce, the tribal is deemed to be the trespasser, and sought to be evicted summarily without even listening to what he has to say. Even the rights of these people to collect MFP, which was duly recognised at the time of the reservation of forests, has not been honoured in its true spirit.[30]

It is noteworthy that the situation in the tribal belts of the North Eastern Region (NER) differs from that of central, eastern and south India. Except Tripura, Assam and Manipur, this region did not experience much immigration even in the colonial days. And although in more recent times, alienation of land and other resources has occurred (despite the provisions of the VIth Schedule and Inner Line Regulations), it has not been as widespread as in rest of the country, in particular the central-eastern tribal belt. Tribals in the NER control their survival resources (82 percent are cultivators as against 52 percent in central-eastern India and 36 percent in the peninsular south). The tribals are a majority in Arunachal Pradesh, Nagaland, Mizoram and Meghalaya and the tribal struggles in this region, have, therefore, little to do with land alienation or expropriation of resources by the state, and are more focussed on political autonomy.[31]

As per EAS Sarma, former Commissioner of Tribal Welfare, alienation of the tribals from the land and forests and the consequent loss of livelihood, oppression and exploitation, are at the core of the tribal militancy. He has observed:

> I am totally against violence of any kind and a firm believer in the democratic process.....but LWE is a secondary issue. How many tribals even know there is a Government? Their only experience of the state is the forest guard, police, and contractors. The Vth Schedule of the Constitution (Article 244) grants tribals complete rights over their traditional land and forests and prohibits private companies from mining on their land. This constitutional schedule was upheld by the Samata Judgement of the Apex Court (1997). If successive Governments lived by the spirit of the Constitution and this judgment, tribal discontent would automatically recede.[32]

While it is true that a small number of tribals have benefitted from the welfare measures of the state and emerged as influential strata within the tribal society, a majority of them are being deprived of their livelihoods against their wishes. Millions of them have been on the move in the last several decades, making way for development projects, industrial activities and forest conservation, to allow the processes of development to proceed unhindered and to make good for the (often) short-sighted policies of the state. Displaced and disoriented, the experiences of these communities were described by Elwin as "loss of nerve". Resettlement, when it does happen, is a painful experience and the conditions in the resettlement sites are often so abysmal that a majority of the people want to return to their otherwise difficult lives, to their villages, kin groups, forests, rivers, Gods, who they know and trust, and who they can depend on in good times and bad.

Notes

1. Government of India, MHA, Lok Sabha, unstarred question No. 828, answered March 01, 2016 [http://mha1.nic.in/par2013/par2016-pdfs/ls-010316/828.pdf]
2. Shereen Ratnagar, *Being Tribal* (Delhi : Primus Books, 2010).
3. Verrier Elwin (1902–64) was an English anthropologist, ethnologist and tribal activist, who began his career in India as a Christian missionary. He dedicated his life for the tribal cause and is best known for his early work with the Baigas and Gonds of central India.

4. Elwin Verrier, *The Tribal World of Verrier Elwin- Selected Writings (*OUP).
5. °Examples are cited in respect of the Gonds (The Gondi or Gond people are a Dravidian people of central India, spread over MP, eastern Maharashtra, Chhattisgarh, UP, Telangana and western Odisha. With over four million people, they are the largest tribe in central India) and Baigas only (Baiga is a tribe found in MP, UP, Chhattisgarh and Jharkhand. The largest number of Baigas is found in Baiga-chuk in Mandla district and Balaghat district of Madhya Pradesh), due to the constraints of space and scope of the paper.
6. 'Berar was a province of British India. In 1936, with the establishment of the legislative assembly of the 'Central Provinces and Berar', the territory was renamed the Central Provinces and Berar. It is now part of Maharashtra (part of Vidarbha region).
7. Alpa Shah, *In the Shadows of the State, Shadowy Practices* (Oxford, 2010).
8. Ramchandra Guha, *Savaging the Civilized – Verrier Elwin, his Tribals and India* (Chicago University Press, 1999).
9. Ramchandra Guha, "Adivasis, Naxalites, and Indian Democracy", EPW, August 2007.
10. Report of the National Commission for Scheduled Castes and Scheduled Tribes, Seventh Report 2001-02, 2004.
11. Walter Fernandes, "Forests and Tribals : Informal Economy, Dependence and Management Traditions", in Mrinal Miri ed., *In Continuity and Change in Tribal Society,* 1998.
12. Amba Prasad, *Indian Railways* (Bombay, 1960).
13. J Gallagher, and Seal, "Britain and India Between the Wars", *Modern Asian Studies,* 1981, p. 15.
14. Nandini Sundar, *Subalterns and Sovereigns: An Anthropological History of Basta* 1854-2006, (2007).
15. Ramchandra Guha, "Forestry in British and post-British India: A Historical Analysis", *Economic and Ppolitical Weekly,* October 29,1983.
16. Shubhranshu Choudhary, "Weaning the Support Base of Maoists", a talk during CLAWS National Security Workshop, September 2014.
17. Virginius Xaxa, "Transformation of Tribes in India: Terms of Discourse', *Economic and Political Weekly*, June 12, 1999.
18. Ramchandra Guha, "Forest Policy and the People", *Frontier,* March 1982.
19. http://www.downtoearth.org.in/interviews/independent-india-worse-for-tribals-38299
20. V. Raghaviah, "Tribal Revolts", report by Andhra Rashtra Adimajati Seva Sangh, Nellore, 1971.
21. Asha Krishnakumar, "How the Tribal Revolt Began?", *Frontline,* Vol. 21, Issue 19, September 11, 2004.
22. Mohan Guruswamy, "The Heart of our Darkness", in Gurmeet Kanwal and Dhruv Katoch, eds., *Naxal Violence - the Threat Within* (2012).
23. Ibid.
24. http://india_resource.tripod.com/Adivasi.html

25. Nandini Sundar, "Bastar, Maoism and Salwa Judum", EPW, July 22, 2006.
26. Arunabha Gosh, "Probing the Jharkhand Question", EPW, May 04, 1991.
27. Indra Munshi, "On Drinking and Drunkenness: History of Liquor in Colonial India", EPW, September 16, 1996, and Shereen Ratnagar, *Being Tribal* (Primus Books, 2006).
28. Madhav Gadgil and Ramchandra Guha, *This Fissured Land: An Ecological History of India (*OUP, 1992).
29. Report, International Work Group for Indigenous Affairs, "Adivasis – Indigenous Peoples in India, A Brief Situationer, South Asian Regions", 1998.
30. Bharat Dogra, "Tribal Discontent:Timely Warning", EPW April 07, 1990.
31. Jaganath Pathy and Pariyaram M Chacko, eds., *Tribe, Religion and Nation in the Coxtent of the Indian State: Tribal Communities in Social Change* (Sage Publications, 1998).
32. Shoma Choudhari, "Weapons of Mass Desperation", *Tehelka*, October 03, 2009.

3. GOVERNING THE TRIBALS

Colonial State and After[1]

The British faced the strongest challenge in the form of resistance from the people, when they endeavoured making inroads in tribal areas, they were forced to retreat. The fiction of 'exclusion' was created for camouflaging the ignominy of their defeat and retreat and, also for continuing their covert operations to tame the people in the wild, into subjugation. The British started insidious operations to make their presence felt in these areas and also to acquire a sort of command over their resources, especially the forests. This led to serious conflicts in many areas. Small gains of the government's initiatives were formally incorporated into various regulations and finally consolidated in the Government of India Act, 1919.

The Simon Commission recommended a comprehensive scheme of 'excluded' and 'partially excluded' areas. The scheme envisaged that the Centre must "ensure the protection of simple tribal communities from the economic subjugation of their neighbours, freedom to pursue their traditional methods of livelihood and follow their ancestral customs and traditions" and "assist the people suitably so as to enable them to manage their affairs in the changing situation".

Accordingly, special provisions were made in the Government of India Act, 1935, to the effect that no Act of the federal or the provincial legislature would apply to these areas except on the directions of the Governor. Hence, the Governor was endowed with extensive powers: (a) to make such exceptions and modifications, as he considered necessary, while extending the said

Acts; and (b) to make regulations for peace and good governance of the concerned areas.

Thus, the traditional system of governance of the tribal people remained uninterfered with by the new regime. The new sovereign, however, reserved the right to intervene, through the office of Governor, thereby retaining the authority to exploit, for ulterior benefits, the resources of these areas.

Adoption of Constitution: Criminalisation of Tribals

The basic structure of governance of the colonial era remained unchanged. The Gandhian idea of the village republic, at the time of adoption of the Constitution, did not move beyond formalities. The formal frame for the tribal areas in the Constitution followed broadly the design of the Government of India Act, 1935.The Governor continued to enjoy unlimited authority with regard to annulment and amendment of any law of the Centre or the state, but with a vital difference. Whereas earlier, no law became applicable to these (scheduled) areas without the Governor's directions, now the extension of laws came to be automatic. Their application, however, could be annulled or suitably amended by the Governor through a notification; which, sadly, is yet to be done even once in independent India.

The crucial change with regard to the application of laws to scheduled areas proved to be catastrophic. It marked the eclipse of the virtual self-governance of the tribals and the beginning of a new era of confrontation between the state and the people. The general laws of the land flooded the hitherto excluded areas with the adoption of the Constitution. No one appears to have noticed this invisible deluge, let alone evaluated its implications for the tribals. The concerned Governors seriously defaulted in their duties, as envisaged in the Vth Schedule of Article 244. Consequently, entire tribal communities became law breakers the moment the Constitution came into force, leading to "criminalisation of the tribal people" in the name of the law. It has rendered them haplessly vulnerable in all dealings with the outside world, including ironically, the system that was designed for their protection and advancement.[2]

The Tribal Identity

A number of factors have contributed towards the evolution of the tribals as a unified and common entity, thereby ignoring their independent characteristics. The 19th century in India, a period that marked a number of policies and events, also served to unite a wide variety of communities living in India's forests and hills. As brought out earlier, one set of policies comprised those that extended state control over land and forests, via revenue collection. This state of expansion was enabled and accompanied by a new influx of exploitative state officials from outside the region; moneylenders and landlords, forming the trinity of "sarkar, sahukar and zamindar".

At the time of independence in 1947, the question of how to incorporate the tribals into the independent nation was a crucial concern. A school of thought represented by the puritan and reformer sociologist GS Ghurye, concluded that the proper description of these people must refer to their place in or near Hindu society; he felt that the colonial policy of 'divide and rule' had isolated the tribes of India. In contrast to Ghurye, others sought to protect these tribes from aggressive and insensitive outsiders. A prominent voice on this line was that of Verrier Elwin, who took the view that anthropology must lead to administrative reform and improve the living conditions of the people. Elwin's actions to protect the tribals, at helping them deal with the onslaught of modernity at their own pace, had a significant effect on the tribal protection policies of Nehru.

The SCs' (Dalits') economic deprivation was linked to their low ritual status, and an erasure of differences was the eventual goal for them. The STs, however, were exoticised and seen as requiring long-term protection and development. Thus, besides affirmative action policies, the tribal areas (erstwhile protected and now scheduled) further benefitted from being treated as separate administrative entities, in order to protect their rights over their lands, forests and water. Article 244 of the Constitution demarcated Vth and VIth Schedule areas, thus, carrying over the principles of the Scheduled District Act of 1874, which excluded the scheduled areas from the operation of ordinary laws in British India.

More than 400 communities comprising about 8 percent of India's population have been designated as Scheduled Tribes under Article 342 of the Constitution. The basic distinguishing feature of the tribal people, compared to other people, is their association with a habitat or territory. Their habitats comprise largely sparsely populated, resource rich, remote, hilly and forest regions. As we have seen, these communities enjoyed undisturbed command over their respective territories. Their customs and traditions provided the frame of reference for self-governance in open forums of village assemblies. The natural resources of these territories, that were located at the margin of mainstream agricultural civilisations, at that point in time, were not of much significance for the people in the mainstream.

This frame of relationship left the tribals by themselves, distinctly different from the rest. Accordingly, the tribal people have remained largely outside the pale of influence of the political centres of power. Even today, since the tribals are dispersed over vast tracts, they do not constitute substantial vote banks in terms of numbers of seats. Resultantly, the political parties do not endeavour to woo them for electoral gains[3], as also, no tribal leader of national or even regional repute has been able to emerge as part of the political landscape of independent India.

Scheduling of Areas: An Exercise in Superficiality

The Vth Schedule was expected to hold the key, especially in the early phase of the directed change, in the hitherto excluded and partially excluded areas. Two orders were accordingly issued by the President in 1950 declaring certain areas as scheduled areas, in the states of Andhra Pradesh, Bihar, Gujarat, Madhya Pradesh,

Maharashtra, Odisha, Punjab, and Rajasthan. This exercise of the scheduling of areas was rather perfunctory. It can be judged by the fact that the 'excluded' areas of Mirzapur district in Uttar Pradesh did not find a place in this list for the simple reason that the people living therein were not included in the Presidential Order of STs. In Bastar, the largest tribal tract of the country, only two and half tehsils out of eight were scheduled. In the states of West Bengal, Karnataka, Tamil Nadu and Kerala, which have some of the most vulnerable tribal communities, no area was scheduled. This exclusion of areas has often led to social unrest, as in the case of the recent tribals' demand in Kerala. Such gaps have allowed space to the Maoists to take advantage of the yearnings of the people.[4]

The routine handling of scheduling of areas, envisaged as the very foundation of resilient governance, was ominous. The Vth Schedule remained a grand edifice, largely decorative, and with little real content. It is said that these aspects did not claim the attention of the concerned authorities, including the Governors, who were vested with all the authority to intervene for the benefit of the people, but have never done so. The omissions have proved to be catastrophic.[5]

State Forced Development

India adopted the path of planned economic development, beginning with the consolidation of schemes taken up under the 'Grow More Food Campaign' and some irrigation projects in the rural areas. Special multi-purpose projects were also taken up in a few tribal areas, following the example of Community Development Blocks, but with an additional premise that these areas needed special care and higher investments. This resulted in permanent loss to the community of benefits which accrue to the the resource rich areas as a result of development. These resource rich areas that should have received more in terms of benefit to the inhabitants were treated at par with any sub-region since the plan was implemented in a strait-jacketed manner and was not region specific.

This pattern of development not only had economic consequences, but also far-reaching socio-political implications. The urban centres, which wield political, administrative and economic authority, are totally outside the purview of the traditional authority of the tribal community. This is the biggest cause of resentment among the tribal people. The urban pockets that should have functioned as growth centres, tend to become centres of exploitation, casting a deep imprint on the mass psyche of the tribals. The proportion of the tribal people in the urban centres in India, except in the northeastern region, is hardly 10 to 15 percent.

Over the years, industry became the leading sector, as the pace of development quickened. Unlike in the earlier years following independence, these resource rich areas gradually acquired centrality in the country's emerging economic matrix. The hitherto prevalent harmonious frame of 'marginal areas and marginal people' got disturbed as the tribal areas were drawn into the new economy. Ironically, the state itself, with its leading role in national development, became an interested party vis-à-vis the people whose protection and advancement were its constitutional responsibility, with extraordinary powers placed in the hands of the executive.[6]

Till the 1970s, the general programmes of development by the government had little success. This was followed by a new genre of special projects promoted by the government for specific groups like small and marginal farmers, agricultural workers, etc. The projects missed the main objective. The focus of attention in these projects ironically remained on the individual, ignoring the community and its leadership that typified the tribal society. The vital issue of protecting the tribal people against their 'neighbours' and the new powerful adversary, the state, was missed in the state's bid for short-term solutions, making the tribals more dissatisfied and agitated.

In the wake of successive failures of a variety of programmes and unrest growing unabated, a new strategy for tribal development was adopted in the early 1970s, popularly known as Tribal Sub-Plan (TSP) strategy. But, from its very inception, the fervour of the TSP started waning. The biggest default was in respect of scheduling of areas and use of the potential of the Vth Schedule. The tribal majority areas identified in the first phase in the states of Madhya Pradesh (including Chhattisgarh), Bihar (including Jharkhand), Odisha, Rajasthan, Himachal Pradesh, Gujarat and Maharashtra were all included in the Vth Schedule by presidential orders, but no action has been taken in respect of areas identified later during the Sixth Plan and included in the TSP. Similarly, the TSP areas in the states of West Bengal, Kerala, Karnataka and Tamil Nadu have not been scheduled till date.

The reasons for this neglect of the Vth Schedule are deeper. With a mechanism for devolution of funds, the message of the new tribal policy was loud and clear. Adventurers of all hues became active to get engrossed in the money game. The milieu was characterised by a 'free for all' spirit, in the wake of the denigration of the traditional system of self-governance and no effective action by the state in terms of the constitutional mandate. The first part of the new strategy, therefore, was rendered inoperative after a bold start. The government has been reverting to the game of figures, money spent, people benefitted, roads laid out, etc. The nodal ministries started dabbling in specific schemes that destroyed the organic structure of the TSPs.

The TSP has been continuously neglected by the government, primarily due to lack of unanimity amongst the Centre and the states. The annual review of the state of administration in the scheduled areas, as a parallel process of a plan exercise that was crucial in the TSP strategy, did not start as per the commitment of the union before the 7th Finance Commission (FC). The 8th FC expressed its inability to assess the needs of the scheduled areas separately because the concerned states had not presented the necessary details. Even this sharp comment had no effect in any quarter and the issue itself was simply dropped by the 9th FC from its agenda, with no question raised from any quarter;

probably those having stakes had no voice even in the form of representation. In sum, in the absence of effective protection of the state as envisioned under the Vth Schedule, and as a direct consequence of the disregard and exclusion of the community from the formal frame, the policy of development with a torrential flow of money through rusted and leaking channels, has made the whole exercise dysfunctional.[7]

This confused situation has prevailed despite the socialist foundations of the goals enshrined in the Constitution. Since, the early 1990s, there has been a sea-change in the tenor of governance. The Vth Schedule areas are endowed with the richest natural resources in the country. The structural transformation that is being currently forced in these areas in the name of development totally ignores the natural rights of the tribal communities over their habitats which they have been traditionally occupying. The main problem is that the people whose homelands were ravaged to extract nature's bounty got little or nothing of it. Even the meagre royalties that the states receive are mostly expended by the bureaucracy on themselves, as salaries.[8] As far as benefits to the affected population are concerned, no policies to include legal and constitutional provisions have been able to dent the colonial psyche of the administration.

When the livelihood resources of people are put to alternative uses such as industry, or are ravaged through mining, the tribals are left to fend for themselves totally unprepared. This manifests because the incongruous laws recognise only 'recorded' entitlements, which are not there; they have no place for the ground reality, including community usage. It results in barbaric and relentless displacement, destitution and frequent resistance to the state.

Since its formation, like many of the special tenancy Acts in Adivasi areas, the Vth Schedule has been under constant threat of amendments in order to allow transfer of tribal lands to non-tribals and corporate bodies. The state continues to entice investors and entrepreneurs by providing them with a conducive environment.

In this frame, the nature of the enterprise—private or public sector—makes no difference in the people's position. The people are totally helpless and at the mercy of the system. The state, on its part, has not been able to prepare even the broad parameters for ensuring equity in the process of structural transformation of the local economy.

The latest threat to these areas has been the formation of Special Economic Zones (SEZs) which give special legal rights to private companies, allowing them to buy land; and it is the tribal lands that are targeted for acquisition. The audit report of the Comptroller and Auditor General (CAG), in November 2014, has questioned the performance of the policy, underscoring that in six states of India, close to 5,500 hectares of land acquired for 52 SEZs were subsequently denotified and diverted for commercial purposes – leaving several questions unanswered.[9]

In view of the resultant dissatisfaction and unrest, especially, in the rural areas, other competing forces have surfaced to seduce the tribal youth, manifesting in the form of the Naxal insurgency. Seeing them as a potent revolutionary force, as harbourers of 'elementary aspects of peasant insurgency', whose class consciousness needs to be developed, the Naxalites have viewed the tribal areas as an ideal base for their movement.

Recommendations Towards Good Governance

Emphatic Governmental Approach to Protective Legislations

The state's response to continued unrest and social dissension in areas predominated by the SCs and STs was to formulate four protective laws. These four Acts are the PESA (Panchayat Extension to Scheduled Areas) Act 1996, NREGA (National Rural Employment Guarantee Act) 2005, the ST and other Traditional Forest Dwellers (Recognition of Forest Rights) Act 2006 and Right to Fair Compensation and Transparency in Land Acquisition, Rehabilitation and Resettlement Act, 2013[10] (incorporating the National Rehabilitation and Resettlement Policy, 2007).

Genuine and effective implementation of the mentioned constitutional provisions is warranted. If the provisions of the Constitution had been implemented in some measure, if not in both letter and spirit, the present situation would not have come about. In 1999, the Government of India even issued a draft National Policy on Tribals[11] to address the developmental needs of the tribal people. Special emphasis was laid on education, forestry, healthcare, languages, resettlement and land rights. The draft was meant to be circulated among Members of Parliament (MPs), Members of Legislative Assemblies (MLAs) and civil society groups. A Cabinet Committee on Tribal Affairs was meant to constantly review the policy. Little has happened since. The draft policy is still a draft, which means there is no policy[12]. The Land Act is currently on the back-burner and there are frequent reports in the media regarding attempts to dilute the Forest Rights Act (FRA), 2006.[13] The governmental approach to the entire issue has to undergo a paradigm shift.

Cohesion Amongst Institutions Working for Tribal Rights

There are many custodians of the interests of SCs, STs and marginalised groups viz., the Tribal Advisory Council in the states, National Commission for SCs and STs, National Human Rights Commission, National Commission for Women, National Commission for the Rights of Children and National Commission for Minorities. There is neither clear focus nor dynamic coordination among all these institutions. By and large, their recommendations have not received any serious attention by the legislatures or the executive. The Expert Group constituted by the Planning Commission had recommended consultations among all these bodies and launching of joint initiatives for concerted and compulsory action on their joint recommendations. To make these commissions effective, they should be given powers of investigation and to pass orders which they could enforce.[14]

Land Related Measures

Land reform laws provide for land access to Adivasis, through redistribution of land. Efforts at implementation of ceiling laws stopped about two to three decades ago, as if there was no possibility of identifying ceiling surplus land thereafter. A serious effort must be made to reinvigorate the process, so that ceiling surplus land thereby obtained is made available for distribution amongst the vulnerable sections. Land Tribunal or Fast Track Courts under Article 323-B of the Constitution need to be set up for expeditious disposal of the ceiling cases. A comprehensive land settlement survey has not been undertaken since the British left India.[15] The government has been trying to digitise land records and make them more easily accessible since the late 1990s, under the National Land Records Modernisation Programme (NLRMP), which has not been able to make substantial progress. Modern technology of the Geographic Information System (GIS) and satellite imagery needs to be duly incorporated.

Old cases should be unearthed and fresh inquiries conducted. Since the landowners have already had decades to manipulate and create false documents, no cut-off dates for reopening the old cases should be prescribed. Also, correct and updated land records are crucial for the security of land rights. Failure to maintain proper records and ensure land rights has led to the proliferation of disputes for the legitimate rights of the landholders, resulting in discontent. Modernisation of the land administration system, including a crash programme of updating of land records, computerisation of textual and spatial records and integration of the registration office should be taken up on priority, with due assistance by the central government .

Livelihood Security

SCs and STs are the two groups that have truly taken advantage of the employment being offered under shemes like the Mahatma Gandhi National Rural Employment Guarantee Act (MGNREGA). The SCs and STs account for 14 and 8 percent of the population respectively, but their share in households that received employment under MGNREGA in the year 2012-13 has been almost 40 percent.[16]; and in relation to the SCs, the scheme has been more beneficial to the STs. Therefore, it is recommended that the resource depleted areas with a high incidence of distressed and involuntary migration and malnutrition be identified for genuine implementation under MGNREGA as the first priority.

There has been no dearth of programmes related to rural development and poverty alleviation. The Ministry of Rural Development (MoRD) administers them from the Centre. At the field level, there is a large disconnect among these programmes. In order to foster the ideological goal of capturing state power through violence, the basic programmes of the extremists relate to elimination of poverty, deprivation and alienation of the poor and landless. Even the government has acknowledged the fact that it is the 'lack of' or 'absence of' governance in the so-called 'Red Corridor' that is the most salient aspect behind the insurgency challenge.To reduce the anger of the people, it is necessary that they should feel that they are a part of the mainstream of Indian society. What is necessary is to saturate these districts with proper and sound implementation of the existing programmes by ensuring their convergence at both the apex and implementation levels, with emphasis at the Gram Sabha (GS)/Panchayat levels.

Administrative Reorganisations

Reorganisation of the administrative arrangement should aim at supplanting the current non-accessible bureaucracy by the three-tier Panchayat bodies, with level-to-level correspondence and interaction with the current administrative structure. The bureaucracy at each level should be directly accountable to the corresponding tier of the elected Panchayat bodies. The Panchayat at each tier should be strengthened by posting of the appropriate level of general and technical service officers. Regulatory functions like revenue, police, forest and labour should be directly accountable to Panchayati Raj Institutions (PRIs), for their actions and performance.

One major deficiency of the existing administrative arrangements is the absence of a justice administration system in the rural areas. The current system is expensive and complicated. Invariably, the tribals get involved in the system as the accused and defendants rather than seekers of their rights and entitlements. A system of justice and grievance redressal, which is simple, inexpensive, responsive and accessible should be made an integral part of governance. In the scheduled areas, Nyaya Panchayats could be modelled, aligned with the GS. Their acceptance in the tribal society would be not that difficult since traditionally, their dispute settlement mechanism and justice system has existed within the confines of their society. Cadre management of these administrative structures needs to be decentralised from the state level to the district level, and if necessary, even lower, thus, empowering the local governing bodies, and, thereby, ushering in capacity building for the GS. The GS should be legally and operationally empowered to conduct social audits of tribal development programmes to enforce the people's participation, and transparency and accountability of the implementing agencies and officials.

A Dedicated Service Cadre[17]

As a macro measure, a better civil administration structure must come up in place of the one present. Perhaps it is time to constitute a new All India Service, similar to the former Indian Frontier Administrative Service (IFAS). The IFAS was an eclectic group of officers drawn from various arms of the government [18*].All tribal majority areas must be consolidated into administrative divisions whose authority must be vested with the democratically chosen leadership. This body could be called the Adivasi Mahapanchayat, functioning as a largely autonomous institution. Instead of the state capital controlled government, the instruments of public administration dealing with education, health, irrigation, roads and land records must be handed over to local government structures. The police must also be made answerable to local elected officials and not be a law unto themselves.

Economics of Exploitation: For Benefits and Consent

The local community must get all the royalties for the minerals extracted from their areas. Till recently, the royalty paid by the extractors was a meagre Rs. 27 per metric tonne. While it has been announced that this has now been raised to 10 percent of the market price, it is learned that in reality this has been raised just tenfold to Rs. 270 per tonne.[19] The cost of extraction is estimated to be not more than Rs. 250 per tonne. The export price has never fallen below Rs. 1,500 per tonne. In February 2010, the landed price per tonne of Indian iron ore in China was $128, which is over Rs. 6,000 per tonne.[20] So one can imagine the margins the private and state owned exporters are raking in.

The economics of steel manufacturing was reported by the *Businessworld* of July 31, 2010, in its story on the financial dire straits in respect of Ispat Industries, the steel company owned by Arcelor Mittal. Ispat's Rs. 12,000 crore steel plant at Dolvi, Maharashtra, financed with huge dollops of investments by government owned financial institutions like the Industrial Development Bank of India (IDBI) has piled up a staggering debt of Rs. 6,800 crore. While some of this can be attributed to mismanagement, the economics of the industry based on cheap iron ore was against Ispat Industries. The article detailed how Ispat could never earn profits unless it had its own "captive" mines like Tata Steel, Steel Authority of India Limited (SAIL) and others. The average price of this iron ore, when imported, as was by Ispat, was about Rs. 6,000 per tonne, while, if derived from 'captive" mines, it would cost merely about Rs. 500-550 per tonne. The implications of this price difference should be obvious; however, what perhaps was not so obvious was that this was essentially profit extracted from the nation's mineral reserves, which mostly lie in the tribal homelands and which by constitutional rights should be theirs.[21] Ultimately, it is the poor Adivasi who pays for it with his home and hearth, and gets no credit for it!

Enhanced royalty of a relatively smaller amount of over Rs. 4,600 crore,[22] accrued to the state government's coffers, with little or none to trickle down. It now needs to be mandated by law that for minerals extracted in the tribal areas, the royalty received should be entirely earmarked to the local administration. Only the local governing bodies, as empowered by the PESA Act, should be vested with the power to give mineral exploitation licences to corporations.

If land is required for industrialisation, the prices must be fixed to the satisfaction of local government authorities and not arbitrarily set by distant bureaucrats to suit the convenience of the investing corporation. We cannot have any more episodes like that in Kalinga Nagar[23] where the Tatas got tribal lands at a fraction of their market value. The locals have been getting nothing but the most menial jobs and in return their hitherto pristine environment is ravaged beyond recognition, with the streams choked with the debris of excavation. With reference to promise of jobs to the locals, unless the clause is included as part of the Comprehensive Economic Cooperation Agreement (CECA) in the case of foreign companies like POSCO, the corporate is within its rights to deny any respectable job openings – a fact that is often missed out while weighing the promises by the state.[24]

In 2007, the Andhra Pradesh government signed agreements with Jindal South West (JSW) of the Jindal group and the Anrak company of Ras-al-Khaimah to mine bauxite in the Araku valley in the eastern district of Vizagapatam. This is estimated to displace over 100,000 tribals while creating jobs for a mere 400. The state government expects to receive a royalty of Rs. 64.5 crore while the two companies are slated to make a profit of an amount of Rs. 1,260 crore and Rs. 2,350 crore respectively[25]. If natural resources must be exploited for development, then the local communities which bear the brunt of the suffering and burden due to displacement and pollution, must benefit the most. This is possible only when the public administration system is decentralised to ensure that local governments feel responsible for their people – commensurate with the provisions of the Vth Schedule.

The real tragedy of the matter is that it is not as if the authorities are not aware of the oppression and exploitation of our tribal people. The Supreme Court, while dealing with a case relating to the acquisition of tribal land in Sundergarh district of Odisha by the Mahanadi Coalfields Ltd., a Government of India enterprise, found that people whose lands were taken two decades ago, had still not been paid any compensation. In a stunning rebuke to the government, a bench of the court comprising Justices Aftab Alam and BS Mohanty termed its development policies as "blinkered" and held it responsible for "fuelling extreme discontent and giving rise to Naxalism and militancy"[26].

Ailing Scheduled Castes Plan (SCP) and Tribal Sub-Plan (TSP) and Reinvigoration

The public resource management needs to be based on equitable development, and two aspects are crucial towards this. One concerns distribution of available public resources proportionate to the needs of the area and the affected communities. The other relates to the efficient utilisation of whatever resources are allocated. The existing financial arrangements have neglected them in both ways. The gap between the SCs/STs and the rest of the population is large and widening. This gap needs to be bridged. The SCP was introduced by the Planning Commission in 1979 and the TSP in 1974 as special programmes, with the objectives of bridging the development gap. They were intended to deliver direct benefits to the Dalits and Adivasis because the universal social and economic welfare programmes of the Planning Commission remained inadequate for these sections of the population.

However, despite their being in place for the last several decades, the government has either chosen to not to allocate funds under the SCP and TSP or has diverted the funds towards other generic development orders.[27] The government has been evasive in the following manner in allocating funds under the SCP and TSP:

- In preparation of the union budget, the Department of Economic Affairs under the Ministry of Finance asks the

Planning Commission[28] to chart out the expenditure for the Fiscal Year (FY) on the basis of taxes collected. The commission, in turn, asks the ministries to send proposals of their budget expenditures. The ministries, while sending proposals, have not been listing out separate expenditure under the SCP and TSP, alongwith their general plan of expenditure. As a result, the Planning Commission has had to allocate funds under these schemes only after the budget is approved. Many ministries have not been allocating any funds under the SCP and TSP.

- Most of the ministries are underallocating – even if funds are being allocated under the SCP and TSP.
- The actual expenditure is much less than even the underallocated amounts under these sub-plans. Also, most of the money allocated under these sub-plans is spent on general programmes like the Food Security Programme, Sarva Shiksha Abhiyan, etc; which, in many cases, are shown under these sub-plans. While doing so, it is conveniently forgotten that the two sub-plans were introduced only because universal programmes could not adequately improve the social and economic stigma attached to the SCs/STs.
- The amounts declared under the sub-plans are also used for purposes that have no direct impact on the population that is aimed to be targeted. A case in point has been the diversion of funds earmarked for SCs/STs to develop infrastucture for the Commonwealth Games, by the Delhi government, as admitted by P Chidambaram in the Rajya Sabha September 2010.[29]

The National Coalition for SCP-TSP Legislation, an umbrella organisation of Dalit and Adivasi groups, recently tabulated [using budget documents and the Right to Information (RTI)] the funds denied to the Dalits and tribals from the Seventh to the Twelfth Five-Year Plans (till 2014-15) in the union budget. The final numbers were found to be a whopping Rs. 5,27,723.72 crore. It is safe to say that more than 60 percent of the due amount was denied to the marginalised sections of society.[30]

As far as the Dalit and tribal population is concerned, vis-à-vis SCP and TSP, the following aspects warrant the attention of the policy-makers

- There is a requirement of constituting a Development Council comprising ex-officio and nominated members for the purpose of planning, allocation and utilisation of the budget.
- A nodal agency is recommended to be created, to make the government more accountable.
- Funds for the SCs/STs should be allocated well in advance and meant only for projects/schemes directly affecting the SCs/STs.
- Consultation with 'primary stakeholders' belonging to PRIs or those at the district levels, should be mandatory as a policy, prior to deciding the expenditure under these programmes.
- The funds in the SCP and TSP should be made 'non-lapsable and non-divertible', as is the case with funds with the Ministry of Development of Northeastern Region (DoNER).

The union government's Ministry of Tribal Affairs (MoTA) had released a draft Bill in November 2013, for the implementation of the TSP, to complement the SCP Bill released in June 2013. Both Bills recommended statutory status for these programmes and were important steps forward in making them stronger. They also recommended institutionalisation of accountability mechanisms in case of non-implementation of these programmes. The status of these Bills as on date, is not clear.

State Response: Need to Look beyond 'Security' and 'Development'

The public policy perspective on the Maoist movement is overwhelmingly preoccupied with incidents of violence that take place in these areas and with its ideological underpinnings. Though it does concede that the area suffers from deficient development and people have unaddressed grievances, it views the movement as the greatest internal security threat. Accordingly, the attention of the government is concentrated on curbing violence and maintaining public order to achieve normalcy. While area development is also being speeded up, the security-centric view accords primacy to security operations. The contextualising of violence is missing from this perspective. Many a times, security measures have further alienated the population. Also, in the past, the strategy of the security forces to curb violence has encouraged the formation of tribal squads to fight the Naxalites, with a view to reduce the risks for the state. This, in the past, had fostered fratricidal conflicts in which ultimately the tribals suffer. Those tribals who were unattached to either the Naxalites or those opposing them, became victims of violence by all the agencies.

The strategy should be to position an empowered task force of specially picked up responsive officials to execute all protection and development programmes for the people's benefit and to redress their grievances. This is the best strategy to eliminate the influence of radical leftist groups. The authorities should encourage civil society groups, having knowledge of, and sympathy with, the local tribals in assisting this task force for wider participation of the people in the implementation of development plans.

Mobilising the support of the people is also absolutely essential to weaken the support base of the Maoists. The political parties are not playing their role in this regard. The representatives of the major political parties have virtually abdicated their responsibilities. There is an obvious vacant space that requires to be occupied by grassroots political activities to provide the tribals with an alternative, other than the means advocated by the Maoists.

A strategy of constructive management of conflict requires two key measures. At its present stage, priority should be accorded to search out creative policies that bridge the gaps between state interests and those of the tribal communities. The tribes are not opposed to development. All that they want is to control the pace and influence, its pattern and direction so that they are enabled to prevent its damaging effects and can enjoy some of its benefits. The autonomy and control over the natural resources which these people seek is consistent with national development. The administration at the grassroots should be made to participate through PESA.

Ensuring a life of respect and dignity for the Dalits, Adivasis, women and the poor in general, is not a task that can be left to the working out of a few laws. A concerted effort through the education system and the cultural media needs to be taken up. The administration needs to be sensitised to the inadequacies and their unacceptability. Government personnel exhibiting an attitude of indifference towards these issues must be deemed to have committed misconduct and proceeded against accordingly.

Mere provision of reservations for the SCs, STs, Other Backward Classes (OBCs) and women in the local bodies does not amount to empowerment. Consequential steps need to be taken to ensure that they are actually able to exercise the responsibilities placed upon them, and that their powers are not appropriated by the dominant sections. In situations where the elected representatives from these communities are threatened or subjected to violence, they should accordingly be protected by the administration.

The law enforcing mechanism, in terms of local policing in the affected areas, would need to be strengthened. Some of the suggested measures could be: additional police stations / outposts; filling up police vacancies and improving police-population ratio; modernisation measures; a thorough training in counter-insurgency including cultural orientation of troops; fostering unit cohesion amongst the Central Armed Police Forces (CAPFs); incentives for personnel posted in these areas; hands down leadership of high order, etc. There is an urgent need to introduce long overdue police reforms and, in tandem, making local governing bodies stakeholders in upholding law and order.

Notes

1. B D Sharma, "The State and the Scheduled Tribes: Past, Present and Future", in Mehrotra Santosh, ed., *Countering Naxalism with Development* (New Delhi: Sage Publications, 2014.
2. Ibid.
3. Jairam Ramesh's talk, "Tribals and Insurgency", Nehru Memorial Lecture, 2013.
4. R Krishnakumar, "The Adivasi Struggle", *Frontline*, Vol. 18, Issue 21, October 13-26, 2001.
5. Ibid.
6. Sharma, n. 1.
7. Ibid.
8. Mohan Guruswamy, "The Heart of our Darkness", in Gurmeet Kanwal and Dhruv Katoch, eds., *Naxal Violence – The Threat Within* (New Delhi: KW Publishers, 2012).
9. Himanshu Upadhya, "SEZ Today, Gone Tomorrow!", *India Together*, February 03, 2015.
10. The government intends introducing amendments to this Act and has promulgated an ordinance in this regard in December 2014. The matter stands referred to the Joint Parliamentary Committee and is likely to come up for discussions during the Parliament's Winter Session of 2016. Aspects related to the amendment, in relation to the existing Act are not covered in this paper and can be accessed at http://www.claws.in/1324/the-land-act-exercising-caution-to-allay-social-unrest-shashank-ranjan.html
11. http://www.prsindia.org/uploads/media/1167469383/bill53_2007010353_Draft_National_Policy_on_Tribals
12. Ibid.
13. Nitin Sethi, "Ministry Changes Stance on Tribals' Forest Rights", *Business Standard,* New Delhi, June 29, 2016.
14. http://planningcommission.nic.in/reports/publications/rep_dce.pdf
15. Barun Mitra and Mitra Madhumita, "Renovating Land Management", Bibek Debroy, Ashley Tellis and Trevor Reece, eds., *Getting India Back on Track – An Action Agenda for Reform* (New Delhi: Random House India, 2014).
16. Neelakshi Mann, "A Boon in the Rural Landscape", *The Times of India*, February 18, 2013.
17. Ibid.
18. A special service known as the Indian Frontier Administrative Service was established in 1957, to administer the northeastern states. This service was doing a commendable job of adequately administering the northeastern states with due regard to the cultural and tribal sensitivities of the people. The IFAS was abolished in the latter half of the Sixties and merged into the Indian Administrative Service (IAS).
19. "The CCEA Approves 10 per cent Royalty on Iron Ore", PTI Report, August 2009.

20. Shankar Raghuraman, "Ironic? Story of the Great Indian Loot", *The Times of India* (Hyderabad), June 05, 2010.
21. "Gasping for Breath", *Businessworld*, July 31, 2010.
22. Ibid.
23. Tata Steel signed an MoU with the Odisha government for the Kalingnagar project in November 2004. More than five years on, 300 families are yet to be moved from the site. The project saw violent agitation against land acquisition in 2006, when police firing killed 14 tribals. Human rights activists have blamed industrial projects for displacing tribals, a cause taken up by the Naxalites on a war-footing, literally. According to a recent Citigroup report, the tribals are among the main victims of displacement. Although they comprise 9 per cent of the population, their land is 40 per cent of the land acquired till date.
24. Prabhash Ranjan, "POSCO Paradox", *The Financial Express*, August 27, 2010. "For instance, according to some media reports, the Odisha Government wants POSCO to reserve jobs for the local population at different levels like the semi-skilled and the managerial levels. This is a major issue in renewing the MoU with POSCO (the first MoU lapsed in June 2010). When the India-Korea CECA outlaws the imposition of any requirement on a foreign investor to reserve jobs at the senior managerial level, how will the Odisha Government insist on such reservations? Even if the Odisha Government is able to persuade POSCO to reserve managerial jobs for the locals, other state governments may not be similarly successful when the adoption of such measures is outlawed—either by a Bilateral Investment Treaty (BIT) or by a CECA".
25. G Arunkumar, "Development? 1 Lac to Lose Land, Jobs for 400", *The Times of India* (Hyderabad), June 05, 2010.
26. Dhananjaya Mahapatra, TNN, "Skewed Growth to Blame for Rise of Naxals: SC", *The Times of India* (New Delhi), July 21, 2010.
27. http ://www.frontline.in/social-issues/giving-dalits-their-due/article5596960.ece
28. The functions of the newly constituted NITI Aayog are yet to be made clear in this regard.
29. http://timesofindia.indiatimes.com/india/Chidambaram-admits-Delhi-govt-erred-in-diverting-SC/ST-funds-to-Games/articleshow/6469604.cms
30. http://www.kractivist.org/the-great-Adivasi-dalit-rip-off-denial-and-diversion-of-plan-fund-wtfnews/

4. PANCHAYAT EXTENSION TO SCHEDULED AREAS (PESA) ACT: TOWARDS EMPOWERING THE GRASSROOTS

Panchayati Raj Institutions (PRIs) were mandated in the Constitution through the 73rd Amendment in 1993 – a time when neo-liberalism was in its ascendancy. An important pillar of this ideology was a transformation in the thinking about the role of the state, and a shift in the focus from government to governance. A distinction was attempted between 'steering' and 'rowing', and it was reasoned that the government must confine itself to giving directions and framing policy while empowering communities to serve themselves. Subsequently, a special effort was made to provide the tribals the opportunity to exercise their right to self-governance through the enactment in 1996 of a special law known as the PESA – bringing in the 73rd Constitutional Amendment to cover the Vth Schedule areas.

This chapter explores the functioning of the PESA Act, 1996, and related facets towards governance in the tribal areas coming under the Vth Schedule. This landmark Act recognised the cultural and economic vulnerability of tribals as also their distinct character, and the historic injustices meted to them. Its passage—an Act of great political commitment—attempted to shift the balance of power towards the communities by providing a mechanism for self-protection and self-governance. By recognising that tribal communities are 'competent' to self-govern, in effect, the validity of their way of life and value systems was recognised. However, today i.e. even two decades after its enactment, it is universally acknowledged that the Act has much to achieve on its promise of securing the people's participation.

An attempt is made to look at the failure of PESA and the 'alternate mobilisation' that has happened.This is evidenced in the series of reports the government has commissioned from time to time, which pointed to the deepening marginalisation of the affected Adivasi communities. The Act, according to Dileep Singh Bhuria, the Chairman of the committee that worked on it, could "mark the beginning of a new era in the history of tribal people. Having lived since generations in a close and dependent relationship with nature in mostly resource rich areas, they were paying an inordinate and often devastating price for India's chosen development model". There exists a complex intersection of what would be justifiably called governance failure and alienation, and its co-terminous relationship with the phenomenon of LWE.

PESA recognised the Gram Sabha (GS) [a habitation was the natural unit of the community, and its adult members constitute the GS, as against the elected Gram Panchayat (GP)] to be pre-eminent. The GS was recognised as being competent to act on a range of powers, to include:

- The power to prevent alienation of land and to take appropriate action to restore any unlawfully alienated land of tribals.
- The ownership of Minor Forest Produce (MFP).
- The power to enforce prohibition, or to regulate or restrict the sale and consumption of any intoxicant.
- The power to exercise control over moneylending to the tribals.
- The power to exercise control over institutions and functionaries in all social sectors.
- The power to control local plans, and resources for such plans including tribal sub-plans.
- The power of prior recommendation in granting licences or mining leases for minor minerals as well as for grant of concessions for the exploitation of minor minerals by auction.
- The right to be consulted on matters of land acquisition.

PESA, thus, constructed tribal self-governance around certain key features. The first feature through Section 4 (b) fundamentally departs from the colonial principle by affirming that an organic self-governing community rather than an administrative unit like a village is the basic unit of self-governance.

PESA also recognises a habitation to be a natural unit of the community, whose adult members constitute the GS. In Section 4 (d) and 4 (m)(ii), communities are declared competent to safeguard and preserve their culture and tradition, exercise command over natural resources, enjoy ownership of Minor Forest Produce (MFP) and adjudicate their disputes. Under Section 4 (m)(vi), the village assembly is empowered to monitor all state institutions within its jurisdiction e.g. schools, health centres etc, with the functionaries under its control.

Section 4 (i), (j), (k) and (l) marks a departure from colonial laws like the Land Acquisition Act and Forest and Mining Acts that lay down that communities must be consulted on acquisition of, or access to, land and land-based resources. They also affirm that the tribal community has the capability and competence to pass judgment on, and act in its wisdom to put an end to all exploitative relations, including land alienation, moneylending, market relations and alcohol trade. This establishes the supremacy of the GS, whose power cannot be usurped by a superior body.

Thus, PESA is a unique legislation, often described as a Constitution within the Constitution, which attempts to bring together in a single frame two totally different worlds: the simple system of tribal communities governed by their respective customs and traditions, and the formal system of the state, governed exclusively by laws.

However, since it was passed, the experience of PESA has been tragically stilted. The legislative and executive work, which state governments were to undertake, remains incomplete. Further, as the above reading of the law shows, PESA envisaged a radical shift in the balance of power – from the state apparatus and from economic and political elites, to the community, which can exercise this wide range of powers meaningfully only when it has access to adequate information and capabilities, in alliance with other arms of the state.

The aforesaid aspects have been given inadequate attention. In a way, thus, the entire effort of all organs of government ought to have been directed towards building up the necessary capabilities such that the 'constitutional/statutory' competence mandated in the communities gets fullest play. This does not seem to have happened and the agenda of self-governance remains postponed.

Given that the challenges to the tribal community's way of life have severely intensified in the past decade with a liberalising economy, wooing of private capital for industry, profitable rush for natural resources (in particular, minerals and land) along with the phenomenon of LWE, the neglect of PESA becomes even more catastrophic.

The Unfinished Legislative Agenda

When passed in 1996, PESA envisaged that the nine states with Vth Schedule areas would enact their own legislations devolving power to their respective tribal communities, as well as amend pre-existing laws to bring them in harmony with PESA within a year. The states have varyingly adopted the PESA provisions in their respective Panchayat Acts.

To begin with, since PESA is founded on a 'self-governed village community' component, participatory democracy (the second component) inheres in the principle of a face-to-face self-governing community, like two sides of a coin. While some states have reworked the definition of a village in their Panchayat legislations, on the ground, the administrations continue to practise their earlier revenue definitions of a village. This effectively precludes the functioning of a 'face-to-face' community as envisaged in the Act and eliminates the likelihood of the functioning of an empowered GS.

In many instances, the states have diluted PESA's power in the wording of their legislations, and the rules governing their implementation. Barring Madhya Pradesh and Chhattisgarh, most state legislations have given the bulk of the powers to the GPs, and not to the GSs. This runs contrary to Section 4 (n) of PESA. Moreover, neither the state legislations nor the rules adequately address how communities may exercise their powers with regard to the issues of land, displacement, liquor, and so on. They have also failed to put in place redressal mechanisms that communities can access, when these powers are violated.

On the other hand, some state Acts, in fact, even put barriers to a GS' powers under PESA. For example, Sub-section 10.8 of Jharkhand 2001 GP Act says that the powers of the GS defined in Section 10(1.a) i.e. formulating schemes for economic development, and section 10(5) i.e. powers of the GS in scheduled areas, will not affect the rules and jurisdiction of the government. Sub-section 10.9 states that "the state Government by ordinary or by special order will be able to enhance the powers of the GS and withdraw them as well." Similar provisions are there in the Act's Sections 75(d), 76(d) and 77, which outline the rights and duties of the village Panchayat, Panchayat Samiti and District Panchayats.[1] In these sections also, the same conditions have been repeated, thus, ensuring that the government retains effective powers, rather than the GS. Without the rules, the operation of PESA on the ground becomes null and void and in such situations, Panchayats work as extensions of the bureaucracy, rather than as representatives of the people.

Comparative analysis of implementation of the Act suggest that the legislations in the states of Madhya Pradesh and Chattisgarh are nearest to the original provisions of PESA. Other states have significant legislative work left to undertake to actualise the Act. However, all the states are faring poorly on implementing these provisions meaningfully. It is tragic that in none of the states, the Governor, who is accorded limitless powers by the Constitution to ensure the upholding of PESA, has monitored or intervened. There seems to be no explanation for these widespread delays other than the fact that PESA is low on the political and executive agenda. It is believed that cultural factors and the legacy of exploitation in the states also militate against a reformist law like PESA.[2]

In December 2009, the Ministry of Panchayati Raj sent to the nine state governments, a set of draft PESA rules as a potential template, but this was not accompanied by a timeframe for action. While these draft rules are laid out mandating the devolution of power to the community, the draft document does not list any punitive measures for violation of rules. In the light of the PESA experience of the past 20 years, it is unlikely that these rules, unless accompanied by well thought-out punitive measures or redressal mechanisms will have their intended effect of empowering the community.

The Challenges

Resources

The sale of tribal lands to non-tribals in the Vth Schedule areas is prohibited. However, transfers continue to take place and have become more pronounced in the post-liberalisation era. The principal reasons are: transfer through fraudulent means, unrecorded transfers on the basis of oral transactions, transfers by misrepresentation of facts and misstating the purpose, forcible occupation of tribal lands, etc. So far, the colonial-era version of the Land Act (of 1894), that preceded the latest Act of 2013, had been widely misused on the ground to forcibly acquire individual and community land for private industry. In several cases, the practice of the state government is to sign high profile Memorandums of Understandings (MoUs) with corporate houses[3] and then proceed to deploy the Land Acquisition Act to ostensibly acquire the land for the state industrial corporation. This body then simply leases the land to the private corporation – a complete travesty of the term "acquisition for a public purpose", as sanctioned by the Act.

In some cases, administrations run through the motions of a PESA consultation, but in no instance has the opposition expressed by the tribal communities to the acquisition of their land resulted in a plan for industry being halted, suggesting the disempowerment of the GS. A source of dissatisfaction has been the inadequacy of 'in lieu' grants to the locals who part with their lands. These people often cannot take advantage of the overspecialised employment opportunities in the new industry because of their low literacy levels, and face the prospect of being reduced to informal, casual labour. The argument that industry brings prosperity is not applicable in these areas; for instance, in Dantewada, the National Mineral Development Corporation has run the country's largest iron ore mine for five decades, but not even one tribal has moved beyond Class IV employment, as the entire operation has been outsourced.[4]Nor is there a recognition that sometimes communities might simply not want to part with their land, no matter how attractive the compensation, because it disrupts their way of life.

When it comes to acquiring mineral resources for industry, the stakes are similarly loaded against the functioning of the PESA Act. The past decade has witnessed a boom in mining. Yet, there is no legal framework in place for communities to dissent to such activity in their area if they so desire, or to secure a direct stake in the earnings, through instruments such as jobs or debentures. Successive governments have systematically ignored the Samata judgment[5], to the severe disadvantage of the tribal communities. The order's highlights are worth reiterating here to indicate how the country could have adopted a model of sustainable mining, which was respectful of the tribal communities living in mineral-rich areas, and, thus, avoided many of the conflicts witnessed on the ground today. The great boom in mining — for example, in the past years, companies paid a royalty to the state of Rs. 26 per tonne of iron ore, selling it for over 100 times that, or an average of Rs. 3,000 per tonne—that means that the profits run into crores of rupees. As per a school of thought, there is a great financial incentive to ignore the PESA law and the Samata judgment, or ensure that they do not get in the way.

Forest Rights

The Scheduled Tribes and Other Traditional Forest Dwellers (Recognition of Forest Rights) Act, 2006 (FRA) was a result of the polity responding to the protracted struggles by the tribal communities and movements to assert their rights over the forest lands that they were traditionally dependent on. The Act turned the colonial forest policy, which had established the rights of the state over the forests over the traditional rights of the community, on its head. Further, by recognising the validity of the GS to give effect to these rights, this Act has great synergy with PESA's provisions. However, continuing bureaucratic control, resistant attitudes of the Forest Department (FD) officials to give ownership to communities, and inadequate efforts at awareness have led to the slow implementation of the Act. The law lays down a clear three-stage process for the recognition of the people's rights. It also defines what constitutes admissible evidence. The FD has a role at the district and sub-divisional levels, but only as one of the parties involved, without any 'decision-making' or 'veto' powers. However, the FD has made every effort to give itself illegal veto powers to deny rights. In most states, the department is refusing to be present at the time of verification by the Forest Rights Committee, and then demanding that the claim be rejected at the screening stage as they did not attend.

The Forest Rights Act requires that all rights be recognised through a transparent, public process, where the GS or village assembly is central. Instead of following that process, government officers have been seen imposing their own diktats. GS are being deliberately called at the Panchayat level or even larger units in Andhra Pradesh, Chhattisgarh and elsewhere – where they are too large for the Adivasis and forest dwellers to have their voices heard. This is in direct violation of the Act.[6]

Class Differentiations in Adivasi Society

With the growing socio-economic differentiation within and across Adivasi communities, marked by the growth of rural elites within them,[7] there is also an exclusion of those who are poorer or whose voice is weaker. These elite within the Adivasi society have benefited by the government's spending by becoming the voice of their respective community and acquiring the role of middle men. This arrangement is convenient for the political class and the bureaucracy, as also, many a times, aligned to the extremists.

LWE and PESA Areas

Out of total 108 PESA districts, 42 districts are LWE affected.[8] While the senior leadership of the party is mostly drawn from non-tribal communities, most of the rank and file are Adivasis, hailing from local villages. The extremist movement has built on the grievances emanating from the non-implementation of PESA.Some analysts consider the resurgence and spread of LWE as a phenomenon of tribal self-assertion. They point to the co-incidence in the rise of economic reforms and the deepening of the Maoist movement. As per a senior politician, "PESA has not yet been honestly implemented in a single district yet. If it were, we would have solved the Naxal problem".[9]

Recommendations Towards Enabling PESA

Participatory Decision-Making

Displacement, as well as loss of access to forest and water resources because of mining and industry, are urgent threats not just to local livelihoods, but also to notions of democratic and fair governance in PESA areas. There have been demands by the people's organisations that the discussion on it be accompanied by a White Paper on displacement, in particular in the Vth Schedule areas. Other views from the ground have even suggested that a moratorium on acquisition and involuntary displacement in PESA areas be declared, till there is an analysis of the costs and benefits that have accrued to the tribal communities through the process of industrialisation. Till such exercises happen, the efforts should be to make the processes of change participatory, rather than violative.

The MoUs signed by the state governments with industrial houses, including mining companies should be reexamined in a public exercise, with the affected GS at the centre of this enquiry.

Environmental Concerns

The Environmental Impact Assessment (EIA) stage of a proposed industrial or mining project is critical in the fate of a tribal community given the possible consequences of such projects – from complete displacement to irreversible ecological damage. But the manner of carrying out the EIA runs contrary to the provisions of PESA read together with the Scheduled Tribes and Other Forest Dwellers Recognition of Forest Rights Act. That both are Acts of the Indian Parliament and the former is meant to supersede any legislation that is not in consonance with it, requires recognition and reiteration. In order to make this devolution meaningful, each state with PESA areas should set up a panel of environmental experts whose services should be available to the GS in the process of giving consent to or dissenting against a project. Details of the panel members should be widely publicised and made known to all the GS in the PESA areas.

Democratic Activism

PESA's principal contribution lies in supplying an institutional mechanism for addressing issues and conflict resolution through an open, transparent and deliberative manner. However, due to its failure in implementation at the ground level, conflicts get compounded, creating fertile ground for alternative mobilisations. The retrieval of the democratic space through the operation of the institutional mechanisms mandated by PESA is an absolute necessity for other developmental implications of PESA to find fuller expression. To ensure that the GS actually meets and becomes a vibrant force of participatory democracy, there is a need to facilitate this process by forming a dedicated cadre of social mobilisers at each GP level. They should also be involved in spreading greater awareness of laws such as PESA and various flagship programmes of the government. Civil society organisations, political parties and NGOs can play a decisive role in this context.

Aggressive Development: A Bane

Through the past years, some sections of the government have stated that the PESA areas will see "an injection of speedy and aggressive development". However, this approach suggests continuing bureaucratic control and ignores the principles of self-governance and community control over resources, as enshrined in PESA. In the current context of the people's mistrust of the state, the term 'aggressive development' needs to be abandoned, and if not, then clearly defined for the consent of the community. Through devolution to the GS, a model of participatory and community-centric development should be nurtured, as opposed to 'aggressive development' from above. In the words of one analyst, "welfare schemes are important, but taken alone, they do not complete our transformation from subjects to citizens. There is no way of having genuinely inclusive governance in rural India without strengthening the PRIs".[10]

Face-to-Face Community Administration

One major impediment in operationalising PESA is the absence of the proper administrative definition of the village that is in consonance with the Act. All the states, without exception, have continued with their earlier revenue definition of the village. Thereby, not only does a village at times consist of 10-12 scattered hamlets, but several revenue villages are clubbed together to form a Gram Panchayat. This effectively precludes the functioning of a 'face-to-face' community administration, as envisaged in PESA.

Traditional Non-Timber Forest Produce (TNTFP)[11]

TNTFP policies have often been aimed at maximising state revenues and not the welfare of the gatherers. To enhance the issue bargaining power of Adivasi collectors, they were organised in Self-Help Groups (SHGs). However, these SHGs could not wield much influence on the terms of the trade for long. Local traders deployed a variety of tactics to ensure that the SHGs were unviable as traders, and gave little additional value to collectors through aggregation and collective bargaining. In some cases where the SHGs were persistent, the traders, through unscrupulous practices, ensured that these SHGs lost credit amongst their members. There is a need to visualise a new and powerful institution in the 'social entrepreneurship' mode to help the primary collectors climb up the value chain and retain more value (the Maoists have often stepped in to provide relief to collectors by ensuring appropriate prices). Such an institution must have the requisite capacity to absorb the inevitable losses in the initial years when it will have to take risks and counter the entrenched trading interests with competitive actions. It is eminently possible to come up with a roadmap to make the NTFP, commercially profitable for primary gatherers, ably supported by the compliance of PESA by the tribal society.

Institutionalised Mechanism of Conflict Resolution[12]

There is also a need to facilitate creation of an institutional mechanism of conflict resolution – of the kind that exists across the world in countries that have faced conflicts over use of natural resources, especially in the context of indigenous people. A conflict resolution framework designed to suit our specific circumstances would help mitigate conflicts before they reach a point of no return. By creating a win-win scenario for all the stakeholders concerned, conflicts that become breeding grounds for Maoism can thereby be taken care of. Enactment of PESA shall have a major role to play in the proceedings, since the ownership of consent, as far as the local population is concerned, shall lie with the GS and for the reason that the nature of challenge that the sub-components of LWE pose, varies from region to region.

Notes

1. Ajay Dandekar and Chitrangada Choudhary, "PESA, LWE and Governance: Concerns and Challenges in India's Tribal Districts", IRMA Report, Ministry of Panchayati Raj, 2010.
2. Ibid.
3. Government of Jharkhand , 'List of MoUs Signed for Mega Investment', 2008, http://www.jharkhandonline.gov.in/DEPTDOCUUPLOAD/uploads/13/D200813070.pdf, IANS, "Chhattisgarh Needs 52,800 Acres for Industry", March 23, 2010.
4. Ashutosh Bhardwaj, "The Bastar Tragedy, Farce – Truth is the First Casualty in This War", *The Indian Express*, April 21, 2016.
5. http://www.samataindia.org.in/documents/SAMATA_EDIT1.PDF
6. Ibid.
7. Alpa Shah, "Shadowy Practices – Development As Corruption", *In the Shadows of the State-Indigenous Politics, Environmentalism, and Insurgency in Jharkhand, India* (OUP, 2010).
8. Lok Sabha Unstarred Question No. +5525, Answered by MoS, MHA, Sh. Haribhai Parathibhai Choudhary, April 28, 2016, http://mha1.nic.in/par2013/par2015-pdfs/ls-280415/5525.pdf
9. Digvijay Singh, "In Conversation with Mani Shankar Aiyar on Pachayati Raj", UTV Bloomberg, November 2009.
10. PB Mehta, "Subjects to Citizens", *The Indian Express*, July 16, 2009.
11. 12th Five-Year Plan, Social Sectors, Vol. III, Planning Commission, 2014, GoI.
12. Ibid.

5. THE SORDID SAGA OF DISPLACEMENT

When people are displaced in the national interest, the usual argument is that someone has to pay for the larger good. That 'someone,' however, is always the rural or urban poor or the tribal, and the notion of 'national interest' is at times extremely vague. Contrary to the common perception that a project displaces the 'few' and benefits the 'many', the cumulative picture since independence is somewhat sombre.

The 29th report of the Commissioner for SCs and STs published in 1989 says, "...whereas tribal people constitute 7.5 per cent of the population in India, more than 40 percent of those displaced are tribals". Roughly one in every ten Indian tribals is displaced. In some projects, tribals account for more than 80 per cent of the displaced. Walter Fernandes estimates that tribals may account for about 59 per cent of the displaced.[1]

Despite its conservative estimate, the Planning Commission in its mid-term appraisal report of 2000 says that development projects have displaced 25 million people since 1950, of whom 40 per cent have been tribals. Less than half of them have been rehabilitated; the rest have been pauperised by the development process. Those moving out do not get the benefits of the projects. Jagannath Pathy of South Gujarat University points out that though many hydroelectricity projects are located in tribal areas, no more than 5 percent of tribal land is assured of irrigation.[2] Many of them cannot even purchase power. In mineral-rich states like Chhattisgarh, Odisha and Jharkhand, the number of MoUs the government has signed with private companies threatens to displace thousands of people, mostly tribals, who inhabited these regions even before the concept of nation-states had dawned.

Resettlement of people – if at all carried out – tends to be on distant sites in culturally different regions, which brings about its own hardships. Thayer Scudder, who has studied development induced forced relocation in India, claims that there are various cultural, social and psychological stresses that displaced individuals face as a result of the breakdown of their socio-economic way of life. As cultural and biological diversity are closely correlated, the destruction of local ecosystems can often lead to a form of cultural genocide. The resistance also stems from their unwillingness to undertake a forced migration, known to bring a marked fall in social status.

Questioning the Development Model

In our country, mega projects have symbolised the breaking of the colonial chain of underdevelopment. However, from the start, ideological sceptics, including followers of Gandhi, challenged this model of development. This alternative view questioned the model of development that equated progress merely with increased production of goods and services and digits of GDP. It demanded that the human, social and environmental impact of such developmental interventions be carefully assessed. This demand was based on the conviction that much more important than merely how much was produced were questions about what was produced, how it was produced, at what cost, and for whom.

Besides the model of modern progress, the protests have also highlighted the aspirations of indigenous and backward communities with respect to 'development'. In states like Jharkhand, tribal leaders (often in collusion with the Maoists) have challenged the modern altar of development and proposed an almost parallel system of what they call progressive society where all classes and communities will be treated equally. This tussle between living standards, age-old culture and traditions and the way of life imposed upon them after displacement has forced them to take up cudgels against the state. They are demanding a say in the planning and development process, and measures to address the grave social consequences for the disadvantaged.

The protests over evictions initially took up the issue of resettlement. But in the mid-1990s, the protests began to challenge the development model, its economic benefits and social repercussions such as displacement, in a wider perspective. These protests question the presumption that displacement is inevitable, that the location of any large project or plant is purely a technical outcome of factors relating to topography and the resource potential of the region. The data shows that displacement has affected the country's tribal and rural poor more than any other section of the population. The disproportionately heavy burden of forced migration placed on the shoulders of the most vulnerable sections suggests that development and displacement are not merely technical and politically neutral decisions. Instead, they are sacrifices imposed on the weak by the economically, socially and politically strong classes. Protest, therefore, is the only resort, often leading to a protracted resistance to the state.

Displacement, Rehabilitation and Resettlement: The Way Ahead?

At the heart of any development project entailing large scale displacement must ideally be a commitment to avoid, or at least minimise, evictions. This must be the focus of developmental policies that follow the acquisition of land. In order to do this, the onus is on the government to prove and justify that 'alternative public purpose' and 'less displacing options' are not available in the first place, calling, in turn, for transparency. Unfortunately, the 'would be' oustees are the last to know about the projects that evict them. It is rare for the potential oustees to be consulted in the planning stages, though one would expect that they would be kept informed about the project and their eviction. Bureaucratic lassitude keeps them in the dark about the phasing of rehabilitation and resettlement. The contents of the compensation package, entitlements and choices are hardly ever made known to the displaced communities.

Ideally, the planning process must entail a realistic assessment of human and social costs to determine the actual cost-benefit ratios of a project. Planning should not imply manipulating figures to prove that the projects are economically viable; rather it should aim at avoiding misery. A common flaw in the current approach – uprooting people and then trying to relocate them to a new site – is that the decision-making is left to the government and the project authorities, to an extent.[3]

Once the planning process of the projects is over, the rehabilitation packages must simultaneously be worked out. However, this is not done in most cases, even in states like Maharashtra that have better statutes than most as far as rehabilitation goes. This lacuna is a direct consequence of the absence of a national legislation. Currently, it is not legally binding on the government or the respective project authorities to integrate rehabilitation with the project plan.

As some researchers point out, the incremental approach of allowing land acquisition and project construction activities to proceed parallel to displacement and rehabilitation has led to ad hoc, and project by project, minimal rehabilitation. Generally, the official stand is that relocation itself is rehabilitation, if at all it is carried out. The cash component of the compensation aside, rehabilitation currently does not so much mention livelihood options for the displaced. Add to this, the scanty budgetary provisions made for rehabilitation. Every project, without exception, reflects the same story of official neglect and abdication of responsibility towards the rehabilitation of the evicted people.

Irrespective of the money granted as compensation, the same always remains undervalued, being premised on the current and not the end value of the land (after the fructification of the intended project), leading to resentment and dissatisfaction. The disbursement of compensation does not imply a step forward in resettlement. What it does mean is that middlemen – from land acquisition officers to tehsildars and patwaris – materialise to take cuts in the compensation doles. In the tribal areas where the oustees are predominantly illiterate, cases of corruption in the distribution of compensation abound. Studies have shown that lack of knowledge about their legal rights leaves the displaced vulnerable to cheating and fraud.

Disbursement of compensation is not without its own problems. The common practice is to compensate a displaced family for the fixed assets it loses, such as land. As mentioned earlier, the calculations are done on the basis of prevailing market rates, as against the value of the land after project implementation. The prevailing rates are calculated as an average of the registered sale prices of land of similar quality and location in the preceding three or five years. It is an open secret that in our country, most land transactions are undervalued to evade registration fees. An oustee, therefore, is offered a rate much lower than the market price. In the scheduled areas, the problem is compounded by the fact that the law restricts the sale of land by tribals to non-tribals, leading to further reduction of the market price of land and, thereby, the compensation. Also, the landless do not get compensated unless they fight for their rights.

Another phenomenon that has been noticed is that land prices around project sites shoot up sharply because of the enhanced demand for land. Thus, the compensation received by the oustees does not help them to purchase similar cultivable land elsewhere. The government could play a role; in that it could help the oustees procure alternative land at a cheaper price, say by enacting a legislation that gives them concessions. It could revamp the process of distribution of compensation in order to end red-tapism and check corruption. There is great scope for enhancing compensation measures, because, as things stand today, expenditure on rehabilitation is much lower compared to the actual project costs.

Additionally, if revenue records are maintained and updated properly by the patwari, it would ensure that the compensation process is streamlined. This would also make tenants, sharecroppers, farm labourers and artisans eligible to receive compensation. These are the most vulnerable sections of the displaced: people who cannot furnish legal titles to claim compensation. The value of land and the interest on it, calculated on the date of the gazette notification, is liable to be paid only from the date of taking possession up to the date of payment of full compensation. The government does not consider escalation of the market price of land between the time of notification and the date of actual possession.

Once the displaced get compensated, their lack of experience in handling big sums of money proves dangerous – they are susceptible to be exploited by fraudulent banks and middlemen. The evacuees buy material goods instead of investing the money in future needs. This is a typical problem: the displaced suffer irrevocable destitution and penury as they squander in months, weeks or even days what could have been their security for the rest of their lives.

The absence of a comprehensive rehabilitation plan, the undervalued compensation amount and the inability to negotiate the market economy together pose serious hurdles to the oustees in securing alternative cultivable land. Since switching over to other avenues of livelihood is often difficult – and the government is aware of this – the cash compensation tends to end up being used as a temporary means of subsistence. Land as compensation, has been suggested in the National Relief and Rehabilitation Policy, 2007 – the same needs to be strictly followed to allay the dissatisfaction which is more than genuine. However, since it is a shrinking resource, the track record of land for land compensation is dismal. Under the existing statutes, it is not legally a binding condition for the government .

Unnecessary delay in the rehabilitation of the displaced could be avoided if the resettlement proceeds simultaneously with the project. Finally, when the rehabilitation is done, the resettlement sites are often found to be inhospitable in a number of ways. The locations are chosen in such a way that the oustees fail to find alternatives of livelihood there. Little effort is made to recreate the lost habitats; the emphasis is more on building structures not of a significant nature. In the wake of reluctance to adopt and operationalise a land for land policy, the challenge for the project authorities and state governments under pressure to rehabilitate oustees is to find non-agricultural livelihoods. Most states have failed to foster successful strategies to offer employment options to the oustees and, resultantly, the stress is more on giving cash compensation[4].

Another frequently neglected problem is the opposition of host populations to the oustees resettled in their villages. A case in point is the typical and closed nature of tribal societies that have lived in harmony with nature in their respective habitations. Relocation hampers the way of life of these people and wedges in a deep sense of insecurity, when they move out of the lands where they and their ancestors were born – making them vulnerable. Rampant adjustment challenges on the part of the oustees and host population prevail, leading to frictions that often flare up, as also provide a fertile ground for anti-national elements to tap on. The disoriented and unsettled displaced people are always in a disadvantageous position in such conflicts because they are termed as outsiders. Their economic fragility weakens them further.

Anomalies of this kind are deep-rooted in the functioning of the government,not simply because of the lackadaisical approach of those who run it, but also because of the long legacy of colonial laws that abet arbitrary decision-making and unequal sharing of the benefits of development; always uprooting the poor, never the rich.A growth model that listens to people who live on the lands that are targeted shall have to be evolved, on the issues of what they need and want from the growth. It would entail taking democracy very seriously. If this is accepted, the protests have to be seen in a new light. There are no Maoists holding up Vedanta in Odisha or the Tatas in Chhattisgarh. These mutinies will have to be carefully heard. Our democracy, in which we take pride, cannot afford to brush aside the people's concerns, in the name of a 'considered' decision taken in Delhi or in the state capital. Once we accept the local veto over development decisions, the tough part begins. For, this means seriously engaging with people to find ways that benefit all. It means sharing revenue from the minerals with the villagers, changing priorities, empowering local governance, implementing constitutional provisions, etc.

Notes

1. Walter Fernandes, "Power and Powerless: Development Projects and Displacements of Tribals", *Social Action*, Vol. 41, 1991.
2. P Sainath, *Everybody Loves a Good Drought* (New Delhi: Penguin Books India, 1996).
3. Jaideep Hardikar, *Evading Responsibilities, A Village Awaits Doomsday* (Penguin Books, 2013).
4. Ibid.

6. TRIBAL RESURGENCE: TIME TO RESET PERSPECTIVE

The New Stage of Maoist Insurgency

Our elite's understanding of the Maoist movement lags far behind the unfolding historical process on the ground. Many scholars and former civil servants have indeed tried to present fresh insights to take this discussion forward, but, unfortunately, they, at best, plead for greater sympathy for the tribals and better governance by the state agencies. At the same time, the dominant voices in the government, political parties and media continue to insist on more effective security measures to liquidate the rebels. Such policies, over the last so many years, have failed to bring peace and contain the violence. There are three trends in the politics of the Maoists movement in contemporary India which have still not been acknowledged by the state agencies and most analysts.

Firstly, during the past decade and more, the Maoists have been far more involved in the big mass movement issues of land, forest rights and basic civil liberties of tribal people and peasants rather than the traditional programmes of armed struggle against class enemies such as landlords in specific areas. In spite of being committed to the seizure of state power and pursuing an anti-feudal and anti-colonial revolution, they had come to realise that such struggles had to be carried out concretely through people's movements on issues that directly affected their everyday life and those that they were taking up on their own or through other political and social movements.

A few decades ago, these could be regarded as less important priorities or even reformist. But the onslaught of an overdrive measure towards state forced development, which was materially felt by people in the course of the massive initiatives of the state and the corporates to exploit the mining and forest resources, created a new situation. As has been brought out earlier, this caused extensive displacement and loss of livelihoods, accompanied by high-handedness on the part of the state to facilitate this process.

In Jharkhand, Chhattisgarh and Odisha, social and political movements against displacements caused by mining and related industries, predated the political arrival of the Maoists. Such resistance movements were led by Gandhian, socialist, environmental, tribal rights groups, etc, to defend the local people's rights. The democratic space was largely used to protest against state policies. The twin developments of state coercion and announcement with mega mining projects, often without consultation with the local population, made the Maoists pitch in as saviours of the tribals. State action to treat the movements of the local people as a law and order issue made matters worse. In many areas such as Narayanpatna in Koraput, when a peaceful movement demanding restoration of the tribal people's land as per the law was subjected to repression, many of the tribal activists sought the support of the Maoists or the Maoists pitched in, taking advantage of the situation. Over the past two decades, the pattern in the tribal areas has been that of a 'state backed' and often non-transparent corporate acquisition of natural resources, that has emerged as the central issue. The above was compounded by the prevalent (historical) alienation that the tribals have gone through for ages.

Given the situation, development initiatives by government agencies through the employment and health schemes such as Mahatma Gandhi National Rural Employment Guarantee Act (MGNREGA), National Rural Health Missiion (NRHM), Integrated Action Plan (IAP), etc have hardly been effective, as far as their pace is concerned. There are enough agencies in the affected areas, including the Maoists, who benefit from such projects, financially as also by not letting these materialise. Also, while such initiatives by the government are getting vigorous, the Maoists too have endeavoured to expand to new areas with new recruits. The reasons being that the Adivasis and peasants have come to question the development strategy of the Indian state and are engaged in defending their rights over land and natural resources. But their struggle is for their right to define their own development path and not be victims of an imposed path of corporate globalisation.

No doubt, laws had been made to empower the tribal villages under PESA to decide on the location of projects, and the FRA did provide many substantive land and forest rights to the tribals. However, the implementation of these on the ground has been a challenge, as was brought out earlier. Also, these concessions were overwhelmed by the major industrialisation drive under globalisation. This is what is being challenged by the mobilised spectrum of the vast tribal and rural population.

To meet the challenge of unmet tribal rights, the current industrialisation strategy must be opened up for reconsideration and only then there may be some possibility of winning the confidence of the people in the movement areas. The trust of the people in the states has to be developed by continuous engagement, and civil society can play a significant role in this regard.

Secondly, as per the trends of the conditions in the movement areas, the Maoist movement remained a pre-organisational movement from the Naxalbari uprising in 1967 till the early 1990s, with many groups in different areas operating along diverse strategic and tactical lines. The Maoist movement during this phase derived its strength mainly from its ideology of anti-feudal, anti-colonial revolution which had a material basis in the contradictions of the agrarian economy and the structure of India.

Therefore, with the ideology and its spread over different regions, the movement lived on, despite the state pressures, since it coincided with the existing socio-economic paradigm that affected the man at the grassroots—the village poor. During the late 1990s and later, the CPI (M-L) and the PWG made significant advances in organisation building in Andhra Pradesh and Bihar. In 2004, when the formation of the CPI (Maoist) was announced, they had evolved into an organisational movement phase. They now had a Polit Bureau (PB), Central Committee (CC), Regional Committees as also the People's Liberation Guerrilla Army (PLGA), spokespersons, journals, websites and international linkages.

What was noteworthy was that many aspects of the pre-organisational character of the movement persisted even after 2004. These included the dispersed nature of its armed cadres, the autonomy enjoyed by local units, the existence of relationships and the unity of programmes amongst various groups. The movement, thus, combined the strengths of both organised and pre-organised ideological movements. Unless this special situation is comprehended, one cannot understand how the Maoist movement has continued to expand its influence, even after almost 50 years. The social basis of the Maoist ideology was now articulated in very clear terms in the struggle of the Adivasis and peasants, against corporate globalisation.

Thirdly, there has been a growing and widespread consciousness amongst the common people everywhere that they are entitled to certain human rights which no one can deprive them of. As the people's consciousness about their rights the grown and the movements of the Adivasis, Dalits, women, oppressed minorities, etc have carried on with their struggles for their legitimate entitlements and demands, a new state of political awakening has emerged, all across the globe, including in India.

The Constitution of India and some of the important laws and judicial decisions became the 'weapons of the oppressed'. Often, on the basis of such laws, civil liberty groups and civil society organisations approached the judiciary and got some relief in a few cases like the Binayak Sen issue, Salwa Judum, Niyamgiri, etc. The important point to note is that this deepening of human rights and entitlements consciousness in India is being, though slowly, acknowledged by many, including the policy-makers.

Adivasi Awakening and Emergence of New Politics

The rising trend of Adivasi awakening is a defining characteristic of contemporary India. There is an unprecedented scale of assertion of not only of the right to livelihood, but also the right to dignity and the right to selfhood, amongst the Adivasis. The political upsurge in tribal India in defence of right to land and forests reflects this new awakening which is a positive sign of the democratic transformation of modern India, which ironically is not always treated as a positive phenomenon. Instead of making development a fundamental premise to discuss the subject and engage the people, the Adivasi awakening is seen as a disruption of India's growth story.

The new awakening is the cumulative outcome of many historical processes and centuries of struggles against colonial domination, and not the result of the Naxalite movement. In fact, the Maoists have reoriented their politics to respond to this new awakening for their ulterior motives. For one thing, the new level of political consciousness amongst the Adivasis demands a reconsideration of all previous formulations.

It shows the emergence of a new politics that ends the era of treating the Adivasis as objects of welfare and assimilation, and begins an era of treating them as subjects and the agency of self-determination; thereby heralding the comprehensive emancipation of all oppressed people. An acknowledgement of this new phenomenon will lead to a serious indictment of the prevailing state policies despite measures like the FRA. It also calls for the adoption of a fresh outlook on the part of the civil society and academia on politics and development.

Questioning the Perspectives of the State, Civil Society and Academia

Independent India had the clear objective of slow assimilation of the Adivasis into the mainstream society. Nehru's 'Panchsheel' on Adivasi welfare, the reservation of seats for STs in the legislatures and civil services and even the TSP, providing for special allocation of funds in every department of the government, were a part of this overall strategy. The vantage point for the state policies was, thus, one of governance and welfare, ignoring the socio-cultural aspects.

While these welfare measures through the state apparatus and under the provisions of the Vth Schedule were being implemented, the exploitation of forest and mining resources by indigenous and foreign capital persisted. As the years went by, the state strategy failed to cope with the aspirations of the tribal people, who remained poor and marginalised.

The vantage point for the dominant state machinery and civil society was inherited from the colonial state, to treat the Adivasis as poor brethren, deserving special support. The upper caste, mainstream 'brahmanic culture' was projected as the automatic process of acculturation in the history of the Adivasis, just as Western education was promoted as the common goal for all Indians. European colonialism had colonised the non-Western world for what it considered its 'civilising mission'. In the same vein, the non-tribal upper class, the upper class elite of India considered it their duty to be 'civilising the savage' Adivasis. But the days of such patronage seem to be over in the current era of people's rights. Victor Hugo can undoubtedly be invoked in the context—he had said, "Nothing is more powerful than an idea whose time has come", and, indeed, it has.

Even after decades of electoral politics and our glorious democratic legacy, none of the major political parties has either allowed or facilitated the emergence of a significant tribal political leadership capable of influencing national level policy-making. The Adivasi leaders remain the protégés of the upper caste or middle class leaders in the various states. Also, the Adivasis have been rendered voiceless because their numbers, being spread over a large area, do not affect or influence any political outcome. The political system has failed the Adivasis in making their voice critical in national policy-making.

Anthropologists and social scientists generally recognised the dignity of the Adivasis and their customs while engaging in in-depth analysis of the uniqueness of the various tribal groups. While some of the colonial scholars assessed the tribal practices against European civilisational norms, a few others discovered the logic and reasons behind many tribal practices. This section, though a minority, engaged in deeper understanding of the knowledge and environmental philosophy of the Adivasis and argued the case of taking them seriously and with respect, as an alternative system as part of the human civilisation. However, all their strenuous efforts ended up merely being an input into the dominant policy-making of the state. Their work failed to persuade civil society and the state to reexamine its patronising attitude and go beyond its welfare and assimilation strategy.

The operative consequences of these approaches did include many laudable initiatives in independent India, for example:

- Transfer of tribal land to non-tribals was forbidden by the law in practically all the states. But, in practice, massive land transfers continued unabated, circumventing the law.
- The Panchayati Raj system under the 73rd Amendment of the Constitution was extended under the PESA Act, 1996, but its very important provisions were hardly implemented or were manipulated to suit the state or the corporate interests. Not a single state has notified the conceptualised PESA Act, so far.
- FRA, 2006, was another major step to restore the rights to land and forests to the tribals and other forest dwellers. The implementation has so far been tardy and attempts are continuously being made to dilute the provisions.
- The developmental policies to include education and health did make special provisions for the Adivasis, with positive consequences. But the basic social indicators show vast disparity between the Adivasis and Dalits, on the one hand, and the rest of the society, on the other.

Thus, on the whole, as a result of these approaches and policies, the Adivasis remained the victims of cumulative deprivation in contemporary India.

Adivasi Swaraj and the Right to Earth

If seen as separate from the Maoists' machinations, in recent times, all the Adivasi movements – Niyamgiri, Jagatsinghpur (POSCO), Kalinganagar, Lanjigarh, etc – were peaceful democratic struggles by the local tribal population. Other than the aspects of Maoists exploiting the alienation and unrest, it may be mentioned that even though all such movements started as protest movements against specific projects, they grew into movements raising fundamental issues of the development strategy, of the consequences of globalisation for the marginalised sections, and the larger human rights issues of self-determination. Along with this, there emerged a transformation towards the 'rightful' demand of a new right – the 'Right to Earth'.

The people's movements in the Adivasi areas affirmed the rights of the Adivasis to exercise control over their land and other natural and cultural resources, and share it with others only on mutually agreed terms. The entire philosophy underlying the anti-colonial struggle was indeed this. Extending Gandhi's concept of Swaraj, one can suggest that this is the right which can fulfill the urges of self-realisation of the people in an area, including the Adivasi region. It is recognition of this right that led to the provision in the PESA that without consultation with GS, no land could be acquired in a village, in a scheduled area – for any project.

The provisions have been violated, with government officials, FD personnel, etc often forcing, manipulating and sabotaging such meetings. For instance, in the case of the POSCO project in Jagatsinghpura, two GS had clearly decreed against the project, yet the government succeeded in meeting the formal requirement by manipulating the process and was determined to go ahead with the project. The POSCO Pratirodh Samiti, however, persisted with its strong mobilisation and the project stands stranded as of now. Similar has been the saga of the Niyamgiri mining project.

'Right to Earth' is not just a narrow defence of local rights to land, but is a defining right to evolve a mode of transformation and manage it according to the interests of the locals. No doubt, the local community has to be transformed at the same time, so that the heirarchical structure of the village does not perpetuate existing inequalities, as was the scepticism of Ambedkar.

The unrest in the tribal areas, when seen separated from the Maoists' movement, brings out the following drivers of the conflict, pointing to an Adivasi Swaraj:

- The Naxalites have adjusted their strategy in the light of the local conditions.
- Adivasi awakening challenged the developmental paradigm in totality and not merely its capitalist class character—that the process and pace of change has to be decided by the local Adivasis, in conformity with their socio-economic and political goals, environmental philosophy and culture. This is far broader than the Marxist understanding of the proletariat or Mao's United Front (peasant-workers) movements.
- The totality of the Adivasis' struggle tradition may include armed struggle, but does not ignore the vast areas of open democratic, political, economic, social and cultural struggle. They have inherited the great civilisational legacies of the Adivasi civilisation, the positive elements of which they must preserve and develop. The knowledge system of the Adivasis deserves as much respect as any other knowledge system.
- The perspective on the relationship between humans and nature which gives rise to a host of environmental questions is yet another dimension of Adivasi awakening.
- Yet another emerging phenomenon is that there are local systems of religious beliefs other than the major religions of the world. Many Adivasis are listing themselves as members of their local religious community, rather than the recognised mainstream religions.

Thus, the Adivasi Swaraj raises a number of issues which are equally significant for the democratic transformation of Indian society as a whole. Political movements need to espouse the Adivasi cause and these movements can enrich themselves by fully integrating themselves with this process of Adivasi awakening, and participate in the new politics of the people's democratic revolution of the present times. The state, civil society and academia can find liberative possibilities if they recognise the full magnitude of the evolving process of Adivasi resurgence, which is much more than merely a violent challenge to authority.

Concluding Recommendations vis-à-vis the Tribal Narrative

The Maoists want a military conflict as it brings more Adivasis into their fold. Also, as often stated by male members of the party's non-Adivasi leadership, the polarising hardships created by military conflict are desirable since they hold the opportunity of swelling the party's ranks.

The state's best bet is in ensuring that it wins over the Adivasis to its side. By solely concentrating on Adivasi empowerment, much of the wind can be taken out of the Maoists' sail. We ought to acknowledge the routine stymieing of democracy and governance in Adivasi India—the context that nurtures the current *avataar* of the five-decade-old rebellion. If the Indian establishment wishes to counter the violent challenge of the Maoists in the long run, it cannot sidestep a hard look at why it stands so discredited in the Adivasis' eyes across central and eastern India. The state must also act to uphold and defend democratic values in numerous Adivasi blocks where the Maoists do not challenge the writ of the state.

Fast-Track the Forest Rights Act

From the Adivasi perspective, the 2006 Forest Rights Act (FRA) was arguably the most meaningful legislation of independent India. It overturned the colonial notions of the state as the owner of the forest, and recognised the Adivasis and other forest-inhabitants as rightful cultivators of forest produce and key actors in forest conservation. But the states have been reluctant to cede control—as per the government 's latest status report (April 2013), under 50 percent of land title claims filed by villagers in Chhattisgarh, Jharkhand, Maharashtra and Odisha have resulted in titles. On the ground, this translates into deliberate neglect. In a mid-May interview with one of the columnists, residents of a Gond village in Odisha's forested coal belt said they had filed FRA claims in 2010 but there was no administrative action to process them. Instead, forest officials had been making rounds of the village with officials of a private mining company. The other important aspect of the law—giving Adivasi communities the right to market their forest produce—has been implemented in only a handful of villages across India.[1]

Stop Criminalising Legitimate Spaces of Expression and Protest

A wide spectrum of non-violent Adivasi movements today exists on the ground, agitating on multiple issues, including forced displacement, the loss of access to natural resources, the absence of meaningful economic and social rehabilitation, below-minimum wages, indebtedness, etc. Many of these struggles get little public or media attention. The state's common reaction is to unwelcome such resistance. This scuttles the democratic space and prepares the ground for the violent elements like the Naxals to step in and highjack the movement.

Attention to Justice

The criminal justice system as it exists today is loaded against the Adivasi. On the one hand, there is little recognition for crimes—from police atrocities to cheating and forced displacement—committed against the Adivasi. In the state's exuberance to control the Maoist menace, the Adivasis are routinely picked up and imprisoned, spending years in a hostile system they can make little sense of. Court proceedings often take place in a language they do not understand, the official legal aid system takes little interest in them, and private lawyers who can get them bail are beyond their reach. There is a need to undertake a dedicated review of Adivasi undertrials, and act on its findings, to create a distinctive legal aid programme for Adivasis with funds from the TSP budget and to institute criminal charges on Adivasi complaints. The criminal justice system vis-à-vis the LWE challenge and related aspects of alienation of Adivasis is discussed in detail, subsequently.

Hold Businesses Accountable

Among the leading violators of human rights in India's Adivasi belt are businesses, in particular mining corporations that have made an unparalleled entry into these areas over the past decade. This presence will only expand in the coming years, but there is alarmingly little attention by the state on the profound implications of this for the vulnerable communities on the ground. Corporate misdemeanours range from intimidating the GS, falsifying records, fixing public hearings, nurturing land speculation and alienation, bribing politicians, the bureaucracy and the district media to facilitate violations, sapping natural resources, including groundwater, and polluting, without any notion of having to pay for it. All of these are open secrets through various levels of government. Yet a blind eye is turned since the consequences of these violations are primarily borne by the Adivasis. Businesses operating in Adivasi areas need to be held accountable to a code of conduct, with clear principles of responsibility and accountability.

Address the Policy Collision Between Mining and Adivasi Rights

There is a nascent but overdue debate within the government on how mining in its current form is incompatible with the constitutional provisions for the Adivasis. V Kishore Chandra Deo, the most engaged Tribal Affairs Minister India has seen in a long time, has repeatedly pointed to the crisis of confidence and trust in Adivasi areas that mining is causing. He took this position most strongly in a letter on April 04, 2013, to the Governors of all Adivasi populated states, men of power who have routinely ignored their constitutional mandate of ensuring 'peace and good governance' in Adivasi areas. Deo's concerns over mining have been publicly seconded by his colleague Jairam Ramesh. What is the larger strategic plan for our mineral resources and where might we draw the line on the social and economic costs that, Adivasis bear for our extractive industries? These are the questions that need to be answered in an honest spirit.[2]

Don't Patronise the Adivasi

The Adivasis are not our 'backward' siblings but full and equal citizens confronted with, and living through, enormous inequality and injustice. It needs to be recognised that Adivasi societies are home to deep and distinctive traditions, which add to the diversity that India takes pride in. They also possess an evolved ecological awareness, acquired over generations of managing their environments and livelihoods— knowledge systems that arguably rival those of the most celebrated "development experts". If the rest of India had the humility to listen, the Adivasi communities could gave valuable policy insights on how we could avoid replicating the fate of China, which has gravely damaged its environment on the path to economic progress. The Adivasis don't have to be looked down upon for "staying aloof from the mainstream of modern society".[3] The fundamental issue seeking resolution is not Adivasi difference, but mitigating the inequality and injustice that compromise democratic values for them at every turn.

The Maoists have occupied the space left by the government, to exploit the tribals for their ulterior motives. Maoism cannot be termed as a tribal movement; the tribals came in, much before the Maoists, in terms of time. It is a matter of sinister irony that Maoists guns were needed for the government to wake up to the formidable 'developmental challenges' in the tribal areas. However, the tribals are caught between the vicious war between the state and the Maoists and require to be bailed out – for the *Maoists' intentions are to be defeated and, tribal aspirations are to be nurtured.*

Notes

1. Chitrangada Chowdhary and Ajay Dandekar, "The Exclusive Adivasi Challenge", *Outlook,* June 23, 2013.
2. Ibid.
3. Ibid.

SECTION TWO
Sustenance of the Rebellion

7. MAOISTS' ORGANISATIONAL SET-UP

Over the past decade or so, the Maoists have evolved from a motley outfit of rebels into a well organised insurgent group. Even if there is no strictly defined structure, it is a very efficient set-up that is capable of sustaining itself by means of a well oiled undeground machinery that caters for a highly complex system of recruitment, training and logistics. Indeed, provisioning of arms, ammunition, clothing, food, medicines, communications, intelligence and printing and distribution of propaganda material, in order to manage between 11,000 to 14,000 armed cadres over nearly one-seventh of the country, covering the most underdeveloped areas, in complete secrecy, is no mean managerial undertaking.

The CPI (Maoist) is headed by its General Secretary, Muppala Lakshmana Rao alias Ganapathy[1]. The outfit's organisational structure is hierarchical. At the apex is the all-powerful Central Committee (CC). As of January 2014, it is believed that the CC consists of 17 members. A smaller core group of seven people constitute the Polit Bureau (PB), which is at the apex of the entire structure.

The Regional Bureau (RB)—a conglomerate of areas in different states— reports to the CC. The State Committee (SC) and its equivalent Special Zone Committee (SZC) report to the RB. Each SC / SZC is responsible for all activities of the outfit within its jurisdiction. Each state is further divided into zones and sub-zones, below which are District Committees / Division Committees (DCs/DVCs). Below the district / dsivision level, there are Squad Area Committees (SACs), which are responsible for activities within a cluster of villages in which the guerrilla squad operates. A village/town cell is at the bottom of the hierarchy.

In tune with the Communist practice and their stated goals, the executive arm of the rebellion is structured around the party leadership and its armed wing that is manned by the hardcore cadres of the People's Liberation Guerrilla Army (PLGA). Proclaimed as raised in December 2000, the PLGA consists of young men and women who are drafted either by persuasion to the so-called cause of protecting their society or by conscription; freedom from hunger and a sense of power acting as strong incentives. A seven-member Central Military Commission (CMC) is at the apex of the Maoist military machine, i.e. the PLGA. There is also a Military Commission corresponding to each of the committees mentioned above.

The Maoist propaganda machinery is guided by the Central Propaganda Bureau (CPB), whose members are also members of the CC. The CPB is responsible for dissemination of all internal circulars of the CPI (Maoist), as well as distribution of its periodicals with varied publication schedules, such as monthly, half-yearly or annual.

All the major decisions are taken by the CC after a careful assessment of their pros and cons. The CC then leaves it to the individual field-level commanders to plan and execute the decisions. After every major action—an attack on a police station, looting an armoury or killing of an important public person or a well protected security official—a detailed de-briefing is conducted to assess strengths, mistakes and weaknesses and, thus, learn lessons for future tactics.

The CPI (Maoist) gathers intelligence in pursuit of its activities, and has a dedicated intelliegence wing, which was once headed by Patel Sudhakar Reddy and later by Sakhamuri Appa Rao, both of whom were killed in separate encounters with the Andhra Pradesh Police. Also, there is enough indication that, sooner than later, there are plans to institute a Disciplinary Committee[2].

Recruitment and its Drivers

According to Bimal, a Central Committee member, the Maoists have "a party controlled mechanism under which they receive proposals from the locals. After obtaining the consent of the parents of applicants, they forward the proposals to one of our committees. It vets them and takes a final call on whether or not to recruit, based on the person's antecedents, class and disposition towards others in his or her village"[3].

Last known, the armed, underground strength of the CPI (Maoist) was approximately 13,000 fighters, both men and women. Besides, there are an estimated 50,000 overground supporters/ sympathisers[4].

The cadre comprises people from various backgrounds—caste, economic and professional. Thus, the guerrillas include those from STs or Adivasis, SCs or Dalits, Backwards Castes (BCs), and Forward Castes (FCs). According to the Constitution of the CPI (Maoist),[5] there are prescribed norms for granting membership to cadres. People belonging to the working class and agriculture labourers are put on observation, which in Maoist parlance is known as the 'candidature period' before being granted membership.

According to an arrested senior and top leader of the CPI (Maoist), women comprise 40 per cent of the total cadre strength of the Maoists[6]. The cadre composition would depend upon the demography of the state, and is largely representative of the caste composition of that state. Thus, it can be noticed that while BCs form the majority of the cadres in Andhra Pradesh, STs would form the majority in a significantly tribal inhabited state like Chhattisgarh or Jharkhand.

Besides, there have been infrequent reports of children being members of the underground. Though their exact numbers are not known, it is believed that children in Andhra Pradesh, Bihar, Jharkhand, Odisha and Chhattisgarh are involved in the outfit's activities. Largely, they are used for intelligence collection. Known as Bal Sangham, which is a banned organisation in states such as Chhattisgarh and Odisha, its members are not fielded in the fight against the security forces until they reach the age of 17, though they could be admitted upon attaining the age of 16 and accorded "full time" membership[7].

While there have been reports of conscription in the Bastar region of Chhattisgarh,[8] by and large, the recruitment into the rebel fold has been voluntary. Men and women join the underground cadre for a number of reasons. For instance, Suneetha, then of an 'impressionable age', joined the group because she was inspired by a moving song—*O veera vanitha*!—that was sung by a visiting squad in her village. Besides, she was also influenced by her uncle who was a squad member. Also, it is not uncommon for villagers, especially the youth, to get stirred into joining the group after listening to fiery speeches made by local-level squad commanders and leaders against exploitation and oppression by the rich, high-caste landlords, or neglect by the government [9].

Bharati, the wife of Polem Sudarshan Reddy, former Warangal District Committee Secretary (DCS) of the rebels and later DCS of Nizamabad, simply followed her husband's footsteps. After her husband was killed in an encounter with the police, she surrendered in 2003. Similarly, the wife of Anupuram Komaraiah, member of the flagship North Telengana Special Zone Committee (NTSZC), too, followed her husband a few years after he went underground. She, too, later surrendered to the police after Komaraiah was killed in a police encounter[10].

Thus, as there are various reasons for different individuals joining the rebel fold, similarly, there is a variety of reasons for their quitting the outfit. For instance, in the case of Sudhakar mentioned above, he decided to quit the underground after he was taken seriously ill following a malaria attack. He was frustrated as the rebel leadership did not provide him with proper medical treatment, and he was rendered immobile. He had joined for the cause, inspired in good measure by the ideology of the outfit, but soon got disillusioned. This prodded him to leave the underground, after spending 20 years in the rebel ranks, complete his studies, get married and settle down to a peaceful life.

In the case of Bharati and the other woman cadre, she got disillusioned with the outfit and its ideology after her husband was killed in an encounter with the police. So, she decided to quit. Also, in a good number of cases, the male cadre (husband) is constantly persuaded by the female cadre (wife) that they should come overground and lead a normal life[11].

Then there is hard core of unarmed cadres scattered in villages and towns, living routine lives while undertaking intelligence, propaganda, logistics and financial management tasks, off and on as a second occupation. The unarmed hard core cadres who lead a double life within the society are said to be numbering close to 50,000 or so[12].

These estimations of the Maoists' strength are just conjectures since there is much joining in and dropping out from a rebellion so decentralised and fluid. Also, there are the vast multitudes of 'supporters' and 'sympathisers' who pitch in with occasional and odd jobs while maintaining a healthy distance from the Maoists as well as the police. Finally, in the periphery of the rebellion structure are the supporters who assist the organisation according to their trade or skill, when called for.

There is much migration among these three tiers and also frequent dropouts, so it is difficult to specify the numbers – it is generally believed that out of 11,000 to 14,000 armed and waiting to be armed, 3,000 are armed cadres who are deployed with the party's political set-up at various levels in groups of 15 to 25. Known as 'Jan Militia', these cadres provide the muscle needed to enforce the Maoist diktats, including abduction, extortion, murder, and so on.[13] The rest of the armed cadres are organised into 'sections' or 'squads', and 'platoons', as part of the PLGA.

The Cadre

The tribals who are brought up in nature's cradle, their way of life being rooted in harmony with the environment, taking from nature only what is required for sustenance – are generally known to be a satisfied lot, until cornered. They abhor anarchy, vandalism or clever manipulations. Presently, however, being at the wrong end of the system and subjected to subtle Maoist brainwashing for decades, they repose not an iota of trust in the state and the 'outsiders' who govern them.

Repeatedly taken for a ride through false offers and promises, and arrogant rejection of their concerns by the state, the depth of mistrust among them is such that even visibly true cases of Maoist high-handedness are summarily laughed off as nothing but concocted propaganda of the manipulative exploiters to distract them. And, importantly, for the state, the vice versa is not happening. It is in this backdrop that it could be said that the biggest motivation for these tribals to go into the Maoists' fold is not ideology of any sort – *per se*.

A candidate or potential recruit has to be sponsored and approved only after detailed scrutiny over his demeanour – a disadvantaged background and some knowledge of Communist ideology helps. Forbidden any form of vice and put under observation, the 'candidature period' for middle peasants, petty bourgeoisie and the urban middle class is one year, whereas those belonging to the other classes have to wait for two years[14]. Also, according to the the Maoists Constitution, rich and upper caste persons are not taken into the rebel fold until they hand over all their property to the outfit.

Once in, the personnel management practices of the Maoists take over to assimilate them into the rebellion. The recruits are put through training under a mentor to develop simple competencies, tested many times, assessed and promoted as per the progress made. On the sidelines, there is a continuous process of socialisation to develop mutual bonding[15].

Leadership

The top spot in the hierarchy is reserved for the ideologues. However, even after the merger of the PWG and the MCC in 2004, no charismatic central leader has emerged. There is, of course, a PB at the national level, of fluid composition and latent formal authority that is tenanted by iconic leaders, in their 50s and 60s, belonging to the old school. These ideologues operate on the borderline of law and lawlessness, propagating a range of complex socio-political theories – much of it out of tune with the times though – to predict certain victory of the proletariat rebellion, formulate strategies from time to time and disseminate the broad directions that the struggle must move towards.

These ideologies find solidarity from many individuals as well as organised groups of genuine social activists and socialist intellectuals who promote varying shades of radical agenda as necessary, to maintain sanity in any society. By purpose or otherwise, many a times, the articulations of these groups go to serve the more sinister aspects of the Maoists' agenda. Then there are individuals and groups who, with relevant convictions but dubious methodologies, tend to make common cause with the insurgent activities and thereby subvert the people's sentiments.

It is pertinent to note that the Maoist ideologues in professing to capture state power, are committed to do so only by the means of 'armed insurrection' – no other method would do. They justify this diabolic single-mindedness by stating that the present unjust and exploitative order cannot be changed by any other means because those who could do so are the ones who are the beneficiaries of this diseased system.

When it comes to justifying the bloodbath and anarchy that must accompany the armed struggle and, consequently, the invariable devastation that the society must suffer for many decades to follow, these ideologues offer no coherent response. They either get agitated or solemn when further pushed to explain as to how, after power has been captured by the armed struggle, the ills and injustices of the present order will be obliterated. The obvious answer, that every change will be brought about by the arbitrary diktats of a rank Communist dictator and enforced through mass elimination of 'class enemies' probably shakes their conscience. The leadership is aware that the world has changed so much that the formulations of the 1920s and 1930s have no place in today's scheme of things. The grave and deep faultlines of their ideology have been dealt with in the subsequent sections of this chapter.

Groups of highly articulate Maoists of proven worth, man committees at the zonal or regional levels, and coordinate the activities in the areas falling under their beat. These leaders manage collection and disbursement of funds, distribution of weapons and other wherewithal, operation of the logistic chain, dissemination of intelligence, and issuance of routine directions. The RCs function in coordination with party cells in towns and cities and are often restructured to maintain cover-up and flexibility, for longevity. The entire middle level executive commanders, the cutting edge leaders, are small town graduates and drop-outs in their early middle age, mostly belonging to Andhra Pradesh, Telangana, Bihar, Odisha and West Bengal.

In another significant development, the tribals, who were earlier unable to fit into the role of frontline leadership at the platoon or dalam levels, are increasingly assuming that responsibility. Many of them have, in a short span of time, assumed a legendary reputation for audacity and cunning while retaining compassion towards their ward. Most middle level leaders are fiercely motivated, however thare are some who may be attracted by power and wealth.[16] Area commanders are the mainstay of the movement. These individuals have good tactical skills and are able to control the insurgent operations more efficiently. These commanders are assisted by platoon and dalam commanders, found to be modest in their proficiency but dutiful to the core.

The leadership of the CPI (Maoist) largely hails from the FC. However, some of the leaders also belong to the BC, SC and ST. Presently, there is no woman member in the CC. Earlier, Sheela Marandi and Anuradha Ghandy were members of the Central Committee. While the former is the wife of Prasanth Bose alias Kishanji, the No. 2 in the outfit and general secretary of the erstwhile MCCI; the latter, now deceased, was the wife of Kobad Ghandy alias Rajan, who headed the Central Propaganda Bureau (CPB) until he was arrested in September 2009 in Delhi and is presently in Tihar jail.

In fact, the CC, as mentioned, is headed by Muppala Lakshmana Rao alias Ganapathy, a *Velama* by caste. Ironically, at that time the then PW—the precursor to the present day CPI (Maoist)—gained popularity because it fought and put to an end the inhumane oppression of the *Velama* landlords *(doras)*. On the other hand, the Maoist military machine is headed by Nambala Kesava Rao alias Basava Raju[17].

The Maoist leadership has consistently denounced parliamentary politics as a sham, and is unflinchingly committed to waging an armed revolution to capture political power. At the same time, the leadership consistently opposes American "imperialism", Indian hegemony in the South Asian region, and the policies of the US-led Brettonwood institutions. It contends that LPG (liberalisation-privatisation- globalisation) has been detrimental to the interests of the Indian agrarian economy.

The CPI (Maoist) leadership is quite authoritarian and takes a serious view of lack of professionalism, indiscipline and loose behaviour / moral conduct. The leadership has not always been cohesive. Ideological differences leading to dissent, personality clashes, professional deficiency and personal weakness are some of the issues that plague the leadership; cohesiveness has not always been easy to achieve. Over 20 months after the merger of the PWG and MCCI, the PB advised the leaders and commanders to achieve complete unity within the ranks and desist from displaying tendencies of being supportive to, or favouring, comrades of their respective erstwhile organisations—PWG or MCCI, as the case may be.[18]

In 2003, Manik, the then West Bengal State Committee Secretary of the erstwhile PWG, quit the organisation owing to differences on the line to be adopted by the outfit. In 2006, there was a vertical split in the Karnataka state unit of the CPI (Maoist), with a majority of the urban cadres, under the leadership of State Committee Secretary Sundaramurthy, quitting the outfit, insisting that the emphasis should be on building the urban movement, rather than focussing on rural areas[19]. Further, in August 2012, Sabyasachi Panda alias Sunil Das, secretary of the Odisha State Organising Committee (OSOC) wrote a scathing letter criticising the highest leadship while resigning from his post and membership of the outfit. The founder of the PWG, Kondapalli Seetharamaiah, was expelled from the organisation as he failed to provide strong leadership and indulged in notorious activities. His wife, Koteswaramma, in an interview[20] to *Hans India*, Hyderabad, bluntly stated that he deserted her for the wife of a guerrilla squad member who was killed in an encounter with the security forces.

On January 02, 2008, Lanka Papi Reddy alias Lachanna, a native of Warangal district, Andhra Pradesh, CC member, surrendered to the authorities in Andhra Pradesh. Lachanna was earlier Secretary of the Dandakaranya SZC (DKSZC) which is considered to be the fiercest guerrilla zone in the country at present. Lachanna surrendered claiming that he was unwell and was disillusioned with the outfit as it was not adhering to the ideological line and principles of the founding fathers. On the other hand, in a scathing attack through a press release, the CC accused Papi Reddy of being individualistic, lacking in discipline and character and misbehaving with a female comrade[21].

The Structure

As mentioned above, the entire territory under the Maoist influence is organised into 'zones' or 'regions' which more or less relate to one or more state boundaries. Zones are further sub-divided into 'regions' and 'areas'. There are also 'special zones' or 'special regions' which are areas fully 'liberated'. These are the areas governed according to Communist principles and, therefore, require special efforts to oversee the various aspects of routine life of the 'liberated' inhabitants, such as matters related to occupation, health, education, state funded schemes, Public Distribution Scheme (PDS), etc.[22] Actually, the governance is confined to the Maoists' impositions on state sponsored schemes and control over public resources and commercial transactions but little else. Obviously, these areas have a larger concentration of the Maoists, where a loose and make believe replica of a 'people's government ' called 'Jantana Sarkar' is run by duly appointed committees – charged with various portfolios like education, health, development, etc.[23]

At the region and area levels, in conformity with the standard Communist practice, the structure stands on the two pillars of 'military' and 'civil' wings. The armed power is treated as an intrinsic part of the political tool and is meant to be used to secure political goals. Subservience of the military wing to the party is absolute while the pitfalls of misunderstanding and rivalry are avoided by incorporating leaders of both the civil and military wings into the decision-making political body, referred to as 'committee'. Accordingly, the committees at various levels are composed of PLGA leaders as well as the civil wing members of the 'party cells'. In other words, at each level, a large number of members are common to both the various committees and commissions (of the commensurate military wing). This arrangement ensures that the PLGA, militia and unarmed hard core, all are strictly under the control of party functionaries.

It is intended that while the PLGA provides the hard power to topple the existing system, the civil wing will create the right environment to bring about the political change. However, in the current stage of the Maoist rebellion in India, there is no formal segregation between the two and the PLGA has not yet emerged as a distict part of the political structure. The division between the PLGA and the civil wing leadership is, therefore, blurred[24].

Committees control the basic units, platoons, dalams or dastas. Though there is no fixed rule as such, a platoon is the armed cadre group forming part of the PLGA, while dalams or dastas refer to the armed militia who shadow the political activities like mass education, fund collection, jan adalats, etc. Thus, it can be said that under the committees at the zonal and area levels, insurgent operations are led by platoons or dalam commanders. Recently, some Maoist commanders have experimented with the creation of PLGA companies, by clubbing a number of platoons, but the trial, reportedly, has not yet succeeded because of limited training amongst the commanders as well as the cadres in managing larger bodies; dividing the operational plans into segments and assigning sub-tasks to separate platoons is still preferred[25].

When it comes to the all-India level, the authority of the intellectual ideologues over the PB is never absolute. The PB and the chain of controlling hierarchy, as reported often, are neither formally structured nor functional at all times and posseses fluid membership. The organisational chain is not sacrosanct – varying from region to region and time to time. Often, the direction from the higher commanders to the area leadership is moulded as per the local situations, for implementation.

It would be not off the mark to infer that interdependency rather than a formal chain of command (as had functioned in the Communist insurgencies in Russia, China and Vietnam) is the basis of hierarchical relationships within the current Maoist structure. This interdependency is manifested in the central and zonal committee level coordination of insurgency operations and propaganda. The aspect of interdependency also plays a crucial role in management of funds and weaponry at the all-India level. In other words, the area and regional commanders are guided by the central hierarchy, but when it comes to the administration and execution of rebel activities, they enjoy complete autonomy. Thus, the Maoists have overcome their inherent organisational weakness by instilling a considerable amount of flexibility. The abovementioned mutual interdependency as against a monolithic structure makes the rebellion a complicated matter to clamp down upon[26]. Also, vis-à-vis the people from different regions joining the Maoist ranks, often the local aspirations vary and, thus, defy unity amongst cadres spread over the wide area of Maoist influence.

Thus, there are nearly a dozen fairly strong parallel factions that operate in smaller areas of their influence and chart their own deviations from the main Maoist agenda. The 'People's Union of Civil Liberties' (PUCL), 'Tritiya Sammelan Prastuti Committee', 'CPI (ML) Liberation', 'Jan Pratirodh Sangharsh Manch', 'Pratirodh Bahini', 'Marxist-Leninist Committee', etc are some of the factions that operate in different parts. While adhering to the Maoist methods of extortion and impositions, these factions adopt locally popular and profitable exceptions in dealing with the people based on the prevalent caste, tribal or class considerations. To some extent, dealing with state institutions such as elections, state sponsored schemes and private enterprises also varies. The lure of controlling the collections also plays a major role towards the varying practices, depending on the respective influence. In general, though all factions avoid presenting a fractured front to the government, the divisions amongst the factions, especially in Jharkhand, have often manifested in a sort of gang war amongst them. Initially, when the state was carved out of Bihar, the state police was poorer in terms of wherewithal and often ended up supporting one faction against the other; a precedence that has led to further deterioration in the present security situation, given the criminalisation of the factions that are more inclined to finances than ideology.[27]

As far as the overall military organisation is concerned, after the merger (in 2004), the Maoists have revamped the CMC. In tandem, they promulgated the creation of two regional commands – Western and Eastern. The creation of these commands is the first step in a deliberate scheme to upgrade the insurgency in intensity as well as spread. Reportedly, the Western Command has been tasked to resuscitate the fledging party cells which have managed to retain their modest existence along the Western Ghats region and in the states of Kerala, Tamil Nadu and Karnataka.

The Maoists have also announced their intent of renewing their efforts through both these commands to expand their areas of clandestine activities as well as area of influence. The announcement also speaks of consolidating the scattered Maoist bases in rural areas into what are referred to as 'guerrilla zones'. This initiative, as per the local interpretations, points to heightened armed actions to expel whatever vestige of the state's presence is there, and in doing so, expand the existing Compact Revolutionary Zones (CRZs) where the Maoists run their so-called parallel government.[28] Under the Regional Commands function the State Military Commissions

(SMCs), which exercise command and control over the PLGA groups in the areas of their operational responsibility. Actually, the SMC is little more than a list of area commanders who actually plan, lead and execute the armed actions.

In line with orthodox Communist practice, the armed cadres are supposedly organised into three: categories; the 'main force' which is the PLGA itself, the 'secondary force' consisting of the 'guerrilla squads' or 'action teams' which assist the party functionaries in enforcing the Maoist diktats; and the 'base force' that refers to the part-time cadres who man the camps or possible intelligence and logistics support from their villages and towns. These distinctions are, however, not overtly apparent and there are frequent revisions of the roles amongst these three categories[29].

Being fluid in composition and somewhat latent in terms of influence on insurgent activities, the Maoist political and military structure does not attract much deliberate discussion among the security establishment. The focus is more on individual leaders rather than on the organisational set-up. This may be a relevant course at the present levels of insurgency. It is felt that the insurgency has not reached the threshold when its organisational structure starts playing a catalytic or force multiplying role. In other words, the insurgency remains guided by individual middle level commanders – notwithstanding the notional overarch of the high sounding political and military bodies. As a corollary, most of the affected state governments consider these organisational structures to be merely the backdrop to the insurgency; a kind of formal heirarchy which remains dormant while the insurgent activities at the ground levels are controlled by individual members in their individual capacities.

Similarly, the PB, the rebel commands and military commissions attract public attention only when the central government now and then announces the adoption of concrete steps to disrupt the insurgents' command and control structure and issues advisories to the states to take concrete counter measures. This situation leads to playing down of the dangers posed; and considering the relative invisibility of the Maoists' purported political and military structure, there is a temptation to undermine the mentioned facet. But close observation reveals that these seemingly fantastic and elaborate structures are gradually and shakily, evolving into reality. It needs to be noted that although the structures discussed above do not have the trappings of formal establishments yet, the purpose of the rebellion as well the operational control and logistic sustenance of the insurgency is being met fairly successfully, more or less. This is no mean achievement for any clandestinely organised armed group that has operateed for decades over such a vast expanse of region. It would, therefore, be wise to take serious note of the rebellion's organisational structure.

Military strategies to deal with the insurgency should be created based on an understanding of the nature of the rebel threat and the structure of the rebel organisations. In a nutshell, the Maoist organisations can be considered to be composed of four elements, organised in concentric circles, with the leaders at the centre bull's eye, operational elements in the second ring, supporters in the third and sympathisers in the fourth. Each has a very different role in the organisation and a different degree of commitment to the cause. Ultimately, neutralising each group will require a different strategy.

The leaders provide direction and serve as a source of inspiration for the group and its followers. They may serve only as the titular heads or may have an operational role as well. Regardless, these are hardened, committed individuals who are not likely to be dissuaded from their activities—they should be hunted down.

The second of the circles is the operational component where the elements responsible for conducting insurgent strikes reside. These individuals may act on the direction of the leaders, get operational support from the parent organisation or may only draw inspiration from the organisational leaders. These operational elements are dedicated individuals, and, like the leaders, are unlikely to be easily persuaded to give up their beliefs or their violent ideology. For such individuals, only pre-attack intervention by intelligence or law enforcement agencies is likely to be effective.

Operational supporters are contained in the third concentric circle. These individuals may have a hand in providing a range of support activities to the operational elements. Such support could include providing money, pre-attack information or accommodation, help with identification documents like passports, or even weapons. The degree of commitment may vary greatly within this group, from highly committed to generally interested in supporting the cause but not willing to actively support, or take part in, any planned violent activity.

The final concentric circle consists of those best described as sympathisers. They take no active part in supporting or executing operations. They have empathy for the cause and may even see an attack as justified in retribution for perceived past injustice. They are part of the rebellion's broader ideological community but are not active participants in any aspect of an attack. Since they are part of that community, though, the people in this group are potentially well-positioned to play an important role in countering terrorist activities — i.e. if they can be persuaded.

The point of dividing terrorist organisations in this manner is to illustrate that the terrorist problem cannot be solved through a set of 'strait-jacketed' measures that treat the four groups as a single entity. Rather, separate strategies must be developed to address each of the components. The goal should be to isolate the supporters and sympathisers from the leaders and operational elements, thus, depriving would-be rebels of important tangible and psychological support.[30] It is only through such a comprehensive and measured strategy that addresses the various components of a terrorist network that the state can effectively deal with the insurgent threat.

Notes

1. Ganapathy is a native of Bheerpur village, Karimnagar district, Andhra Pradesh. A teacher by profession, Ganapathy joined the Naxalite movement in the 1970s, and was second-in-command to Kondapalli Seetharamaiah, the founder of the CPI (ML) (PW), popularly known as the PWG, whom he ousted in 1992, and went on to become the PWG's leader. In 2004, the PWG merged with the Maoist Communist Centre of India (MCCI). The amalgam was christened Communist Party of India (Maoist) or CPI (Maoist).
2. PV Ramana, "Understanding India's Maoists- Select Documents", Introduction, (IDSA, Pentagon Press, 2014).
3. *Mint* (New Delhi), May 29, 2009.
4. Ibid.
5. Ibid.
6. Misir Besra, a member of the Central Military Commission of the CPI (Maoist), while speaking to mediapersons, cited by PV Ramana in his work.
7. See *Hindustan Times* (New Delhi), March 21, 2008; and P V Ramana, "Child Combatants in the People's War Group", accessible at http://www.ipcs.org/nmt_militaryIndex2.jsp?action=showView&kValue=1058&military=1016&status=article&mod=b
8. Ibid.
9. Ibid.
10. He was killed on April 25, 2003, in an encounter with the police in Karimnagar district. Komaraiah was a member of the North Telengana Special Zone Committee (NTSZC). See www.rediff.com/news/2003/apr/26ap.htm
11. Ramana, n.2.
12. Gautam Banerjee, *Impressions: The Maoist Dispensation: Reign of the Red Rebellion* (Lancer, 2013).
13. Namrata Goswami, *Indian National Security and Counterinsurgency: The Use of Force v/s Non Violent Response* (Routledge, 2015).
14. Ibid.
15. Ibid.
16. Ibid.
17. Ibid.
18. Ibid.
19. K Srinivas Reddy, "Karnataka Naxal Movement Splits", *The Hindu*, February 14, 2007. The splinter group termed itself as Maoist Coordination Committee (MCC).
20. See MMA Sarma, "The Eternal Communist", interview with Kondapalli Koteswaramma, wife of Seetharamaiah, *Hans India* (Hyderabad), November 07, 2012.
21. Ibid.
22. The Maoists lay claim over the region they call Dandakaranya (DK)—a vast region with slices taken from five different states – embracing parts of Madhya

Pradesh, Maharashtra, Telangana, Chhattisgarh and Odisha. People of several tribes such as Gond, Madia, Govari, Kondu, Kondareddy, Nayakapu, Dorla, Muria (Koya), and Baiga as well as Odiya tribes of Puruja, Gudijursa, Butar, Durva, etc, live in DK.

23. Ibid.
24. Bannerjee, n.12.
25. Ibid.
26. Ibid.
27. Anumeha Yadav, "In Jharkhand, Armed Groups Backed by the Police to Fight Maoists have Turned on the People", Scroll.in, July 14, 2014.
28. Bannerjee, n.12.
29. Ibid.
30. http://www.rand.org/about/people/g/gerstein_daniel_m.html

8. PROLIFERATION FOR WAR-FIGHTING: WEAPONS, EXPLOSIVES AND FINANCE

The present manifestation of LWE in India is predominantly in the the deprived regions of east-central India. The traction that the Maoists have been able to extract is mainly due to the existing socio-economic depravity, which the Maoists project as a cause that they fight for. And they have done so by projecting their ideology as the backdrop. As has been brought out in the earlier chapters, in 2004, the two main LWE organisations, the PWG and MCC merged to form the CPI (Maoist), with an estimated strength of over 15,000–20,000 armed cadres.

One consequence of the massive escalation of conflict from the late 1980s was a substantial weapons upgrade characterised by massive enhancements in lethality. The Naxals have used landmines on an extensive scale, using the wire-control method, and inflicted heavy losses on the state security forces. The crucial result of this conflict dynamic is a wholesale militarisation of the movement, a major break with the pattern of the late 1970s when they built a considerable base through mass organisations, especially in Telangana. The civil liberties activist K. Balagopal, who saw the movement at close quarters, became progressively more disillusioned as the military perspective took over and reshaped the nature of the PWG. In 2006, a few years before he died, he described the CPI (Maoist) as a "hit and run movement," underlining precisely these features[1].

Between 2011 and 2016 (upto June 30) around 1,568 civilians and 556 security forces personnel have been killed by the

Maoists in different parts of India[2]. The majority of the civilians killed are tribals, often branded as 'police informers' before being brutally tortured and killed. In fact, the tribal and economically under-privileged sections, whose cause the Maoists claim to espouse, have been the main victims of the so-called 'protracted people's war' of the CPI (Maoist) against the Indian state.[3] The CPI (Maoist) has a strategic game-plan to create a 'United Front' with all like-minded insurgent / terrorist outfits in India. It needs to be remembered that many of these outfits are supported by external forces inimical to India and the CPI (Maoist) considers such alliances as strategic assets[4]. The linkages struck, and aspired to, are the prime facilitators of the evolving militarisation of the movement.

Today, the Maoists have an effective presence in 118 districts in 17 Indian states.[5,6*] The strength of the well-armed PLGA is pitched at 9,000 to 12,000 hardcore cadres, grouped into military companies, platoons, and special squads[7]. An organisation with such strength demands huge amount of money to attain its objectives towards 'armed insurrection'. In this chapter, an attempt has been made to explore the arms and explosives network, and financing of the Maoists, given the ideological and organisational background of the movement in its current *avataar*. An endeavour has also been made to put in series the related aspects of linkages that sustain the CPI (Maoist) as a militant outfit, which was termed as the greatest internal security threat by the former Prime Minister[8].

Ideological and Organisational Context to Maoist Militarism

The Marxist–Leninist ideologues have always believed in armed struggle to achieve political power. The emphasis given to militarisation could be gauged from the following extract taken from the founding documents of the CPI (Maoist):

> A military line has to be formulated, corresponding to the correct political line to achieve revolutionary objectives. The military line should be subordinate to the political line. The

> correct military line takes birth in struggle, develops through struggle and takes a clear shape in the course of struggle. In order to completely smash the state machinery of the exploiting classes or for overthrowing it, the building of the people's army as the organized armed force of the masses is indispensable.[9]

The United Communist Party that led the Telengana struggle of 1946-51, did not create a people's army and was strongly criticised for this lapse. This shortcoming was rectified in the Naxalbari uprising of the Sixties, where armed guerrilla squads were raised to lead the revolution. Since then, the military might of the Maoists has grown to a sizeable force and has shaped into the People's Liberation Guerrilla Army (PLGA). Eventually, as the mass base of the PLGA expands to include various sections of society, the Maoists hope to transform the PLGA into a People's Liberation Army (PLA).

The organisational structure of the CPI (Maoist) has already been analysed in the previous chapter. Notwithstanding, in order to contextualise, certain organisational facets of the PLGA are reiterated. A seven-member Central Military Commission (CMC) is at the apex of the PLGA. There is a Military Commission corresponding to each of the committees at the local levels. Besides, there is an overlap between the political and military structures i.e. while there are separate political and military structures, their membership is common in the largest measure, which amplifies the role that the military has in the entire revolutionary concept of the Maoists.[10] The PLGA is the armed organisation to achieve the revolutionary political tasks by preserving its strength and destroying that of the enemy.

The PLGA consists of three types of forces, viz. primary force (platoons), secondary force (guerrilla squads) and base force (people's militia). The people's militia comprises people who otherwise have a vocation in life and are imparted rudimentary military training for barely a fortnight. As regards the significance of the people's militia in the Maoist scheme of things, it is held that the people's militia is at the very foundation of the PLGA. The armed struggle, they believe, cannot be advanced unless the people's militia is built in a big way and there is mass participation[11]. The thought process indicating that the Maoists have an insatiable quench for acquiring war-like stores to accomplish their overall aim.

Arms Proliferation

In the current South Asian context, the expanding trade in Small Arms and Light Weapons (SALW), mostly illicit, has influenced more than 250 militant and insurgency movements. In geostrategic terms, the Indian market for small arms is interestingly placed between the global black market in Southeast Asia and the surplus of arms in Central Asia. According to the United Nations, India is home to about 40 million firearms. Historically, the primary source for proliferation was the Afghanistan conflict in the late 1970s, complimented on the eastern frontier by the bloodbath of the infamous Khmer regime. More recently, the US led anti-terror campaign in Afghanistan, the long drawn civil conflict in Sri Lanka, instability and fundamentalist struggles in Pakistan, huge state support to terrorist groups from China and Pakistan and the ethnic insurgencies in Myanmar have together created a deadly whirlpool of illicit arms influx.

This supply, obviously, is demanded by requirements amongst the Indian insurgents groups. The external supply is reinforced by growing indigenous sources of illegal arms, especially 'cottage industry' locally produced 'kattas'. Indigenous weapons are cheap, and though low on technology and frills, they remain highly destructive and impossible to trace using ballistic finger printing. Besides, leaks and thefts from state stocks, challenges associated with the licensing process also add to the growing numbers[12].

According to a study by the British NGO Oxfam, in collaboration with Amnesty International and the International Action Network on Small Arms (IANSA), the bulk of illegal arms supplies to India make their way into J&K, Bihar, Chhattisgarh, UP, Jharkhand, Odisha and Madhya Pradesh. The Maoists are the likely end users, thus, creating a major crisis for the states in the "Red Corridor".[13] The Maoists primarily acquire weapons in three different modes i.e. procurement, production and looting / snatching.

Procurement

Linkages

As mentioned earlier, given India's location at the centre of two major international weapon warehouses – Pakistan's North-West Frontier Province (NWFP) and the Southeast Asian arms market—there exist approximately 13 identified gun-running routes close to our northeastern border areas. The CPI (Maoist) has linkages with various insurgent groups from not only India's northeast but also with those operating in J&K and earlier, the Liberation Tigers of Tamil Eelam (LTTE).

The National Investigation Agency (NIA) in July 2011 registered a case arguing that the Manipur-based People's Liberation Army (PLA) had formed an alliance with the Maoists for procuring arms and ammunition. Later, in May 2012, the agency filed a chargesheet in this regard before the special NIA court in Guwahati, against three arrested cadres of the PLA, N. Dilip Singh alias Wangba, Senjam Dhiren Singh alias Raghu and Kh. Arnold Singh alias Becon. Wangba was the self-styled 'chief of external affairs' of the PLA, and was arrested during a raid in Paharganj in New Delhi on October 01, 2011. The other two accused were senior functionaries of PLA working under Wangba, and were arrested on February 04, 2012, from Kolkata, and on April 02, 2012, from Siliguri respectively. According to an NIA press release,[14] the alliance between the CPI (Maoist) and PLA was inked in 2008 after several meetings between the outfits since 2006. Subsequently, the PLA established an office in Kolkata, which played a crucial role in coordinating the deals and meetings with the Maoists.

On August 29, 2012, the Jharkhand Police seized a consignment of arms and ammunition from the areas of Barachatti

Police Station of Gaya district in Bihar and from Chouparan Police, Station in Jharkhand. Two persons, Prafulla Malakar alias Pankaj and Anil Yadav, were arrested. Malakar, a conduit for supplying sophisticated arms to top Communist Party of India-Maoist leaders, was supposed to deliver the consignment to Anil Yadav, who is in charge of the Maoist armoury in Bihar and Jharkhand. Yadav had come with Rs 900,000 to take the delivery. The seizure included a US-made M-16 rifle and 14 cartridges of 5.56 mm, one 9-mm pistol of Italian make, and one lightweight bullet-proof jacket worth Rs 400,000, manufactured in the United Kingdom. Malakar later told interrogators that he had supplied four AK-47 rifles, two AK-56 rifles and three Self-Loading Rifles (SLRs), to Yadav. Significantly, the M-16 rifle, manufactured by Colt Defense, carried a 'US Army property' marking on it. Officials in the Ministry of Home Affairs (MHA) claimed that this was confirmation of the opening of "the northeast arms supply route" to the left wing extremists[15].

The linkages that the CPI (Maoist) has with various outlawed groups facilitate their militarisation, mainly through weapons acquisition. Such linkages have been categorised as fraternal and non-fraternal. The non-fraternal ties are entirely opportunistic, meant to enhance capabilities where ideological compatibility was never a factor[16]. These linkages exist within and outside the country to include the northeast insurgents, Nepali Maoists and LTTE. While speaking in the Lok Sabha, Bandaru Dattatreya, former Union Minister of State for Railways, said on December 10, 1991, that the then People's War Group had acquired 60 AKs and 20 sten guns from the now defunct LTTE[17]. However, the extent to which these linkages have helped the Maoists extremists is not clear. Information on spinoffs in terms of a boost to the militarisation of the Maoists, is scanty. Hence, it is difficult to arrive at a definite conclusion of whether extra-regional linkages have become a regular and reliable source of weapons supply to the Indian Naxalite groups.[18] Nevertheless, the transfer of weapons technology that has led to indigenised production (elaborated in the subsequent section) the can be said to be a direct effect of the evolved linkages, and assumes significance.

Role of China and Pakistan

The covert role of China as a source and facilitator to keep alive the mentioned supply route is too pronounced to be ignored; the dynamic that includes insurgent groups from the northeast and the Maoists. In 2011, the Indian intelligence agencies had come up with reports, revealing the Maoist leaders' secret visits to China's Yunan province for arms training. As per the report, China has set up a weapon manufacturing facility in Myanmar's Kachin province, which produces near-exact replicas of AK 47 rifles which are supplied to the Maoists.[19] Also, in November 2009, the then Home Secretary, GK Pillai, had said that he was confident about the supply of arms from China to the Maoists in India, though he ruled out any direct involvement of the Chinese state actors[20].

Repeated recoveries of Chinese made arms, radio sets, etc from the Naxals is a substantial exposition of Maoist-China linkages, which more often are via the insurgent groups in the northeast region. If seen in the context of the global Communist movement, the CPI (Maoist) is part of the international ultra-left brethren. It is a member of the Coordination Committee of Maoists Parties and Organisations of South Asia (CCOMPOSA), which is believed to have the direct blessings of the Communist Party of China (CPC)[21] and a platform where certain European actors too get involved in funding the CPI (Maoist).

During his interrogation in 2010, the apprehended CPI (Maoist) Bengal Secretary Sudip Chongdar alias Kanchan revealed that the Maoists had been receiving weapons from China through international smuggling routes, facilitated especially by the northeastern groups like the National Socialist Council of Nagaland (Isak-Muivah) [NSCNCIM]. In fact, the arrest of Kanchan was the fallout of the arrests of Anthony Shimray, a senior leader of the NSCN (IM) and Rajkumar Meghen, Chairman of the United National Liberation Front of Manipur. Kanchan, as well as many other senior Maoist leaders, including CC member Kishenji were in touch with the northeast insurgent leaders. A large haul of weapons and communication devices, believed to be part of a Rs. 4.5 crore consignment that was bought from China was also seized during the arrest of Kanchan and other Maoist leaders. Kanchan also revealed that some senior Maoist leaders, including a CC member, had visited China.[22] A report of 2009 says out of the total weapons seized in India from the Maoists, a major amount is of Chinese origin. The General Secretary of the CPI (Maoist), Ganapathy,. in an interview in November 2010, admitted that they purchase weapons from abroad[23].

There have been indicators towards the involvement of Pakistan's Inter-Services Intelligence (ISI) with regards to supply of weapons to Indian insurgent groups, including the Maoists. The strategic think-tank, Stratfor, had come out in 2009-10 that the ISI was trying to forge an alliance with the Maoists in a bid to destabilise the Indian state from within. It was acknowledged that the "Indian Maoists have been meeting with the outlawed Pakistan's militant group Lashkar-e-Taiba (LeT), according to the Director General of Police Chhattisgarh". And "the ISI was providing weapons to Naxalites in exchange for money or other services"[24]. The earliest proof of the alliance of the ISI with the Maoists can be traced to January 2005, when, during a fierce encounter with Chhattisgarh Police, the empty cartridges of nearly 300 bullets fired by the Maoists were found at the site of the encounter. Many of these empties had the markings of a Pakistani ordnance factory, while some others had markings of production in the United Kingdom[25].

Recently, in March–April 2014, ahead of the Lok Sabha polls, a large consignment of weapons had reportedly been smuggled into India from Bangladesh after being shipped from Pakistan. Indian intelligence agencies tracked a boat named *Padma* that was docked at Kutubdia port in Bangladesh in March 2014. The vessel was used to transport the consignment of weapons, which was offloaded at the port before being smuggled into India through the porous border along Bangladesh's Jessore district. The intelligence agencies, however, lost track of the consignment and did not know where it was sent to. They suspected that the weapons could have been intended for insurgent groups, especially the Maoists, who had expressed their resolve to disrupt the polls in the areas controlled by them[26].

Although the abovementioned examples pertain to recent times, the Southeast Asian gun-running route has been active for the last few decades. Initially, it was to sustain NER insurgencies; the shades of Maoist movement augmented the demand, subsequently. In one operation in the Andaman Sea, the complement forces of the (then) Fortress Andaman & Nicobar (FORTRAN) in the highly secretive Operation LEECH 3, captured a huge consignment of war-like stores comprising several RPGs, RLs, MMGs / HMGs, mines, grenades, etc. This haul in the year 1998, was, by far, one of the largest single hauls of arms and ammunition ever captured by the armed forces in sub-conventional operations and almost the entire inventory was of Chinese origin. The executor in the said gun-running was the Arakan Army, a Burmese rebel group having links with China[27].

Production

The Maoists have come a long way from fielding farm implements and country-made weapons, and snatching weapons from the security forces. Apart from procurements, largely facilitated by their linkages, researchers hold the view that the Maoist arsenal is largely indigenous; outright purchase of arms in the grey arms market is only in 'fits and bouts'. Their ingenuity in the manufacture of weapons is noteworthy.[28] On January 10, 2007, the police in Bhopal unearthed an arms-making-cum-R&D unit and seized 25 books on arms published by international publishing houses, detailed drawings of cross-sections of rocket launchers, etc[29].

In September 2012, the NIA chargesheeted Sadnala Ramkrishna alias Techie Anna and four others for waging war against the state as members of the CPI (Maoist) and for illegal manufacture of arms and ammunition. The NIA seized from them cash, ammunition, explosives, Maoist literature, diagrams and parts of rocket launchers and other weapons as evidence. Among the big seizures were 69 crates full of weapons from a Raipur godown and some material from a workshop in Kolkata. From the interrogation reports, it became evident that the agency had struck crucial links of how Maoist cadres get their weapons. It is a supply chain that runs on 'make do' and improvisation. The rebels have been known to be working on it since 2001 and have come a long way since then. The strategy is simple enough: snatch or seize a piece or two from the security forces, field-strip it, diagram its working, fashion the parts using available material and workshop machinery, assemble a piece for testing, and, finally, pass on the knowhow to production units[30].

In 2003, the Andhra Pradesh Police raided a Maoist camp in Malkangiri (Odisha), where two-inch mortar shells and five rockets were to be developed and tested. The cadres escaped, but the blueprints found there left the security agencies worried. The apprehended Maoists weapon experts revealed that some 25 rockets were made in Chennai—costing as low as Rs 950 each. Twenty were distributed to various dalams, five retained for testing. By 2004, these were being test-fired. The pioneer technical experts who worked on the project were Rama Krishna, Tech Madhu, Seenu and Vishwanath. Tech Madhu oversaw the manufacture and distribution of 1,600 rockets and 40 rocket launchers to nine dalams in selected districts. He was given Rs 25 lakh in installments for the purpose. By 2006, Tech Madhu had more or less met the production target, but much of it was seized by the Andhra Pradesh Police. Some of the work was also outsourced[31].

From the late 1980s, the Maoists have been working on building self-sufficiency with regard to weapons. Their technical capabilities have grown and evolved since then. During interrogation, Techie Anna revealed that one of the first technical units was set up in Bangalore in 1989, by him, with some comrades. The aim then was humbler i.e. to manufacture and supply .12 bore guns and ammunition, butts and barrels for .303 rifles, grenades and similar weaponry for the dalams in the forests. There were similar units in urban and semi-urban centres, in the guise of ordinary workshops. The locations of these workshops were changed frequently and the feature of stealth became integral to their weapons acquisition programme, apart from make-do and innovations.

Till the early 1990s, the Maoists in their earlier *avataar* (of PWG) were not focussing on manufacture and used to procure arms from local arms dealers and smugglers. With increasing police pressures and several apprehensions, the Maoists decided to make forays into indigenous production. In 1994, Techie Anna set up a Technical Development Committee (TDC) to coordinate the work of the production units. But this committee failed to live up to the expectations of the top Maoist leaders, so it was disbanded and a Central Technical Committee (CTC) was created in July 2001, to work directly under the Maoists' CMC. This unit was rechristened in 2005 as the Technical Research Arms Manufacturing Unit (TRAM). It was mandated to not only manufacture and supply weaponry but also acquire and develop skills and technology[32]; thus, reaping payoffs from linkages that had been developed over a period of time.

The TRAM comprises five members, with an elected secretary. Three members concentrate on development and production, while the secretary coordinates and strategises the supply of weapons. Members are expected to visit production units twice a year, while TRAM itself convenes a meeting every three months. Once a year, a CMC representative attends the TRAM meetings. Production units are expected to overhaul weapons and conduct repair workshops for the dalams. There are three-member repairing units under each Maoist district committee, with members having to assimilate a full-fledged syllabus during training. As mentioned earlier, the weapon units keep shifting locations[33].

With regards to the rocket launcher programme of the Maoists, a broad timeline from 2003 to 2007, was laid out : "In 2003, police recovered blueprints in a raid; in 2004, the launchers were test-fired; in 2005, the Maoists improved them further; in 2006, a large consignment was ordered, but a good part of it was seized by the police; in 2007, the Bhopal Police busted a key Maoist Research and Development (R&D) unit where both the old and new blueprints were found"[34].

The Maoists envisaged executing "Project Rocket Launchers (RL)" in two phases — "RL–I" and "RL – II".[35] RL–I was a pilot project undertaken ahead of elections to the Andhra Pradesh State Legislative Assembly in 2004. The plan was to manufacture 25 rockets with launch pads at a cost of Rs 950 per rocket. In the process, five rockets each were distributed to Anantapur, Guntur and Nallamala. Five were tested at various locations in Prakasam district, and five were set aside for further trials in order to develop the next version. RL–II was a project for the development of shoulder-fired rockets and launchers. These were tested in September / October 2004, when the Maoists, following the trials, were of the opinion that the rockets were neither effective enough nor accurate, but had nuisance value. After the second set of trials, Tech Madhu was instructed to have 1,600 rockets and 40 rocket launchers manufactured. Accordingly, he headed to Chennai and got 1,550 rockets and 40 RLs manufactured. Tech Madhu was given Rs 35 lakh to execute the plan. Irrespective of these rockets possessing mere nuisance value, presently, in view of the building up of their weapon programme, as and when the Maoists acquire the versatility to manufacture rockets with accuracy, their lethal impact would be enormous[36].

The Maoists also manufacture a range of 'country-made' weapons. Intelligence reports claimed that nearly 500 arms manufacturing units had been established by the Maoists in Chhattisgarh alone. These small sized manufacturing units, often run in huts and cottages deep inside forests, were strategically located to facilitate a smooth supply of weapons and ammunition to the armed squads[37]. A forensic study on the firearms used by the PWG in Andhra Pradesh between 2001–05 revealed that they were firearms that could chamber any type of ammunition available in the Indian markets. Since manufacturing ammunition locally involves complicated technology, for ease of its availability in the markets, the Maoists adapted their weapon manufacturing to suit the requirement.[38] The failure of the state in implementing strict control measures towards marketing of ammunition in large quantities has encouraged the Maoists to be 'calibre flexible'. Of late, paucity of ammunition has been one of the major attributable factors of receding Maoists strikes on the security forces and state agencies, for which they are duly compensating by resorting to Improvised Explosive Device (IED) attacks.[39]

Arms Loot

The looting of weapons from police personnel, civilians and private companies has been a major source of arms for the Maoists, apart from procuring and manufacturing. The Naxalites also loot explosives from mining companies—a constant source of supplies towards manufacturing IEDs. For example, in February 2006, the Maoists looted the Bailadila mining complex. Aided by almost 2,000 villagers, they carried out 20 tonnes of explosives – enough firepower to fuel the insurgency for a protracted duration[40]. A summary of weapons snatched by the Maoists in recent years has been given below. These numbers do not show an even trend and unless complemented by procurement and production, cannot sustain the militarist shade of Maoism.

Table 1: Arms Snatched by Maoists: 2007–15 (up to July 15)

Year	2007	2008	2009	2010	2011	2012	2013	2014	2015
No. of Weapons	233	1,219	217	256	67	38	89	58	36

Source: Ministry of Home Affairs, Government of India

Besides minor incidents of looting and weapon snatching, the Maoists have carried out a few audacious and synchronised large scale attacks in which they accomplished their multifarious aims of gaining moral ascendancy, causing attrition to the state forces and lapping up huge amounts of war-like stores as booty. These have been the Koraput armoury raid (February 06, 2004), Giridih Home Guards armoury raid (November 11, 2005), Jehanabad jail break (November 13, 2005), Nayagarh armoury raid (February 15, 2008) and Balimela attacks (June 29, 2008). These attacks could be seen as a critical aspect of the increasing militarisation of the Maoists.

The growing Maoist violence in central-east India and its potential in other parts of the country multiply the security threats that challenge the state. Several overdue measures such as the need to increase the police-to-population ratio, police reforms and modernisation, etc have found considerable traction. However, one aspect that continues to be relegated to the back-burner is that of illicit small arms trafficking and procurement by armed groups and terrorist outfits.

Gun control is intrinsically linked to counter-insurgency strategies and warrants due attention. In doing so, the state shall have to holistically address the challenge by taking note of all related aspects that have been flagged in the paper, i.e. funding, linkages and weapon manufacturing abilities of the insurgent groups, especially the Maoists, since this has been the longest sustaining insurgency in the country. It is imperative that small arms, both 'licit' and 'illicit', be curbed at the source and in terms of exports, especially through illegal channels. International and transnational regional cooperation has a crucial role to play and effective diplomacy, backed by bipartisan political will is of immense relevance.

The gun-running of the Maoists is a part of the South Asian illegal arms trade in particular and that of the global phenomenon in general. Globally, there is one gun for every ten people on earth; eight million small arms are manufactured yearly; every year, enough bullets are made to kill every human twice.[41] In the long run, the buck stops at the global arms manufacturers who run the military industrial complex.

Maoists' Explosive Proliferation

The mine is the weapon of choice for the Maoists. It is a low cost device with tremendous psychological impact and mine warfare has become an integral part of the Maoists' tactical arsenal. They are said to have learned mine warfare techniques from some renegade LTTE cadres in Bastar and blasted the first landmine in 1989. Widespread use of mines started towards the end of 1990 in Andhra Pradesh and early 2000 in Bastar and continues till date, unabated. Consistent usage of mines, including IEDs, by the Maoists, over the last decade, is summarised below:

Table 8.2: Fatalities and Incidents of Landmine Explosions by Maoists, 2005-15

Year	05'	06'	07'	08'	09'	10'	11'	12'	13'	14'	15'
Incident(s)	11	39	79	48	113	112	40	23	23	19	27 *(till Sept)*
Fatal Casualties	54	106	72	53	123	51	68	56	36	42	13

Source - http://www.satp.org

A counter-insurgent tends to focus on developing technical solutions to counter the IED threat. However, IEDs are a product of human ingenuity, social and administrative organisation. It becomes pertinent to understand the aspects relating to the 'supply chain' of explosives in order to effectively scuttle the sustenance and have an additional avenue for defeating them in the long run. A focus on IED supply requires examining the supply chain or sources that sustain the availability of explosives. The mineral extraction industry in India constitutes the backbone of the supply chain, which facilitates explosives proliferation by a Maoists.

While mineral production is reported from as many as 32 states and union territories, among onshore areas, a few states dominate. Andhra Pradesh (including the present Telangana 12.24 per cent), Odisha (11.85 per cent), Chhattisgarh (9.18 per cent) and Jharkhand (8.79 per cent). Together with the offshore areas, they account for 60 per cent of mineral production in India[42].

Coincidentally, these states comprise the belt where the Maoist movement thrives.

Delving into the socio-economic and political nuances of mining in the region and its connection to the rise of Maoism is beyond the scope of this chapter. The chapter solely looks into the aspect of explosives proliferation by the Maoists and the role that the mining industry has played towards the same. Post the reform years of 1991, the government and the private corporations have vied for access to the mineral wealth. There have been two major sources of supply of explosives to the Maoists; accumulation of explosives from miners and looting from private and government owned mining companies.

Explosives from Mining Industry

Unregulated mining in our country has proliferated at an extraordinary rate. An indicator of the scale of the problem was provided by Mr. B.K. Handique, Union Minister of Mines, who informed Parliament on March 08, 2010, that the state governments had detected 1,61,040 illegal mining activities in 17 states of India between 2006 to 2009. This number represents only a small part of the illegal mining in the country[43]. Explosives cannot be sourced through legal channels by illegal mines—they are sourced illegally and, as a result, there are now extraordinary quantities of unregulated and illegal explosives available in India's conflict zones.

It is important to understand that profit driven unregulated markets do not operate on any sense of principle, and aspects of national security shall be too ambitious to be expected from the profiteers. Illegal mines obtain large quantities of explosives illegally and, given the Maoists' aims, it would seem irresponsible not to assume that the insurgents are doing the same.[44] State governments so far have taken minimal action to prevent illegal mining. Mr. Handique had informed the Parliament on February 23, 2010, that in 1,61,040 cases of illegal mining in 2006-09, the state governments had filed court cases in only 20,646 cases.[45]

Effectively, it is hard to escape the conclusion that state failure to regulate mining is arming the Maoists.

It must be noted that supplies of explosives have to come from somewhere. Here, the mining industry has a case to answer. The evidence suggests that the regulated explosive markets are, in fact, poorly regulated. If one accepts the existing consensus that illegal explosives and detonators are accessed from within India, then one must conclude that the most likely benefactor is the 'regulated' market for explosives i.e. pilferage from the regulated market.

Also, the 'protection industry' under Maoist control has a major role to play. The private mining companies are able to continue to work if they pay 'protection money' to the Maoists. On July 22, 2010, then Home Minister P Chidambaram conceded this arrangement when he stated that "unless the state is able to provide them better security, they will have to pay these rents to protect their investments"[46]. It is common knowledge that Maoist 'taxes' go well beyond cash. Insurgent groups need explosives that the mining companies can provide. The mining companies (both legal and illegal), operating in areas where the state cannot offer security, are in no position to refuse the Maoists and often pay their taxes in terms of explosives.

There exist major lacunae in existing legislations with regards control of explosive material in India. Neither the Explosives Act, 1884[47] nor the Explosives Rules revised in 2008[48] provide for any specific requirement to ensure that explosives sold/sanctioned to the licensees have been used only for lawful activities. There is no provision for monitoring end use of explosives by physical inspection on-site. Rule 24 of the Explosives Rules, 2008,[49] provides only for "maintenance of records and submission of returns". While Rule 128 of the Explosive Rules, 2008,[50] provides for "powers of search and seizures", there is no mechanism for monitoring end use by spot verification of the explosives sold / sanctioned to the licensee. Explosives are sanctioned by the Petroleum and Explosive Safety Organisation[51*] (PESO). India's anti-terror bodies such as the Multi-Agency Centres under the Ministry of Home Affairs or

State Multi-Agency Centres have little idea about the explosives and other materials being sanctioned by PESO.

Pilferage and Loot

On December 23, 2014, Parthibhai Chaudhary, Union Minister of State for Home, informed the Parliament about instances of illegal use of industrial explosives by LWE groups. It was also confirmed by the Jharkhand Police that industrial explosives and detonators pilfered from industries and mines were used by the Maoists against the security forces, in their landmine warfare[52]. The lack of coordination between different government agencies has meant that explosives are easily available to the rebels. While PESO is tasked with monitoring the manufacture, sale and use of explosives and is under the Commerce Ministry, the agencies of the MHA and the state governments that are responsible for law enforcement are entirely out of the loop.

Apart from pilferages that benefit the Maoists, there have been a myriad cases of looting from various mining companies, government or private. More than 15 lakh kg of industrial explosives were stolen between 2010 and 2013 from carelessly guarded warehouses across the country whcih made their way into the hands of the Maoists. The inventory of stolen explosives includes 8.5 lakh kg of nitrate mixture explosives, 5 lakh detonators, 1.3 lakh cartridges for small arms/war rockets and 30,000 safety fuses/cartridges[53].

One of the major cases of plunder took place on February 09, 2006, when the Maoists looted the richest iron mine in India at the Bailadila (40 km south-west of Dantewada) mining complex. The complex stored not only $80 billion-plus worth of mineral deposits, but also the mine's explosives magazine, which held the ammonium nitrate that the miners used to pulverise mountain-sides and loosen the iron ore. Local villagers' participation in this operation was tremendous, reflecting the support that the Maoists were able to garner. Altogether, 2,000 villagers, led by the Maoists, carried away

20 tonnes of explosives— enough firepower to fuel a covert insurgency for a decade.[54] The looting was at its peak during the year 2009-10, wherein, as per the security forces' claim, the Maoists looted over 54,500 kg of explosives.[55] A few of the major looting operations are as given below:

- May 19, 2010, the Maoists hijacked a truck and looted 16.5 tonnes of high-grade ammonium nitrate in Bastar region of Chhattisgarh[56].
- March 10, 2010, the Maoists stopped a tanker and looted over 16 tonnes of ammonium nitrate in Gadchiroli district in Maharashtra[57].
- April 12, 2009, the Maoists attacked the National Aluminum Company's (NALCO's) magazine depot, where explosives used for blasting purposes were stored, in Koraput district in Odisha.[58]
- March 27, 2008, the Maoists raided a mining facility of Steel Authority of India Limited (SAIL) in Dallirajhara area in Durg district of Chhattisgarh, and looted about 2 tonnes of explosives.[59]
- February 09, 2006, the Maoists looted some 20 tonnes of explosives from the National Mineral Development Corporation (NMDC) magazine at Hiroli in Chhattisgarh's Dantewada district, and killed eight Central Industrial Security Force (CISF) personnel[60].

To cut down the availability of explosives in the region, so as to scuttle the supply to the Maoists, the government had solicited suggestions on alternative methods of mining which do not rely on explosive blasting. One of the proposed options was 'mechanised heaving' to remove the topsoil. And since it does not damage the environment, it was a preferred option even with the environmentalists. However, the move did not find much traction, since, as per the experts, alternatives like mechanised heavy-duty rippers (used for heaving) and excavators do not work well in bauxite mining areas in Odisha because of hard soil conditions.

Rippers are also expensive compared to explosives like ammonium nitrate or slurry-based blasting substances[61].

Recommendations

In order to scuttle the source of the supply chain of explosives to the rebels, the government needs to take necessary measures towards the following:

- Declaring a complete ban and providing for enhanced punishment and penalty for illegal mining. Encouragingly, the Mines and Minerals (Development and Regulation) (Amendment) Bill 2015, that was promulgated in January this year has brought in provisions invoking more stringency towards illegal mining.[62]
- Closing all the illegal mining as a matter of national security priority.
- Bringing the sanctioning authority for explosives for mining within the ambit of the security establishment.
- Amending the Explosive Rules of 2008 to provide for mandatory, on the spot end use verification of the explosives obtained by the licensees.

In the rush for acquiring mining leases, many new companies have been born in the past few years. Companies, which already had mines in their possession, signed MoUs to set up new steel plants. These corporates continue to export iron ore and other minerals while their plans for industrial projects to contribute to development of the region, remain on paper. The government should realise that those who have come forward to invest lakhs of crores of rupees in these projects are primarily miners whose chief interest shall remain extracting minerals and not developmental goals[63].

India's lack of action against illegal mining in the last five years can be argued to have changed the nature of the conflict with the Maoists. The Mines and Minerals (Development and Regulation) (Amendments) Bill, 2015, remains silent on security[64]. Sensitivity towards monitoring detonators and explosives is absent; and the mining lobby remains too powerful to allow anyone to subject the industry to government oversight. As long the explosives for mining are not brought within the ambit of the security agencies, India will continue to hand explosives to the Maoists and our endeavours towards refining an all encompassing national counter IED strategy shall remain an unfinished agenda.

Financing the Rebellion

The Maoists finance their activities, in overwhelming measure, through extortion. The Rajya Sabha was informed that the Maoists extort money from a variety of sources to finance their activities. In December 2013, replying to a question, the MoS MHA said, "The main source of funds for the Maoists include(s) extortion from *tendu patta* contractors, infrastructure/development work contractors, businessmen, corporate houses, etc. In addition, they rob banks and public / private property to augment their finances.[65]

In a document titled "Our Financial Policy", the Maoists talk about three types of economic needs that they have, viz. the needs of war, political propaganda and the people. To cater to these needs there are three broad categories of resources, viz. (a) membership fee, levy and contributions from the people; (b) confiscation of the wealth and income of the enemy; and (c) 'revolutionary taxes' collected in guerrilla zones and base areas.[66]

Thus, money is collected from individuals as well as businesses — ranging from petty to big industries. Development works (PWD) contractors, government schemes such as MGNREGA, Indira Awaas Yojana (IAY), mining industry, illegal mining of all minerals, big industries, businessmen, timber contractors, bamboo contractors, contractors dealing in Minor Forest Produce (MFP), small-time shopkeepers, protection racket — including for the cultivation of ganja — PDS, tendu (kendu) leaf contractors, etc. The rebels also levy taxes in their strongholds.[67]

According Vishwaranjan, a former DG Police, Chhattisgarh, the Maoists annually extort a sum of Rs 1,500 crore[68]. Besides, supporters and sympathisers make contributions, while card members pay an annual subscription. According to the 'Constitution' of the CPI (Maoist), "Membership fees are Rs 10 per annum. The concerned unit, after assessing the economic situation of the party member, will fix a monthly party levy"[69]. It is believed that a total of 10 per cent of the funds collected across the country is made available to the PB and CC to meet the expenses of its members; 25-30 per cent of the annual extortion is spent on Research and Development (R&D) to manufacture weapons and fabricate ammunition. The Maoists also spend funds on intelligence gathering and in undertaking development works in their areas of control, though there are no precise estimates about how much this would account for. It is also said that approximately 5 to 10 per cent of the extorted amount is siphoned-off[70].

The CPI (Maoist) does not hide its major sources of funding, that have clearly been outlined in its "Party Constitution" as early as 2004. Chapter 13 of the Constitution deals with "Party Funds". Article 60 states: "The party funds shall be obtained through membership fees, levies, donations, taxes, penalties and the wealth confiscated from enemies." Article 61 adds: "The levy to be paid by party members shall be decided and collected in their respective state committees." Maoists exploit every stage of the industrial cycle, from mining to manufacture and movement of finished products. The method of collection is based on targets given by the CC. This, in turn, is conveyed to the zonal committees. The collections are done by overground workers, and the armed cadres are not involved in the process. The allocated funds are retained at each level, before the balance is sent to the next higher level[71].

To maximise returns, the Maoist insurgency has begun to operate like a franchise. Using force and propaganda, the Maoists create an environment that incentivises and enables others to participate in an extortion ecosystem. In this role as a black market maker, the Maoist insurgency accomplishes two tasks: eroding the ability of the state to govern, and building a substantial war chest. Towards their goal of making money, ethics do not seem to be of any consequence. For example, in Chhattisgarh, several criminal gangs were shaking down businesses and government officials by imitating extortion letters written by the Naxals, who responded to this dilution of their brand with violence against the gangs. They then enforced a simple edict: gangs could extort as long as they did not cut into existing Naxal revenue. Chhattisgarh's criminals now operate within Naxal bounds, give a portion of their revenue, to the insurgency, and seek out new victims, in both the legitimate and illicit economies[72].

The model based on the criminal–Maoist nexus works well in the following manner:

- **Mining:** Government records show 182,000 instances of illegal mining across 17 states, with 30 percent of those being found in the Maoist affected area. There are an estimated 60,000 illegal mines, with 500 million untrained labourers who work in entirely unregulated conditions.[73] These mines are operated by criminal organisations and mafias that also pay into the Maoist revenue pool. Prasoon S. Majumdar, Editor of *Economic Affairs*, estimates that the Naxals receive between 20 and 30 percent of the revenue for each truckload of coal, with 15 percent reserved for corrupt local officialdom.[74]
- **Narcotics:** India is the world's largest legitimate producer of opium for the global pharmaceutical industry. Every year, it issues thousands of permits to farmers to supply the licit demand. Motivated by the potential for massive returns, some farmers operate outside this system, risking the wrath of the security forces. The US State Department estimates that as much as 30 percent of India's opium production is diverted to the black market.[75] Jharkhand is one of the leading states towards the same. The Maoists, noting this opportunity, have stepped in, to provide protection in exchange for a share of the proceeds.

Whereas the state can only levy tax on legitimate enterprises, the Maoists have successfully expanded their revolutionary tax pool to include illicit actors. By creating the opportunity where there was none, the Maoists have sparked a deviant economic engine. They disrupt government operations and provide safe harbours for deviant entrepreneurs to continue their activities unhindered. In exchange, they receive a share of the revenue. This positive feedback loop enables the black market to prosper, the Maoists to build their capacity, and the Indian state to decline.[76]

In the political domain, the Maoists field their candidates in local body elections, so as to accomplish two-fold aims, i.e. gaining political space and controlling the development funds that are allocated. During the Panchayat polls in 2010, as many as 181 Sarpanches and 10,980 Panches were elected unopposed in Bastar division. The highest number of 63 Sarpanches elected unopposed was in Dantewada (now divided into two districts, Dantewada and Sukma), followed by Bijapur (55), Bastar (30), Kanker (20) and Narayanpur (13)[77]. It goes without saying that all these unopposed candidates had Maoist backing.

Another major source of funding is the protection racket that the Maoists patronise in their area of influence. For the Maoist Communist Centre (MCC) led movement in Jharkhand, one of the major financial sources had been the protection that the Naxals sell to the local elites. The MCC's grassroots support was not based on a shared ideology or on violence alone, but on having greater control over what could be termed as a market of protection, in which violence and muscle power was used to sell protection for bargaining for more power and financial benefits.[78] Thus, the nexus that evolved over a period of time, made terrorism, banditry and gangland rivalry all come on the same continuum of selling protection to find more fuel for militarisation.

Notes

1. K Balagopal, "Public Intellectuals in the Chair: All the News we get is Killing and Getting Killed", interview by Vijay Simtha, *Tehelka*, January 21, 2006.
2. http://mha.nic.in/sites/upload_files/mha/files/Lweviolance_15072016.PDF
3. http://mha.nic.in/naxal_new
4. http://mha.nic.in/naxal_new
5. http://www.satp.org/satporgtp/countries/india/database/LWE_conflictmap2015.html
6. 22 – highly affected; 18 – moderately affected; 78 – marginally affected.
7. Rishi Chikara, "People's Liberation Guerilla Army of CPI (Maoist)", Manekshaw Paper, No. 35, CLAWS, 2012.
8. Government of India, Press Information Bureau, Prime Minister's speech to the 2nd meeting of the Standing Committee of the Chief Ministers on Naxalism, April 13, 2006.
9. "Strategy and Tactics of the Indian Revolution, Central Committee, CPI (Maoist)", Chapter 10, adopted on September 21, 2004, at the founding of the party.
10. Ibid.
11. PV Ramana, "Maoist People's Liberation Guerrilla Army", IDSA Comments, December 12, 2011.
12. https://www.academia.edu/207858/Politics_of_Gun_Control_and_Indias_Internal_Security
13. Gurmeet Kanwal and Monika Chansoria, "Small Arms Proliferation in South Asia: A Major Challenge for National Security", Issue Brief No. 18, May 2010, CLAWS.
14. http://www.satp.org/satporgtp/countries/india/maoist/documents/papers/press_21052012.pdf.
15. http://www.satp.org/satporgtp/sair/Archives/sair11/11_14.html
16. PV Ramana, "India's Maoists: Profile and Thought Process", *Understanding India's Maoists: Select Documents*, Section 1 (IDSA, Pentagon Press, 2014), pp. 12-13.
17. http://www.parliamentofindia.nic.in/lsdeb/ls10/ ses2/1910129105.htm#*m08
18. PV Ramana, "Left Wing Extremism in India", ORF Analysis, December 18, 2003.
19. http://www.strategypage.com/htmw/htproc/articles/20120111.aspx
20. http://indianexpress.com/article/india/regional/maoists-get-arms-from-china-not-chinese-govt-pillai/
21. PV Ramana, "Linkages Between Indian and Nepalese Maoists", IDSA Comments, November 09, 2010.
22. Madhuparna Das, "Arrested Maoists Reveal a Supply Chain from China", *Indian Express*, December 08, 2010.

23. https://southasiarev.files.wordpress.com/2010/11/gp-interview_english_full_final.pdf
24. Ben West, "Pakistan and the Naxalite Movement in India", Stratfor, November 18, 2010.
25. "Remnants of Pakistani and British Arms Found at Naxal attack", *The Asian Age* (New Delhi), January 12, 2005.
26. Abhishek Bhalla, "Ghost Boat Smuggles Weapons into India from Pakistan", *Daily Mail*, April 08, 2014.
27. As told to the author by an officer of the Indian Army who was deployed in Andaman & Nicobar and participated in Operation LEECH 3.
28. Ramana n.16, pp. 10.
29. Ibid.
30. Varia Deshpande, "The DIY Maoist Manual", *Outlook*, September 2012.
31. Ibid.
32. Ibid.
33. Ibid.
34. PV Ramana, "Rockets in Maoist Arsenal", IDSA Comment, May 10, 2013.
35. Ibid.
36. Ibid.
37. http://www.satp.org/satporgtp/sair/Archives/sair11/11_14.htm
38. http://bprd.nic.in/writereaddata/linkimages/8935853177-april-june.pdf
39. http://indianexpress.com/article/opinion/columns/bastar-naxal-violence-chhattisgarh-2762696/
40. Jason Miklian, "Fire in the Hole", *Foreign Policy*, August 06, 2010.
41. https://www.youtube.com/watch?v=yZ8pZVtWY0k
42. CP Chandrasekhar, "Liberalising Loot", *Frontline*, Vol 27, Issue 14, July 03–16, 2010.
43. Unstarred Question No.1151 asked by Shri Rajkumar Dhoot and answered on March 08, 2010, in the Rajya Sabha by Shri B.K.Handique, Minister of Mines and Minister of DoNER.
44. Suhas Chakma, "India: Handing Explosives to the Maoists", *Human Rights Report Quarterly*, July–September, 2010.
45. Unstarred Question No.12 asked by Shri Prabhakar Ponnam and answered on February 23, 2010, in the Lok Sabha by Shri B.K.Handique, Minister of Mines and Minister of DoNER.
46. Rohini Singh, ET Bureau, "If Someone can do the Job Better, I Would be the Happiest Person: PC", *Economic Times*, July 22, 2010.
47. http://dipp.nic.in/English/acts_rules/Acts/Explosive_Act_1884.pdf.
48. http://peso.gov.in/Pdf/ExplosiveRules2008.Pdf
49. Ibid.
50. Ibid.
51. PESO comes under the Ministry of Commerce and Industry, Government of India. With an overall objective of ensuring the safety and security of the public and property from fire and explosion, the organisation as a statutory authority is

entrusted with the administration of the Explosives Act, 1884, Petroleum Act, 1934; Inflammable Substances Act, 1952, to include the rules framed under these Acts.

52. Sandeep Pai, "How Maoists got Hold of 15 Lakh kg of Industrial Explosives", *DNA*, March 23, 2015.
53. Section–6, "Results Framework Document (RFD)", PESO, Department of Industrial Policy and Promotion, Ministry of Commerce and Industry, 2012-13.
54. Jason Mikian and Scott Carney, "Fire in the Hole", *Foreign Policy*, August 06, 2010.
55. "Mining and Arming of Maoists", *Human Rights Report Quarterly*, July – September, 2010.
56. Zee News, "Naxals Loot Tonnes of Explosives", May 20, 2010.
57. NDTV, "Maharashtra: Naxals Loot Explosives", March 13, 2010.
58. "Maoists Attack Nalco Mines in Orissa, 2 CISF Jawans Killed", *The Indian Express*, April 13, 2009.
59. "Naxals Loot Explosives from SAIL Mine", *Business Standard,* March 29, 2008.
60. "Maoists Attack PSU Depot, Kill 8 CISF Men", *The Times of India,* February 11, 2006.
61. http://www.downtoearth.org.in/news/mining-explosives-attract-maoists-3510.
62. http://pib.nic.in/newsite/PrintRelease.aspx?relid=114589
63. Prafulla Das, "Miners Paradise", *Frontline*, Vol 27, Issue 14, July 03–16, 2010.
64. http://www.prsindia.org/billtrack/the-mines-and-minerals-development-and-regulation-amendment-bill-2015-3648/
65. GoI, MHA, Rajya Sabha, Unstarred Question No. 1457; answered on December 18, 2013.
66. PV Ramana, "India's Maoists: Financing the War Machinery", IDSA Comments, December 27, 2013.
67. Ibid.
68. Interview of Mr. Vishwaranjan in July 2007, by PV Ramana and referred to in his, book n.16.
69. http://www.bannedthought.net/India/CPI-Maoist-Docs/
70. Ramana n.16, p.10.
71. Vivek Chadha, *Lifeblood of Terrorism – Countering Terror Finance* (IDSA, Bloomsbury), pp. 76-77.
72. https://www.oodaloop.com/security/2012/07/12/weaponizing-markets-indias-naxalite-insurgency/
73. Shaikh Azizur Rahman, "India's Illegal Coal Mines Turn Into Death Pits," *The Washington Times*, November 24, 2006.
74. Prasoon Majumdar, "Our Own Banana Republics!" Indian Institute of Planning and Management, August 26, 2010.
75. http://www.unodc.org/india/en/rajiv_quoted_et.html.
76. http://www.oodaloop.com/security/2012/07/12/weaponizing-markets-indias-naxalite-insurgency/

77. http://www.firstpost.com/india/chhattisgarh-panchayat-polls-naxals-trying-regain-lost-base-2060717.html
78. Alpa Shah, *In the Shadows of the State – Indigenous Politics, Environmentalism and Insurgency in Jharkhand* (OUP, 2010), pp. 165–166.

9. IDEOLOGICAL FAULTLINES: WHY IT LEADS TO NOWHERE

Maoism or Naxalism in India, like any other leftist movement around the globe draws its ideological basis from the Bolshevik revolution. After the success of the Lenin-led revolution in Russia, the intellectual class in many countries started thinking of ushering in a change in their respective nations. Prominent amongst them were Che Guevara, Fidel Castro, Ho Chi Minh and Mao Tse Tung. These leaders became the architects of revolution in their countries, mainly inspired by the model of the Bolshevik revolution.

Vladimir Lenin, who originally was a Marxist, modified Karl Marx's doctrine to become the founder of Leninism. He tweaked Marxism to suit the situation in Russia that prevailed before the Bolshevik revolution. The modifications were made to suit conditions in a society where imperialism was not very strong, where the peasantry was to have a larger role and a revolution that was designed to be an armed insurrection (with the rank and file of the Russian Red Army joining in). Marx had propounded a revolution led by the working class, which could never see the light of day in his lifetime, but for a brief period during the Paris Commune that did not sustain beyond a very short duration.

The Russian backdrop of war weariness (World War I), poor economy, flexible industrialisation and substantial peasantry were the main drivers for Lenin to modify Marxism so that it could suit Russia. The advocacy of the armed nature of the revolution was meant to be potent against the despotic and hegemonic Tsar, who could be overthrown only through such means as against any democratic process. The prime intent was to bestow power into the hands of the exploited and marginalised, irrespective of the configuration. With egalitarianism as its basis, the idea was to enforce societal control over various aspects of governance and nation-building.

As per Leninism, the revolution was to be steered in, over several phases i.e. people's revolution leading to socialism which eventually was to pave the way for Marxism based on the Commune. The call for revolution made by Lenin had mass appeal in the sense that the commoners could identify with the ideological underpinning, bringing in their optimum participation. Lenin's efforts to embrace the burning issues were translated into three slogans (peace, land, bread): "land to the tiller", "bread to the hungry" and "rest to the army". The effective tool of 'mass mobilisation', made Lenin an international icon and inspired 'left revolutions' across the world.

The prevalent conditions in China that provided the background to the Mao-led people's revolution, were marked by a predominant and marginalised peasantry, nascent industrialisation, competing colonial powers (the USA, Japan, France, etc) and a turmoil-ridden society. In such conditions ripe for a revolution, Mao too, like Lenin, opted to take up the societal cause for developing a mass following.

The success of the left revolutions in various parts of the world inspired the political left in India to strive for a similar feat in order to liberate the exploited classes. However, the planning lacked deliberations and efforts were not made to adapt the foreign experience to Indian conditions. Unlike Lenin's methodology of enabling the desired changes in a phased manner, the left political class in India strived to outdo (the prevailing) Capitalism, Imperialism and Feudalism in one stroke.

The inception of the Naxal ideology could be traced to the advocacies of the peasant leader Swami Sahajanand Saraswati, who gave a call for the United Front (Samyukt Morcha) comprising the peasantry and the working class. The movement was dovetailed into the Indian freedom struggle and aimed at the three-pronged objective of peasant revolution, independence and liberation for the downtrodden. An effort towards this was attempted in the Telangana movement. Unfortunately, a united front could not work there mainly due to the weaknesses of the leadership that was divided and dissent-ridden.

Maoists and Mao's Ideological Umbrella: Not to Be

Soon after the Communist Party of India (Marxist) was formed at the Seventh Congress of the Communist Party of India in November 1964, a section of its leaders wanted the party to add armed revolution to its agenda, following the example of China. Prominent among them were Charu Majumdar and Kanu Sanyal. The party leadership did not entirely dismiss the possibility of an armed uprising.

In 1965, Majumdar came out with his famous *Eight Documents*[1], which essentially exhorted the party to fight against revisionism within itself, follow the example of Mao's China, and take up an armed struggle against the state, whilst underlining that action, rather than politics, was the need of the day[2]. The two factions of the party continued to coexist, albeit a little uneasily, under the same banner for a while. Their differences became irreconcilable when the first CPI (M) led United Front government was formed in 1967.

The proponents of Naxalism splintered from the CPI (M) primarily over differences on the issue of future participation in a parliamentary democracy and, more significantly, on the means of carrying forward the 'revolution'. In the monsoon of 1968, Kanu Sanyal led a team of five revolutionaries on a trip to China where they received a warm welcome. It is believed that in their two-and-a-half month stay in China, they even underwent military training.

Back in China, the Chinese Communist Party (CCP) drifted towards a left sectarian position and began characterising India as a neo-colony and client of the imperialists. The Naxalite movement received ideological support from China and saw the emergence of the left extremist leaning and formation of the CPI (ML), in 1970. The official mouthpiece of the CCP, the *People's Daily* published an editorial on July 05, 1967, titled "Spring Thunder Breaks over India", hailing the Naxalbari revolt, arguing that an "armed struggle is the only correct road for the Indian revolution ..." The editorial further went on to state, "A peal of spring thunder has crashed over the land of India. Revolutionary peasants in the Darjeeling area have risen in rebellion. Under the leadership of a revolutionary group of the Indian Communist Party, a red area of rural revolutionary armed struggle has been established in India. This is a development of tremendous significance for the Indian people's revolutionary struggle"[3].

In the beginning of the Naxalite movement, there was mutual rhetorical support between the Maoist regime in China and the Naxalites in India. While there was little evidence of material support (in addition to no indication of such support even today), the advent and growth of the Naxalite movement certainly did serve China's goal of politically weakening its largest neighbour to the south, when viewed through the prism of Sino-Indian relations during the decades of the 1960s and 1970s. With the expectant Chinese prescription, the Naxalites in India adopted the strategy of the Chinese revolution discussed above and portrayed themselves as the "flag bearers of the Chinese line".

Back in China, Mao Zedong came to feel that party leadership in China during the decade of the 1960s was drifting away from ideological purity. Given that his own position had considerably weakened following the failure of his "Great Leap Forward" (1958-60) and the ensuing economic crisis, Mao got together with Defence Minister Lin Biao, to help him attack the current party leadership and reassert authority and control. Resultantly, the Great Proletarian Cultural Revolution was launched in August 1966, at a meeting of the Plenum of the Central Committee. The movement gathered momentum with students forming paramilitary groups called the Red Guards – claiming true understanding of Maoist thought. The flip side to this was the factionalism within the Red Guards battling for supremacy, rendering many Chinese cities on the brink of anarchy by September 1967. Owing to the political chaos, the Chinese economy plummeted, with industrial production for 1968 dropping 12 per cent below that of 1966.[4]

The adverse impact of the Cultural Revolution was felt far and wide by 1969, with nearly 1.5 million people being killed, millions suffering imprisonment, seizure of property, and torture.

The CCP itself went through radical changes in the aftermath of the Cultural Revolution and the subsequent death of both Mao and Zhou Enlai in 1976. Deng Xiaoping regained power in 1977, and controlled China for the next two decades. These political upheavals in Beijing impacted the fragile ideological framework of the CPI (ML) and it could not come to grips with the transition, eventually leading to innumerable splits during the decades of the 1970s and 1980s.

Despite the deviations from Maoist ideology in post-Mao China, Chairman Mao remained above any criticism for the Naxalites and their movement in India. The Naxals attach an almost divine infallibility to Mao, seeking to emulate his analysis, strategies and tactics adopted during the Chinese Revolution, including using weapons to achieve objectives in an Indian context[5]. The desired 'adaptation' of Mao's model to the Indian context has remained elusive; on the part of the Naxalite groups in India, it came to be a blind replication.

Failing to Adapt

While Lenin and Mao suitably contextualised Marxism to the conditions existing in their respective country, the Naxalites have inherently failed to align the imported ideology to the cause of the deprived sections of India. This inability to generate mass mobilisation has been the primary cause of the failure of the movement in India and led to consistent splintering of the LWE groups, since its inception.

The CPI (Maoist) came into existence in 2004. It has shot into the limelight by means of numerous acts of violence and bloodshed, and certainly not owing to any achievements for the tribals or peasants whose cause they claim to uphold. Ever since the movement's inception, India's LWE groups have believed in the 'one size fits all' theory of revolution – and imitating the Chinese module. By doing so, they have failed in reading and inferring the correlation of class forces amongst India's masses.

The simplistic dogma adopted by the LWE ideologues has been that the situation is always ripe for a revolution, and if it succeeded in China, it just needs to be emulated in India at all costs. In this reference, the Naxalites led by Charu Majumdar have often been referred to as 'men in a hurry' – with 'romanticism' becoming the key driver, coupled with their inability to gauge the tempo of mass mobilisation. In the process, the Naxalites committed grave blunders while pursuing their version of revolution, the first among them being rechristening of India as 'Dakshin Desh', China being 'Uttar Desh' and Chairman Mao, the Chairman. Secondly, they pursued relentless and unwarranted class annihilation, thereby segmenting their own home support base[6].

These developments did not go down too well with the masses, and the opportunity to develop the crucial mass base was lost even before coming their way. Besides, in a revolutionary bid to encircle cities from the countryside (as advocated and practised by Mao), the ill-prepared optimists, with urban backgrounds, holed themselves up in cities, and were neutralised. Not surprisingly, with no emphasis on the people's movement, the initial phase of Naxalism triggered by the Naxalbari uprising was smothered in the early years of the 1970s.[7]

Following the Congress of the CPI (M-L) in May 1969, one of its leaders, Souren Bose, went to China with the party documents. China's CCP was strongly critical of the activities of the CPI (M-L) and rejected the latter's claim that "China's Chairman is our Chairman". Considering that India's Naxalite movement was going nowhere and had become a cause of embarrassment, it is reported that the Chinese Communist Party sent a note to Charu Majumdar expressing its reservations over the activities of the CPI (M-L) in 1970-71. Chinese Premier Zhou Enlai reportedly pulled up the Naxal leaders who visited China, for attempting a blind replication of the Chinese model of revolution and feigning united front tactics.

Faulty Interpretation of the Indian Milieu

The Naxalites' characterisation of the Indian bourgeoisie as 'comprador' remains the basic source of its errors. As per a thesis adopted at the Sixth Congress of the Communist International (1928) 'comprador' meant native merchants, engaged in trade with imperialist centres, whose interests are in continuation of imperialist exploitation, acting as agents for exploiting the masses in the colonial countries. To characterise the Indian bourgeoisie as comprador grossly misconstrues the character of the ruling classes that has evolved into a different shade after India's independence [8].

Without understanding the complexity of the evolutionary process of capitalist development in India and mechanically presuming an exact resemblance with pre-revolutionary China, the Naxalites grossly misread the Indian class character. Given that their theoretical understanding about India's capitalist development is totally out of line with reality, the practice of the Maoists has little to do with the people's livelihood and attaining socio-economic justice. While the first and second generations of Naxalites in India (from the late 1960s, through the 1970s and 1980s) were centred on issues pertaining to land reforms, the present generation led by he CPI (Maoist) planks itself on the issues related to the political economy of neo-liberalism. In the fight for tribal rights, they do not believe in organising the tribals for exercising their sovereign rights over land and forest resources or for socio-economic development[9]. Political executions and violence are their practised methodologies and such nihilist anarchism is perpetrated in the name of 'people's war'. The belief that "tribals can only be mobilised under the slogan for a 'protracted people's war' and that policy changes will take place only after a 'revolutionary government ' is established", remains a pipe-dream.

The Communist Party of India, drawing lessons from the Telangana movement, (wrongly) inferred that a socialist revolution in India could only be initiated as a capitalist revolution rather than as a people's revolution. Resultantly, the CPI started supporting the Nehruvian model of mixed economy that had elements of the public and private sectors. This approach did not find appeal amongst the entire party, leading to a split in the CPI and giving rise to the CPI (Marxist), followed by the falling apart of the Charu Mazumdar led faction called the Naxalites. Initially, the anti-establishment political tone of various resistance movements was anti-Congress but later i.e. post 1967, seeing the many non-Congress (left) governments not able to make a mark, it was established that liberation for the marginalised and exploited class could not be merely anti-Congress in nature, but had to be anti-ruling class. In other words, pitching the ruling class versus the rest gained ground and continues to be the tenor of the Naxal movement till today.

As per a school of thought, like China, had Naxalism gained roots in India in the 1930s, things would have been different. By the late 1960s, when the ideology gained a foothold in the country, capitalism had made substantial inroads in India. At that time in history, blind replication of Mao's model, without mass mobilisation, was attempted by Charu Mazumdar, to no avail. In fact, Chinese Premier Zhou Enlai had pulled up one of the Naxal leaders of that time for attempting a blind replication of the Chinese model of revolution.

In the decades of the 1980s and 1990s, a number of groups with Naxal ideology were active, mainly in the two states of Bihar and Andhra Pradesh. The leaders of those times like Vinod Misra, Nagbhushan Patnaik, Nagi Reddy, etc drew the correct lessons from the failure of the preceding phase of Naxalism and laid due emphasis on mass mobilisation. The aspects of class annihilation and armed insurrection were somewhat diluted and saw several sections of the society aligning with the movement, including people from the intelligentsia as also segments belonging to the Jaya Prakash (JP) movement. However, any semblance of a united front (Samyukt Morcha) comprising the peasants and working class was still missing and, therefore, the movement could not be transformed into a populist one. For example, in rural Bihar, social churnings led to caste wars; and class war, as a base of Naxalism, lost ground. Private armies and militias (funded by the rich) belonging to various castes sprang up, resulting in clashes amongst the lower strata of society. A common cause that could have provided a platform for mobilisation was missing, mainly because of the prevailing circumstances of constitutional democracy and equity in spite of being perceived to be lopsided. Within the ambit of the Naxalite movement, a conflict existed between the short and long-term gains of the rural poor. The shorter one being destruction of resources and infrastructure of the establishment and the landed class, which hampered the long-term benefits of amelioration of the conditions of the poor by dissuading investments and development. Incidentally, the said conflict exists till date, which has seen shrinking of the ideological bandwidth of the movement.

Indulging in mindless militarism in the name of revolution, the Maoists have committed gross human rights violations. The present phase of Naxalism in India has no class war as its basis and is primarily directed against the government , with a conspicuously missing ideological edifice to stand upon. The CPI (Maoist) continues to remain in the shadows of the old ideological structure that is not synchronous to the façade of the 'tribal cause' that it claims to champion. As per a former Naxal activist Raghav Sharan Sharma, "Sporadic spates of Naxal violence in the central-east tribal belt of India can be compared to the flicker of a flame before it extinguishes"[10]. Their ideology of an 'armed uprising' makes it totally unacceptable not only to the Indian government, but also places a realm of scepticism around the people who constitute their supposedly 'claimed' support base. The party is able to survive till the time they become a major threat to the sovereignty of the nation[11].

Also, their policy documents appear to be 'Stalinist' with the predominant tone of centralisation and secession; aspects that remain unacceptable not only to the government but also to the people who form their support base. The tribal aim is not to overthrow the Indian state but to succeed in securing unhindered access to resources that *belong to them*, but which the state has been denying them. The tribal struggle is for the right to life, to livelihood and dignity, including freedom from violence and from the racism that much of India displays and practices towards them. The massive alienation of tribal land that has gone on even after independence was something the government could have stopped if it had the will to do so. Whatever the CPI (Maoist) might think, the vast majority of the tribals in India have no conception of "capturing state power," since the state itself is such an abstraction gxcept in terms of harassment by forest officials, neglect by state governments, and violence from the police and paramilitary[12]. The aspirations of the tribals are clearly in a different silo vis-à-vis the ulterior motives of the Naxalites. The government needs to fulfill the former while firmly dealing with the latter.

Notes

1. https://ajadhind.wordpress.com/historic-documents-charu-mazumdar/
2. Suhrid Sankar Chattopadhyay, "End of a Revolution," *Frontline*, Vol. 27, No. 8, April 2010.
3. Ibid.
4. For more details, see Xu Xiaoge, "The 50th National Day of the People's Republic of China" in Linda K. Fuller, ed., *National Days/National Ways: Historical, Political, and Religious Celebrations Around the World* (Greenwood Publishing Group, 2004), p. 80.
5. Nilotpal Basu, "The Tragedy of Maoism", in Prasenjit Bose, ed., *Maoism: A Critique from the Left* (Leftword, May 2010).
6. Shashank Ranjan, "Ideological Faultlines of the Naxal Movement in India", Article 1332, Centre for Land Warfare Studies, June 24, 2015, available at http://www.claws.in/1399/ideological-faultlines-of-the-naxal-movement-in-india-shashank-ranjan.html
7. Ibid.
8. Ibid.
9. The Maoists have conspicuously remained absent in the struggles for forest rights of the tribals waged by various democratic organisations, which led to the enactment of the Forest Rights Act of 2006. Also, unlike the late 1960s when the Naxalites attempted to organise tribal peasant movements, the contemporary Maoists have shown no such inclination.
10. https://www.youtube.com/watch?v=mfKkrQtwPbA
11. Ibid.
12. *Platypus Review*, 26, "The Maoist insurgency in India: End of the Road for Indian Stalinism?", An interview with Jairus Banaji, August 26, 2010.

Section Three
The Perception Paradigm

10. MAOISTS' CLAIMS: "REVOLUTION BY, OF AND FOR THE PEOPLE"[1]

Dandakaranya (DK), the hub of Maoist control, lies in central India. This is a vast region with slices taken from five different states. It embraces parts of Madhya Pradesh, Maharashtra, Telangana, Chhattisgarh and Odisha. People of several tribes such as the Gond, Madia, Govari, Kondu, Kondareddy, Nayakapu, Dorla, Maria (Koya), and Baiga as well as the Odiya tribes of Puruja, Gudijursa, Butar, Durva, etc live in DK.

As per the Maoists' literature, the Adivasis of the DK region have been victims of exploitation of three types[2]:

- The ruling classes have retained the age-old socio-economic structure and backwardness of the people and the region.
- The local people have been subjected to ruthless exploitation by the landlords, traders, usurers and government officials (primarily the Forest Department).
- Exploitation by the multinationals – the comprador-bureaucrat capitalist combine—who have displaced thousands, polluted rivers, cut down their forests and reduced the Adivasis to the existence of beggars.

The Maoist movement in DK commenced against the above-mentioned background in the late 1980s, when a number of CPI (ML) People's War armed activists from Andhra Pradesh, split into groups, and entered Gadchiroli and Bastar to spread the message of revolution. The mentioned area, especially south Bastar, continues to be the stronghold of the Maoists, even today.

Predicament about the Revolution

There was a view prevalent among some of those political workers who entered DK in 1980s, that since there were no classes in DK, there was no need of an agrarian revolution and that the New Democratic Revolution(NDR)[3£] would not be applicable here. Since there existed no feudal system, the NDR was considered to be unsuitable and a new theory was required to be forged. Others held the view that even if there was no feudal system, there was the state that represented the comprador, bourgeoisie and feudal classes. The state, hence, was the enemy and there was to be the NDR[4], as per the Maoists' ideologues steering the movement.

The dilemma with respect to the existence of classes in DK was solved in 1987 when the armed cadres formed Forest Committees. In 1988, the Forest Committees resolved on the basis of investigation that there were classes in DK too, and that the feudal exploitation was in the primitive stage in the region. Various classes, irrespective of their stage of formation, were to be dealt with as per the understanding of the NDR, suited to the local conditions.

Entry in Gadchiroli

Gadchiroli district came into existence in Maharashtra in 1982 with the merger of three taluks – the others being Sirinchanad and Etapalli. Its population then was 700,000 of whom 45 percent were Adivasis. The district covers an area of 15,435 sq km, 80 percent of which was dense forest, primarily the Chandrapur forests. The Maoist activists entered the area in the late 1980s. Most of the forest people owned small plots of land which were not very fertile. They lived in poverty and backwardness, dependent partly on a single crop, rain-fed agriculture and partly on forests for their livelihoods.

The forests, given the abundance of resources, were a source of tremendous revenue for the FD and the government. These forests were exploited by the government for the benefit of big paper mills owned by the comprador big bourgeoisie and big contractors. The net revenue of the FD in 1981 was Rs. 1.10

crore. The contractors and forest officials minted millions from both legal and illegal sales of teak, bamboo, etc[5].

On the other hand, the local villagers had been induced into becoming cheap labour for the FD. They were harassed and exploited in innumerable ways by the contractors and FD employees. These people were once the rulers of the jungles, but had become the wage slaves, while the FD and the contractors had become kings of the forests. The Adivasis had lost many of their rights over the forests. Whether it was grazing cattle, or collecting deadwood as timber, or even mahua flowers to make their traditional drink, they found themselves at the mercy of the forest guards and the police. Paying fines to them and bribes was a common occurrence.

There was a report prepared in 2001 at the initiative of the Maoists, which has the details of changes brought about by the Maoists in Gadchiroli. The field reporter claimed to have visited 60 villages in Gadchiroli to make the report. At every stage of development, the rebels had to fight against forest officers, landlords, security forces, etc by mobilising people on a large scale. Armed squads played an important role in all the stages, backed by various democratic organisations of the Adivasis, women or those dealing with culture[6].

In the preface of the report, the author states; "The revolutionary movement brought about many changes in various sectors in the division in the past two decades....changes occurred in land relations, traditional bonded labour, economic and other forms of exploitation, loan facilities, production relations, rising of the petty bourgeois section, in the living conditions of the people...man-woman working relations, education, health, customary celebrations, and many such things. To put it in one word, the seeds for a fundamental change in the socio-economic and political aspects have been sown. Our revolutionary movement is one of the main reasons for this change"[7].

As per the Maoists' literature, "In Gadchiroli, right from the very beginning, the Maharashtra government dealt with the Maoist movement in a way that had nothing novel about it. On the one hand, it adopted a policy of repression by spending millions of rupees on the creation and mobilisation of police and paramilitary forces; on the other, it initiated 'developmental' works—called economic reforms. The other element of such development activities was the construction of a communication network by making roads connecting large parts of the interior, significantly in those areas where radical struggle had already become a source of headache for the government. The aim was not just to send police / paramilitary convoys, but also to establish a market link and exploit the remote villages in the forest area permanently. Such measures, meant to counter radical movements, affected the society in a big way, such as in the emergence of a minority section who became the beneficiaries of the state sponsored development schemes"[8]. The salient aspects brought out in the report are given in the succeeding paras.

Changes in Land Relations

The changes in land relations were closely tied up with the expansion of the armed squads. The decade of the 1980s was the turning point in the lives of the Adivasis, as the revolutionary movement gained the upper hand. Until 1980, a majority of the peasants were deprived of land rights (pattas). Normally, every peasant was eager to have land rights that empowered him socio-economically and psychologically. Local political leaders extracted money from the peasants promising to provide them with pattas, but pocketed the money and deceived them. Maoist squads mobilised the farmers with the slogan, "land to the tiller" – aligning it with the objectives towards the NDR. The people fought heroically against the FD for rights over land. Between 1981-84, in 40 villages of Gadchiroli district, 20,000 acres of land was brought under agriculture. Migration to these villages, where farmers were free to till without the oppression of the FD, took place by the landless farmers of neighbouring areas.

The land over which possession or ownership was established through the struggle were called 'jabran' land as opposed to 'patta' land. And a time came when, through the emancipation of the peasantry, the area of 'jabran' land was more than that of 'patta' land. As the Maoists gained a foothold through their mass movement over land rights, by the late 1980s, they started declaring the state government as irrelevant – signalling the beginning of an assertion of a new political power. Ideas started getting transformed and mobilisation of peasants on the issue of 'patta' land outlived its utility by 1990, since the inherent aim related to land rights had been achieved.

In a nutshell, vis-à-vis the land relations, three achievements that could be listed were: firstly, as a result of the revolutionary movement, the majority of the poor peasants got new lands; secondly, all new lands were being tilled, and thirdly, due to availability of additional land, fundamental changes took place in land relations, reflected at the base level by way of enhanced standard of living of the erstwhile poor peasantry.

Bonded Labour and Other Forms of Non-Economic Exploitation

In the region, there was a marked difference in the forms of exploitation of the poor Adivasi peasants before and after 1980. As the revolution gained momentum, changes took place. The rural peasantry, however, could not break the traditional exploitation at the hands of the traditional village heads, as much as they broke that of the FD, Revenue Department and police. The backward, exploited peasantry continued to respect the dogmatic traditions, superstitious customs and unscientific practices associated with the Adivasi culture.

However, over a period of time, after the entry of the squads and consolidation of the revolutionary movement, changes started taking shape towards overcoming the traditional chains, too. In Gadchiroli, the movement was based on the support of two tribes, the Koya (Rajagondu) and Gotte (Maria). The influence of the king and traditional heads on the Koyas was relatively less than that on the Maria Adivasis. Until 1990, the Koyas were the main constituents of the guerrilla forces.

Meanwhile, various people's democratic organisations emerged which highlighted several immediate and long-term issues. By 1990, 15,000 peasants formed part of the DK Adivasi Mahila Sangham (KAMS). There were at that time 61 party cells, 64 militias (Gram Raksha Dalams), all of which helped in the propaganda work in a big way. The exploitation by the tribal heads in the villages ended because of the radical movement. Moreover, primary changes in production relations, land relations, increase in production and social changes, came about. The government officials did not dare to come to the villages. Such changes, needless to state, had not been easy to bring about. There were many ups and downs. In Gadchiroli division, various forms of feudal or traditional exploitation had been eliminated; but the tribal head continued to have a say in the super-structural issues of the village. Revolutionary organisations were sometimes not in a position to intervene in the cultural affairs of the village.

Changes in Rural Loan Facilities, Moneylending and Limiting Profits

Previously, the Adivasis had been subjected to various forms of exploitation. It is well known that the non-tribals considered the tribal areas as 'golden ducks'. Many traders came to the tribal hamlets, sold ordinary food and cosmetic material, and pocketed a huge profit. There were also instances when the Adivasis surrendered their prized possessions as well as their land to the outsiders. The story is the same with 'Diku' of Chhotanagpur, 'Payika' of Bastar, 'Koskir' of Abujhmaad, 'Komati' and 'Gandla' of Gadchiroli, etc. These outsiders exploited the Adivasis in several ways.

The sahukars were one of the main exploiters of the rural peasantry. The spread of the revolutionary movement put a brake on their exploitation. 'Famine raids' were organised to loot the granaries of the hoarders and the rich. The party allowed normal traders to carry on with their businesses and also took measures to curb greedy profits. Steps were taken to enforce proper measurements, fixing rates, thereby, limiting profits. The eradication of loans at unreasonable returns was carried out by the revolutionaries by the formation of 'paddy cooperative societies'.

Before the spread of the movement, the Adivasi peasants got government loans only nominally. However, with the consolidation of the revolutionary movement, the government sought to allure the people with 'loan melas' to wean the villagers away from the movement. Various forms of loan schemes were introduced by the government – however, these loans generally went to the rich peasants, people of higher castes and those with connections. In response, the party adopted the policy of convincing the people to boycott 'loan melas'.

Developments in Market and Commercial Activities

There was a considerable increase in the purchasing power of the Adivasis during 1980-2000, mainly due to stabilised production relations and for the end of exploitation, ushered in by the revolutionaries. This led to the growth and expansion of markets. The Maoists enforced wage hikes, at times for certain commodities and services to up to 25 percent. Proper rates of labour wages were demanded and obtained by the revolutionary mass organisations, which fought against exploiters and government officials, demanding these rates for the labour.

The income of the farmers increased, but they still did not have ownership rights over the forests. They started to realise that ownership rights were tied up with the success of the NDR.

Revolutionary Movement and Village Life

The exploitative nexus of the landlord-village head-village priest, with the local king at the helm was very strong before 1980. The mass organisations setup in the wake of the revolutionary movement, started to take control over Panchayat matters as also in the case of disputes or contradictions between village heads and Adivasis. Members of mass organisations and squads met Adivasi families and listened to their grievances. Mass organisations started conducting public meetings which were attended by the erstwhile exploiters as well. Assertion on the part of the poor started. Slowly, the exploiting class stepped down from the leadership, and the poor and middle class peasantry, represented by the guerrillas, took charge.

People's War in DK: The Alternative Model of Development

In the programme of the CPI (ML) adopted at the Party Congress held in May 1970, the accomplishment of the NDR, the essence of which was an agrarian revolution, was declared to be the immediate goal of the revolutionary movement, and this had to be achieved in a semi-feudal and semi-colonial country like India by fighting against feudalism, comprador capitalism and imperialism[9] . The aim was to set up a new democratic society and then create a socialist society. It also charted the major task of an Indian revolution such as "confiscation of the enterprises of the Comprador Bureaucrat Capitalists, implementation of land to the tillers programme, formation of organs of people's political power, development of a new culture and education oriented towards the needs of the people, etc"[10]. It was the new model of development clearly opposed to that championed by the Indian ruling classes.

At the special conference of the CPI (ML) People's War held in 1995, new changes were introduced, most of which were incorporated into the programme of the CPI (Maoist) adopted in 2004 after the merger. Some new aspects, either not addressed or partially addressed earlier, were pointed out at length, such as the caste-based feudal structure, the pro-Hindu bias of the Indian state, Indian expansionism, importance of Adivasis and the need for the formation of a voluntary union of the People's Democratic Federal Republics of India (PDFRI), recognising the rights of self-determination. There was also a clear outline of the picture of the new society they aspired to create[11].

The Naxalbari movement, in the first phase, could not attempt these new social experiments. It is only in the current phase of the Maoist movement that there have been successful attempts at implementing a totally new model of development for the first time in the country. It was attempted first in the DK region in the central part of India[12]; of which Gadchiroli formed a part, as has been discussed earlier.

Apart from the major socio-economic developments carried out (and claimed) by the Maoists that have been discussed earlier, one of the major achievements according to them, has been the 'New System of Justice'. In earlier periods, it was the Adivasi priesthood that acted as the administrative system, running side by side with the Indian administration. Twelve villages made one 'bancha'; forty villages made one 'pargana'; and sixty villages formed one 'patti'. Atop all, there was the tribal king. Each village had a headman, who looked into the village problems and also performed administrative duties. Problems that remained unresolved were referred to higher bodies like the 'pargana' or 'patti'. The decision taken in the higher / highest body was binding on all. Once a decision was taken on any crime, punishment was meted out by taking into consideration the depth and extent of the crime. The judgement was made by the village elders. These elders were called 'Patels' at the village level and 'Manjhi', 'Shandoshes' and 'Bhumiyal' at the higher level. These village judges delivered judgements on various issues such as murders, problems related to marriage, customs, etc. The extent of punishment depended entirely on the whims of the elders. The villagers were terribly afraid of what the punishment might be, and the decision was final and binding on all. In the Adivasi society of yesteryears, the state machinery was rather weak and there was hardly any communication system worth its name. The Adivasi world was totally isolated and people did not have any experience of police or courts even as late as the mid-1970s. All the disputes were settled within the tribal administrative network, irrespective of the gravity of the crime.

It was nearly a decade after the spread of the revolutionary movement in those areas that people's courts came to be established[13]. That was quite natural. The appearance of the people's court presupposes a situation when the revolutionary movement has already taken roots in society. The old village elder-centric Adivasi system of justice had outlived its utility and acceptability, and revolutionary forces had made their strength felt by countering attacks from the state forces. The elementary form of the people's courts, according to the activists, has to be found in the mass organisations themselves[14].

The building of mass organisations and the spread of mass movements followed close on the heels of the revolutionary movement in DK. Peasants and agricultural labourers were organised under mass organisations to fight against exploitation and repression by the village elders. Gradually, the influence of the priests declined and the people turned to the mass organisations for the redressal of their grievances. Thus, the peasants and agricultural workers could resolve their problems, on their own. In place of financial penalty or ostracism, a new system of justice based on mutual cooperation was introduced.

In 1995, the revolutionary movement culminated in the formation of the Gram Rajya Committee (regarded as the present form of the dictatorship of the proletariat), or people's court. With the progress of the movement, the RPC (Revolutionary People's Committee) set up the Department of Justice as one part of it. This department brought in its fold, all the people living in the area covered by the RPC (about 3,000 persons under one RPC). This department consists of 3 to 5 members of both sexes, and has under its supervision, one People's Protection Squad of 7 to 11 members each. Later, these squads came to be known as militias. The Department of Justice was part of the Janatana Sarkar (JS) that had other departments like People's Defence, Finance, Agriculture, Trade and Industry, Education and Culture, Health and Social Welfare, Forest, Public Relations[15].

The Maoists, in their summing up of their experience of their movement in DK, over several decades, arrived at the following conclusions[16].

First, in place of mass organisations, the judicial department of the revolutionary government has started taking steps, even if in a rudimentary form, to resolve the people's problems.

Second, in place of the old Panchayati Raj system wherein the village elders reigned supreme, peasants and agricultural labourers under the new organs of people's power have established their control over various rural affairs.

Third, the age-old judicial system under the village elders has been demolished. In its place, there has emerged a judicial system under the judicial department of the JS or the people's government.

Fourth, the new JS adopts a class outlook and metes out punishment on that basis. Before a prisoner is given a death sentence, a thorough investigation is conducted and the decision on the death sentence is taken only after consultations with the people.

Fifth, the people's authority is not guided by considerations such as selfishness, individual profits, individual likes and dislikes or narrow party interests.

Sixth, new ideas are emerging that should be strengthened to unite the people against the old ideas within the old society and also transform the existing realiy.

Seventh, dogmas in the name of customs and traditions have been done away with, mainly due to the revolutionary march. These traditional customs were but some of the many ropes round the necks of the peasants and their end instilled in the minds of peasants, a sense of liberation from the age-old shackles.

Eighth, with the weakening of old customs, there has been a spread of critical outlook and scientific knowledge.

Ninth, the new system of justice, introduced by the Maoists has made people turn away from the Indian judicial system, thus, providing them with succour.

In a nutshell, as claimed by the Maoists, the most important achievement of the DK struggle is that a new society is being created and is thriving. People oppressed for ages have stood up with their heads held high. The DK region is the scene of numerous social, economic and political experiments, and these became possible because of their inseparable ties with the ongoing armed revolutionary struggle. DK is witnessing what the erstwhile liberated areas of Telangana, Srikakulam, etc could not see and what Charu Mazumdar had dreamt of.

Notes

1. The chapter draws accounts primarily from Maoists' literature and Maoists sympathisers' accounts.
2. Amit Bhattacharya, "Storming the Gates of Heaven – The Maoist Movement in India, a Critical Study" in *The Maoist Movement and Socio-economic Changes* (Setu Prakashani, 2014).
3. The CPI (Maoist) describes India as backward, semi-colonial and semi-feudal. It is committed to Marxism-Leninism-Maoism. Its objective is to wage Protracted People's War (PPW) on the lines propounded by Mao, seize/capture state/ political power and herald an NDR, under the leadership of the agrarian class. This NDR would be conducted through guerrilla warfare by establishing base areas in the villages and then encircling the towns and cities, before the final Long March to capture political power.
4. Report titled, "Various Classes in Bastar – Our Attitude", *Viyukka*, September 2000.
5. Report titled, "Chandrapur Forests: A Stir" in the *Voice of Vanguard*, organ of the Central Committee, Communist Party of India (Marxist-Leninist) (People's War), Vol. I: 7, September 1983, pp. 9-11.
6. Bhupati, "Revolutionary Changes in Gadchiroli in Two Decades", a manuscript report referred to by Bhattacharya, n.2.
7. Ibid.
8. Ibid.
9. The inherent faultlines in interpretation of this principle have been discussed separately in different chapter.
10. "Programme of the Communist Party of India (Marxist-Leninist)" in Suniti Kumar Ghosh, ed., *The Historic Turning Point – A Liberation Anthology*, Vol II, (Calcutta, February 1993), pp. 10-17.
11. "New People's Power in Dandakaranya", a report on the ongoing developmental activities through the New Organs of CPI (ML) (People's Power), Calcutta, December 20, 2000, p. 2.
12. Bhattacharya, n. 2.
13. A people's court is not peculiar to the Indian Communist revolutionary movement. Most of the revolutionary movements in different countries were witness to the formation of people's courts and the meting out of justice.
14. Ibid.
15. Ibid.
16. Ibid.

11. MANAGING PERCEPTIONS FOR THE MAOISTS

The militant groups have a tendency to show an inclination to address the civil society, rather than the state – as an endeavour on their part to strike at the very thought process of the society. Since the Maoists cannot represent themselves, with their leaders in hiding and no sympathisers ready to act as mediators, a section of intelligentsia and activists in the form of front organisations, provide them with the legitimacy they lack and allow them to participate in the lively debate that characterises our society[1]. Given the role of the media and intellectuals in any political order, it primarily rests on the intelligentsia, supported by the media to assist in the people's empowerment by giving a voice to their aspirations and not letting the anti-national ultras hijack a people-centric agenda to swing public perception.

The intelligentsia that includes academia, writers and journalists, enjoy the combined benefits of a democracy to the optimum. By their disposition, they are partly immune to the repressive mechanism of the state till they do not go overboard, as happened in the recent arrest of GN Saibaba, who was charged with allegedly providing logistics, helping in recruitment, and maintaining contact with the Maoist leadership[2].

As remarked by Noam Chomsky, "The history of intellectuals is written by intellectuals, so not surprisingly, they are portrayed as defenders of rights and justice, upholding the highest values and confronting power with admirable courage and integrity"[3]. Therefore, the voice of the intellectuals has tremendous credibility in a society. The ability to investigate issues with intellectual diligence and honesty to expose the falsity propagated by the parties involved, should be the central aspect of an intellectual campaign. Notwithstanding the above, in many of the cases, the intellectual community as a whole is not exactly the harbinger of real social change. Intellectuals do tend to develop vested interests, owing to their prejudices and, often, romanticism.

The CPI (Maoist) has a well-organised United Front, comprising the Tactical United Front (TUF) and Strategic United Front (SUF). The TUF comprises organisations that are opposed to the state for one reason or another. For example, the People's Democratic Front of India (PDFI) was formed in July 2006, through the efforts of a Maoist front organisation known as the Revolutionary Democratic Front (RDF) and on its rolls are public personalities and activists like Medha Patkar, Nandita Haksar, P Vravara Rao, etc. The TUF helps the Maoists put into effect, their consolidation and expansion in the society through overground cadre expansion, carrying out indoctrination campaigns, especially in urban areas, poaching partners for potential leaders and ideologues, serving as a cover from the state and reinforcing the military activities, i.e. the armed struggle[4].

The Maoists consider themselves to be a political organisation, and, hence, the issues concerning the people form part of their agenda. The canvas of the issues they undertake is very wide, with substantial resonance in society. They find the much desired legitimacy, with a section of the intelligentsia and middle class associated with the TUF in some manner, giving them support. They exploit every available forum to voice the concerns of the people and turn it to their advantage. In all this, the ultimate goal remains the armed overthrow of the state and, therefore, it is important to distinguish between hardcore Maoist sympathisers amongst the intelligentsia and those who do not subscribe to the Maoist ideology of 'armed insurrection'. When well known intellectuals and public figures write and speak in support of some pro-people activities of the Maoists,they actually play into the hands of the Maoists.

By influencing the impressionable minds of the young, they further the Maoist agenda[5].

Many a times, intellectual campaigns have degenerated into propaganda when the principles of value and truth are disregarded. One such case has been the initiating and executing of political petitions asking people to support a cause. This is particularly serious when signatures are sought from distinguished persons who are not likely to know the background well enough to give an informed consent. A case in point has been Mahasweta Devi's declared dissociation with Chhatradhar Mahto, once his links with the Maoists came to the fore[6]—the links which she was not privy to, in the beginning, when the endorsement was done. An online forum by the name 'Sanhati', went on to paint the disturbances in the LWE affected areas as a war between the state and the Adivasis – and successfully obtained endorsements without even hinting at the role played by the armed Maoists – colouring the Adivasi resistance as Maoist and all Maoists as Adivasis[7]. In such statements, the picture that is painted remains totally silent on the role played by the CPI (Maoist) and its armed rebellion. In such petitions, the Maoists are mentioned in passing, to plant the idea that the government uses the 'shadow of insurgency' as an excuse to hunt down the marginalised indigenous people. There is always an ill-concealed attempt to paint Maoism in terms of a "desperate resistance of local indigenous people". What is not so transparent from these statements is the condition that has brought about this state of affairs; with armed Maoism at the root.[8]

Adivasis who become Maoists do not do so because they agree with their politics, their ideology or their programme. They do so because 'Maoism' performs some functions in a very immediate sense in their lives. And in the clash between the state and the Maoists, these unfortunate people are sandwiched[9]. What needs to be highlighted here and in similar situations is that it is not Maoism that is the real issue. It is the injustice, which lies at the root of this bane. The fact is that the Maoists have lapped up the tribal agenda for their ulterior motives. The intellectual supporters, perhaps inadvertently, act in conjunction with the Maoists to suitably the mould perceptions of the citizenry.

While the Maoists have built their campaign around the perceived or actual neglect and alienation of the tribals, the state policies have remained inadequate towards creating a favourable perception, in the society in general and amongst the aggrieved population in particular[10]. One of the most neglected areas of the government's counter Maoist approach has been the lack of adequate emphasis on psychological operations.

Towards this, the state has to pitch in the intellectuals inclined against the Maoist ideology to counter the propaganda by the Maoist intelligentsia. Cultivating, moulding and nurturing a favourable opinion shall play a major role and its percolation ought to be inclusive, down to the local levels and not merely confined to 'arm chair musings' and 'prime time debates'.These measures should provide a background to the government's approach to address the prevalent 'trust deficit' amongst the population in the LWE affected areas. Also, the stance which the state supporting intelligentsia takes, has to be based on truth, flowing from a genuine approach by the state to address the aspirations of the aggrieved populace. Lest it ends as a counter-productive exercise, vulnerable to be exploited by the Maoists and the section of intelligentsia backing them.

The state, to counter the Maoists' intellectual propaganda, has often attempted to enforce itself on the Maoist disposed intelligentsia. Any such move to scuttle the voices, in the form of a law and order measure, is laced with the dangers of providing fuel to the opponents of the state's anti-Maoist stand. In the past, front organisations have shown intense resistance to the government's attempt of imposing acts like the Unlawful Activities Prevention Act, 1967 or POTA, to rein in the Maoist sympathisers in the intelligentsia. Any overbearingness of this sort is highly non-workable in the present times of media proliferation. For example, with respect to the recent media leak of the IB Report vis-à-vis foreign funded NGOs, the activist under the allegations, SP

Udaykumar, has voiced his resistance, and plans to file a writ petition against the state[11].

An awareness campaign at the behest of the government needs to expose the fallacy of the Maoists' philosophy, wherein it has to be elaborated that the Maoist forms of resistance are inconsistent with the broader democratic resistance which continuously metamorphoses and strives for the genuine welfare and empowerment of the downtrodden. Given the present state of the nation's evolving economy, complemented by a democratic polity and society, power is certainly not going to flow out of the barrel of a gun.

Notes

1. Faisal Devji, "Why Maoists Want Arundhati Roy & Likes", *The Guardian*, March 09, 2012.
2. PV Ramanna, "CPI (Maoist) and Urban Movement", idsa.in/idsa_comments/CPI_Maoist_and_Urban_Movement_pvramanna.
3. Chomsky, *The Great Soul of Power* (2010).
4. PV Ramana, "Growth of CPI (Maoist)", in Gurmeet Kanwal and Dhruv Katoch, eds., *Naxal Violence: The Threat Within* (New Delhi: KW Publishers), pp. 108 and 109.
5. Ibid.
6. PTI, *Business Standard*, October 07, 2009, "I am unaware whether Chhatradhar is a Maoist. Once, he came to my house with a group of women and crew of a TV channel. When I was told that the women were Maoists, I drove away all of them, including Chhatradhar", said Mahasweta Devi.
7. http:sanhati.com/excerpted/1824.
8. Nirmalangshu Mukherji, "Role of Intellectuals, Maoists in India," in *The Maoists in India, Tribals under Siege* (2013), p.87.
9. Aditya Nigam, "The Rumour of Maoism," *Seminar*, October 2010.
10. Bibhu Prasad Routray, "India's Response to Maoist Growth: Tactics and Strategies", in Kanwal and Katoch, n.4, p.184.
11. Interview with SP Udaykumar, coordinator, People's Movements Against Nuclear Energy, "Our Struggle Was Funded by People", *Frontline*, July 11, 2014.

12. SEEING THROUGH THE MAOIST MYTHS

The chapter contextualises the LWE in east-central India, in terms of exploitation of Adivasi aspirations by the Maoists to foster their the ulterior intentions. Since the inception of LWE in India, splintering and factional rifts have been rampant amongst the Maoists, over issues concerning ideology and leadership. The PWG, which forms the backbone of the CPI (Maoist), was active in Andhra Pradesh, during the decades of the 1980s and 1990s, with its sideline activities in neighbouring Chhattisgarh. By 2006, with pressure on the cadres nearly absolute in Andhra Pradesh, they decided to shift their focus to the forested areas of Chhattisgarh and Jharkhand (by the erstwhile PWG).

The Maoist movement has undergone ideological flip-flops, right from the Charu Mazumdar era. The stress has been on 'annihilating the class enemy', with negligible attention towards any form of mass struggle. Kanu Sanyal, one of the founding fathers of the movement, realised the flaw in the ideology of preferring a bloodbath of 'annihilation' over cultivating a 'mass base'. His advocacy found takers in many of the factions that went on to modify their means and methodologies. Some of them like the CPI (ML) Part Unity (PU) opted for embracing the parliamentary system. However, groups like the MCC (in Bihar) and PWG (in Andhra Pradesh/ Telangana) continued with the murderous politics, later merging to form the CPI (Maoist), in 2004. This umbrella organisation has tapped into the Adivasi dissatisfaction to build a mass base, towards achieving the ultimate goal of 'armed insurrection'.

Myth: Adivasis are Maoists

In the past, due to their history of isolation and exploitation, tribal traditions had acquired a considerable degree of militancy. Resistance movements in the Adivasi belt preceded the advent of the Maoists by centuries. The adopted means of annihilation translated into targeted and often ruthless killings of the landed class (large / middle / small), traders, officials and so-called traitors and informers. It is pertinent to mention here that apart from the few prosperous ones belonging to the category of the declared 'class enemy', a majority of the targeted individuals are from the middle or lower class – mostly, the poor Adivasis.

It would not be unreasonable to infer that the Adivasis have been bearing the brunt, being on both sides of the conflict. This is also to be seen in the light of the fact that the Adivasis constitute the larger part of the rank and file of the CPI (Maoist), led by an exclusive leadership. While orders emanate from essentially a non-Adivasi leadership, hiding safely in their secure bases, it is the Adivasi foot soldiers on the ground who execute the assigned tasks.[1]

Victimisation of the tribals is likely to continue till the state does not see these Adivasis as being different from the Maoists, who have a tremendous pool of human resource at their disposal and will ensure that the fight continues down to the last Adivasi. Also, as long as the Maoists continue with their militarism in the name of the people, the state shall continue its efforts to monopolise violence with perfect moral authority. The Adivasis are trapped in this vicious cycle of conflict, with no stakes in the revolutionary politics of the Maoists.

Myth: Maoists are for Empowerment of the People

The Indian democracy has 'empowerment of the people', as its bottom-line. The Constitution, political parties, media, human rights and minority organisations, etc have all reinforced the democratic fabric of our nation. In spite of several faultlines, India is looked up to as one of the better examples of the functioning democratic models. This soft power that has become characteristic of India, has worked to its advantage on the global platform, which has an obvious bias for equality and liberalism.

The Maoists have 'overthrow' of this democratic polity at the root of their ideology. They undermine and reject the enabling function of democracy manifested in the election system that empowers the marginalised. By exhorting their so-called mass base to boycott the elections, the Maoists deny the people their only instrument of 'exercising and expressing power'. However, the people have often boycotted such diktats in the recent times, by going ahead to exercise their rights; a clear indication of the unsustainability of the Maoist ideology[2]. At times, the Adivasis have also defied the Maoists' call of boycotting Gram Sabha meetings[3].

The fault of the state lies in the growing democratic deficit that has led to the expansion of the Maoists. The electoral democracy in our country has not been able to ensure the people's access to state power. As a result, the concept of the welfare state serving the interests of the population has lost appeal. One can, thus, appreciate the emergence of radical elements like the Maoists, propagating anti-electoral doctrines of 'direct control' of governance, in the name of the people[4].

Answering the question as to why the CPI (Maoist) declines to fight elections and refuses to participate in the democratic process, Maoist leader Ganapathy remarked, "You think raising issues in the Parliament is the democratic way whereas we believe that people are raising their issues in a democratic way through organised protests, supported by us"[5]. The Maoists term parliamentary politics as a 'dog-eat-dog world' and the Parliament as a 'talking shop'.

The Maoist viewpoint on shunning elections as a matter of strategy is surprisingly similar to the anarchist perspective. Anarchists believe that "utilising the state, standing in elections, etc only prepares people to *follow leaders* – it does not encourage the self-activity, self-organisation, direct action and mass struggle required for a social revolution." Likewise, the Indian Maoists also believe that "participation in Parliament does not help in developing the subjective forces; rather it only drives people into legalism and diverts them from intensifying the revolutionary class struggle".[6]

Myth: Maoists are for Adivasi Development

Although vigour in Maoist activities in the neighbouring states of Andhra Pradesh intensified in the years 2004-05, their activities in Chhattisgarh commenced as early as 1979. There have been pockets controlled by the Maoists, in (Dandakaranya), portions of states like Chhattisgarh, Maharashtra, Odisha and Telangana that are claimed to be 'liberated zones', characterised by an absent state or 'governance vacuum areas'[7]. On moving in here, the Maoists took up the Adivasi cause concerning land, forests, livelihood, displacement, mining, etc – primarily to build up and consolidate their (guerrilla) bases. The expansion and expression of the class-based struggle, premised on the tenets of egalitarianism, was a cause of celebration for the Adivasis. In the Maoists, the Adivasis saw somebody who supported them against the oppressive higher class and the state. For the first time, the most marginalised had a chance to move from their consistent betrayal by the dominant classes to genuine 'people's power'[8].

From early years of the 2000s, these regions were directly administered by the Revolutionary People's Committee (Janathana Sarkar). Given the protracted duration that the Maoists have been governing these sub-regions for, the lives of the poor Adivasis have not witnessed any revolution in terms of development and welfare. The Maoists, on the contrary, have widened the gap between the poor and the state; a gap that was already substantial. Especially interesting in the context has been the sizeable amount of revenue that the Maoists generate from their industry of protection, extortion, kidnappings, indirect taxation regime, etc. It is reported that more than 50 percent of the generated income is allocated to military capability building, 12 percent for agriculture, 9 percent for health and merely 0.9 percent towards education.

While the government cannot be absolved of its responsibilities towards the welfare of the Adivasi population in the Maoists' controlled regions, what is being flagged is that by forcing the state out and not doing enough for development, the Maoists are betraying the Adivasis. Recently, an incident came to light when, under the Maoists pressure, the Forest Department employees urged the state government to shun development activities[9].

The exploitative system of contractors and pilferages suits the Maoists. The funds generated thereby are their primary source of income and the enabler for their 'revolution' – and while all this manifests, the poor Adivasis continue to toil at subsistence levels. Arundhati Roy has brought out the corruption and cheating on part of the contractors, vis-à-vis their dealings with the Adivasis[10]. She, however, misses the link manifested in the contractors – Maoists nexus, exploiting the Adivasis to fund the Maoists' war.

The preceding perspective also explains as to why the Maoists never encourage genuine development based on the empowered local governance model which the state stands for; as enshrined in the Indian Constitution through PESA. Empowered GS and cooperatives administered by the local bodies, tend to threaten the system of private contractors, thus, marring the revenue inflow of the Maoists. Also, there have been instances when the Maoists have subverted democracy by forcing contesting candidates to withdraw from local polls, thereby ensuring that their own candidates win in an unopposed manner. This ensures diversion of development funds to the Maoists, through their proxies[11].

It is in the interest of the Maoists that the so-called 'liberated zones' do not open up to the outside world. The influx of state officials, political cadres, service and goods providers, etc could seriously compromise the secrecy, security and inaccessibility of the network of guerrilla bases. In turn, this is used as an alibi by the state officials for not venturing into these areas.

As against the views expressed by the Maoists and their sympathisers, it is not the welfare of the Adivasis but the establishment of guerrilla bases that has been a priority for the Maoists and any semblance of tribal welfare is purely incidental. Thirty years is a long time to set up schools and health centres, achieve competitive wages, etc – the parameters on which, the Maoists have been found wanting.

Myth: Maoists' War is Against Adivasi Exploiters

There is an important and often missed out class dimension to the entire Adivasi identity. The middle class, the educated and well off section of the Adivasi society is distinct from the grassroots Adivasis and tends to marginalise the poor. The initial spread and rise of LWE was supported and propagated by this category of 'rural elite'. This category supported the Maoists not because of a shared ideology, but because it offered better security to them towards accessing the informal economy of the state resources[12].

Most of the research work and analyses concerning the Maoists tends to focus exclusively on their *modus operandi.* Contextualisation of their activities vis-à-vis the prevalent social processes is normally overlooked. The advent and settling down of Maoist cadres from outside into the newer regions, unfolded a typical process. While making forays into rural Jharkhand, the Maoists started 'selling protection' to the rural elite. The rural elite, since it knew the local dynamics well, introduced the Maoists to strategically selected people who further oriented the cadres to the local settings.

The Maoists gained support by practising populist vigilante activities such as 'resolving' local disputes in Jan Adalats. Such activities were carried out in the backdrop of taking up the tribal cause based on the egalitarian left ideology. Over a period of time, as more villages came into their fold, a few youths would be recruited for the Maoist bases in other places, to be trained and armed as members of squads of the underground guerrilla army. The connotation was contrary to the established rhetoric that the Maoists espoused the cause of the poor Adivasis against the exploiters. As a matter of fact, the Maoists gained a foothold in the new areas by aligning with these very exploiters i.e. the rural elite, contractors, etc. The Maoists used them to gain grassroots support and later the agenda of the elite was promoted by the Maoists, as a return favour[13]. And in executing their judicial system, the Maoists obliterated the traditional cohesion that had been inherent for centuries: the uniqueness of the Adivasi culture.

As far as the class of rural elite was concerned, beyond their own elevation within the society hierarchy, they had other pressing motives to support the Maoists. In Jharkhand, abolition of the zamindari in the early 1950s meant that these elites, who faced impoverishment, increasingly attempted to sustain their lifestyles through state resources – either directly (by gaining jobs) or indirectly (through contracts). They created their positions as entrepreneurs who maintained their financial position by participating in the informal economy of development programmes. As a result of their intimate connections to the state officials, they were particularly effective in siphoning off money from the state and, in turn, were of great utility to the Maoists.

To obtain a contract, one needed a patron, a powerful person with leverage over the state officials. One also needed supporters to perform the two-fold functions of threatening competitors as also promoting interests based on muscle power. In effect, there existed a symbiotic equation of offering protection on the part of the Maoists and earning contracts on the part of the rural elite. Also, in this equation, were the crucial links provided by the local politician who was connected with the rural elite. The state officials, with their desire to be on the right side of the local politician, completed the picture.

When the Maoists showed up in Jharkhand, they marketed a very similar kind of protection to the rural elite that local politicians had been offering earlier. The Maoists, thus, became one more group that protected entrepreneurs' illicit access to state resources, and politicians too stood to gain by receding into the background. In fact, as the Maoists gained further support in the respective area, the dividing line between the local officialdom and the Maoists became thinner, with certain officials themselves seeking the Maoists' protection. By cultivating a mutual web of linkages, the Maoists and the local bureaucracy started enjoying a degree of interdependency[14]. As a spinoff, the Maoists got on the right side of the state officialdom. Resultantly, during security crackdowns, the most likely to be arrested were the grassroots party cadres, the Adivasis and not the non-Adivasi leadership.

The Maoists have presented themselves as a dual structure: a visible and an invisible one. The visible power includes their involvement in local politics, its embodiment through the local people and everyday activities; while the invisible power involves the secrets, the vast hidden resources and the capacity for violence[15]. The invisible power is manifested in several ways. Firstly, it was created through an idea of a highly centralised, hierarchical, and organised movement – with the overall purpose to create an expansive Red Corridor. Secondly, the image of immense power was perpetuated through the clandestine nature of the operations, and the circulation of secrets and hidden resources. False names were used and people recruited at the local level had only a vague idea about who else was involved in the hierarchy above their immediate commander. Also, this cloud of secrecy generated uncertainty about the size and spread of the organisation. The belief generated was that the Maoists were omnipresent. Thirdly, rumours added to the myth – block, police and forest officials were all Maoists. Such rumours created the idea that the Maoists were so powerful that they had been increasingly infiltrating the government.[16]

In the chapter, examples have been drawn from the Maoists' controlled areas to bring out the lack of development and how little has been attempted by the Maoists towards the same. Notwithstanding the aforesaid, the prime onus for the penury and backwardness of these Adivasis falls on the state and its policies or the absence of the same. The government is endeavouring to address the issue in a holistic manner. In the current governmental approach, perception management had rightly been dovetailed, which needs to be shaped for busting the Maoist myths.

However, given the historical baggage, the law and order domain still holds primacy in the approach. Unsurprisingly, the logic is that the Maoists are squarely responsible for the conflict and their armed control over a vast area has prevented the state from undertaking developmental and welfare measures. And since the authority of the state is required for development of the Adivasi belt, the priorities over the course to be charted get confused. In the context of the terror by the Maoists cadre, the state often falls into the trap of justifying its attempts to monopolise violence. Given the diverse nature of the Maoist challenge in different regions, flexibility is the need of the times, rather than going for the 'one size fits all' approach.

Notes

1. Nirmalangshu Mukherji, "Examining the Myth of Maoist Concern for Tribal Welfare", countercurrents.org, 2010.
2. www.claws.in/1294/boycotting-the-boycott-masses-maoists-and-democracy-shashank-ranjan.html
3. "Tribal People Defy Maoists' Diktat, Attend Gram Sabhas', *The Hindu*, August 17, 2013.
4. Nirmalagshu Mukherjee, "The Maoists in India – Tribals Under Siege", in *Fragile Democracy* (New Delhi: Amaryllis, 2012).
5. www.satp.org/satporgtp/countries/india/maoist/documents/papers/interview_ganapathy.html
6. Ibid.
7. Talk by Hon'ble Shekhar Dutt, former Governor, Chhattisgarh, on "Naxalite Movement in Chhattisgarh and the Challenges of Governance", January 21, 2015 at VIF.
8. Prakash Loius, *People's Power: The Naxalite Movement in Central Bihar* (Delhi: Wordsmith, 2002).
9. Ashutosh Bhardwaj, "Forest Staff Write to Raman: Stop All Departmental Works in Maoist Hit Areas", *The Indian Express*, March 23, 2015.
10. Arundhati Roy, "Walking with the Comrades: Gandhians with a Gun", *Outlook*, March 29, 2010.
11. Bidyut Mohanty, "Odisha: Panchayat Election Results and their Meaning for the Assembly Poll", *Mainstream*, Vol. l, No. 30, July 14, 2012.
12. Alpa Shah, "In the Shadows of the State", in *The Dark Side of Indigeneity* (OUP, 2010).
13. Ibid.
14. Alpa Shah, "In the Shadows of the State", in *The Terror Within* (OUP, 2010).
15. Ibid.
16. Jonathan Spencer, "Problems in the Analysis of Communal Violence", in *Contributions to Indian Sociology* (1992).

SECTION FOUR
Putting the House in Order: Rising up to the Challengem

13. NATIONAL SECURITY MANAGEMENT CONCERNS

National security, as a state policy, has been an area of neglect in our country. The political class in the country has often been dictated by a partisan approach, thereby neglecting this very crucial part of nation building. National security covers a very wide canvas to include 'human security' as its important facet. In this chapter, however, only the politico-administartive aspects of internal and external security are discussed, with emphasis on the former. There is an urgent need today for the central government to secure appropriate understandings with the states for finalising a National Security Policy (NSP) and putting in place a modern, fully coordinated security management system which can effectively negate any emerging challenge to the security of India, external or internal.

The first generation of India's security analysts, who focussed attention almost entirely on issues relating to external security, had found it convenient and workable to distinguish between issues relating to external and internal security. However, such a segregated approach is no longer practical, particularly with the internal security dynamics, characterised by terrorism and insurgency that interwine with the external dimensions.

As per the provisions in our Constitution, it is the duty of the union to protect every state against external aggression and internal disturbances, although law and order which often overlaps with insurgencies in the state, is a state subject.[1] However, not all the states have so far accepted the central government's authority to enact and enforce federal laws for dealing with acts of terror, cyber offences and other crimes which have pan-India ramifications. The states have also been opposing the Centre's authority to establish new security management agencies with pan-India jurisdiction.

Being a subject on the state list, it has been argued by several state governments that it is the constitutional prerogative of the states to manage law and order within their territories and that the Centre has no basis for interfering in this area. More often, this is as a result of the tendency to protect the respective turfs, wherein the larger picture is neglected in a narrow partisan manner.

Undoubtedly, the states are constitutionally mandated to make all the required laws in regard to the police and public order, take all necessary executive decisions, establish adequate police organisations and manage appropriate security systems within their territories. However, looking back at the serious law and order failures, often involving insurgencies and secessionist rebellions, which have occurred in various parts of the country in the past several decades, it cannot be said that there have been no failures and that all the states have a sustained record of preventing any breach, within their jurisdictions; where the Centre has merely 'pitched in' as a supporter. Of course, the Centre's support role would have been justifiable in an eventuality of the state's strength, which has not been the case.

One of the more significant contributory factors in this context is the states' inability to maintain adequate intelligence organisations and well trained police forces in the required strength to effectively maintain internal security within their resprctive territories. According to the Ministry of Home Affairs Annual Report for 2007-08, there is an over 16 per cent deficiency in the numbers of Indian Police Service (IPS) officers in position as against the sanctioned strengths:

Table 13.1

Sample States	**Sanctioned Strength**	**In Position**	**Percent Deficit**
Bihar	193	159	17.6
Chhattisgarh	81	70	13.5
Jharkhand	110	82	25.5
Odisha	207	84	41.3
Jammu & Kashmir	135	115	14.8
Assam-Meghalaya	153	133	13.0
Manipur-Tripura	121	101	16.5
India	3,886	3,234	16.7

This data may, indeed, understate the magnitude of the crisis in some crucial instances. Odisha, for instance, currently among the states facing an acute Maoist challenge, has a total of 207 sanctioned posts in the IPS ranks; there are presently just 84 officers in place[2].

Police-Population Ratios

According to norms set by the United Nations, a minimum police-to-population ratio of 1:450 should be maintained for 'peace-time policing'. This works out to a ratio of 222 police personnel per 100,000 population. Most Western countries maintain ratios well above this minimum standard: for instance, the ratio is as high as 559 per 100,000 in Italy and 465 per 100,000 in Portugal. Significantly, most of these countries have policing needs that are certainly less demanding or extreme as compared to those confronting India, where the culture of the rule of law is far from entrenched and virtually all compliance needs enforcement. Yet, India's police-to-population ratio stands at a bare 125/100,000, and conditions in the states and areas most afflicted by disorders are often much worse:

Table 13.2

France	205	All India average:	17.6
UK	205	Bihar	13.5
Belgium	358	Jharkhand	25.5
Austria	330	Chhattisgarh	38.3
USA	315	Odisha	14.8
Germany	291	AP	13.0
South Africa	277	UN Recommended Ratio	222
Australia	209		

Thus, some of the states worst afflicted by Maoist violence have the worst police-area ratios. Crucially, despite significant funding from the Centre to the states underwriting the Modernisation of Police Forces (MPFs), Security Related Expenditure (SRE) and augmentation of capacities, a substantial proportion of these funds is unspent or misspent each year[3]. Till as recent as September 2014, the Home Secretary had flagged the issue concerning the police personnel deficiency to the Chief Secretaries of all the states and union territories[4].

The challenges to policing cannot, however, be reduced to these quantitative indices alone. The quality of policing and the integrity of the institutional structures underlying police administration have long been issues of contention. For decades, proposals for police reforms have been kept in abeyance, despite the urgent recommendations of numberless National and State Police Commissions, and notwithstanding the eventual intervention of the Supreme Court in September 2006, with a seven-point directive to immediately secure compliance on a small set of these recommendations. A comprehensive transformation of the Indian police forces into modern, democratic forces would require the implementation of a wide range of these reforms as well as a comprehensive institutional *reinvention*, to equip them for contemporary and evolving challenges, including, particularly, terrorism, insurgency, and sub-conventional warfare[5].

Urgent containment initiatives also need to be launched in the immediate future, and the first stage of such a response relates to a more efficient mobilisation of existing capacities. Immediate steps can be taken to operationalise, retrain and reorient the maximum proportion of available police and intelligence resources, which are currently deployed on fairly wasteful patterns. Major initiatives are also possible to tap civilian resources and populations for surveillance, information-generation and intelligence. The rapid acquisition and augmentation of technical and technological force multipliers can also help enhance the efficiency of responses in the near term.

On many occasions, the states have also displayed a lack of political will to deal with an emerging situation on their own. Instead, the general tendency and practice, which has evolved over the past many years, has been for the affected state to rush to the Union Home Ministry for an urgent deployment of the Central Armed Police Forces (CAPFs) to restore normalcy.

Another factor which has adversely affected internal security management relates to the progressive erosion of the professionalism of the state police. This regrettable decline has taken place because of political interference in the day-to-day functioning of the constabularies. Such interference has, over the years, caused untold damage and most adversely affected the accountability, morale and the very integrity of the state police. The recommendations of the Model Police Act do address the issue to an extent, wherein the suggested regulations were incorporated in terms of appointment, transfers and accountability of the personnel. However, as mentioned earlier, in spite of the Supreme Court's directives in 2006, no state has enacted laws towards the same; at best, the efforts on the part of the states have been to introduce measures that circumvent the apex court's directives[6].

Considering the all pervasive and grave security threats, it is important that the central government takes the most urgent steps for finalising the NSP and the machinery for its administration, in consultation with the state governments; in a non-partisan way. After the National Security Policy (NSP) is finalised, the central government will have to undertake, in collaboration with the states, a countrywide review of the existing security management apparatus and draw up a plan for restructuring and revamping it, within a stipulated timeframe. While playing their part in such an exercise, the states would need to accept the important role they are required to play in the national security management apparatus and demonstrate their unconditional commitment to working closely with each other and with the Centre[7].

For nearly two decades now, there have been repeated pronouncements that the central government is promulgating a law for dealing with identified federal offences and establishing a central agency which would have the authority of taking cognisance of, and investigating, crimes which have serious inter-state and nationwide ramifications for national security. The proposal of setting up the National Counter Terrorism Centre (NCTC), for instance, has continued to be debated for the past several years. A number of states, which have been opposed to the establishment of the NCTC in its proposed form, have suggested that the proposed framework of this body should be entirely revised in consultation with the states. Some other states have urged that the NCTC should not be established through an executive order but through an Act of the Parliament – that it should function under the administrative control of the MHA instead of being controlled by the Intelligence Bureau (IB).

The Government of India, after 26/11, enacted a law to set up the National Investigation Agency (NIA), on the pattern of the FBI of the USA. The aim was to investigate and prosecute terror offences; i.e. only certain specified offences that are committed within the country and which affect national security.

The NIA has no extra-territorial jurisdiction and no powers to probe incidents which occur outside India, as, for example, the attack on the Consulate of India in Herat that took place in May 2014. The NIA Director does not have the powers enjoyed by the

Directors General of Police (DsGP), to permit an investigating officer dealing with a terror crime to seize or attach property. Also, unlike in the case of the CBI, the NIA is not empowered to depute its investigating officers abroad for direct interactions with a foreign agency that is investigating a major terror act which directly or indirectly affects our national security interests.

The NIA's functioning in the past eight years also shows that the police authorities in the states are reluctant and take their own time in handing over to the NIA even major criminal cases which may have serious inter-state and nationwide ramifications. Many offences, including major crimes under the Indian Penal Code (IPC) which may be directly linked to terror activities, have still to be brought under the NIA's jurisdiction. Thus, briefly, the NIA, as presently constituted, does not have the legal authority to take the required action to preempt or prevent a terror crime, even when it functions in coordination with the concerned states. The NIA needs to be fully empowered, on the most immediate basis, if it is to serve the purpose for which it was established[8]. The Centre and the states have to walk a considerable distance towards each other to make such federal agencies more effective so as to play a crucial role as part of the national security apparatus.

The acts of terror and other federal offences cannot be dealt with by the existing security management apparatus; it is necessary that the central government underakes urgent discussions with the Chief Ministers to resolve all doubts and issues raised by the states. Towards this, the MHA could beneficially utilise the aegis of the Inter-State Council (ISC)[9], of which the Prime Minister is the chairperson. Similarly, it would be useful for the central government to consider inducting represetatives of the states in the National Security Advisory Board (NSAB) and the National Security Council (NSC), even if the same is done on a rotational basis. The NCTC should be attempted with all seriousness, in a non–partisan manner.

Some of the doubts voiced by the states about the management of security related issues arise from the style of functioning of the institutions which are exclusively controlled by the central government and the NIA too, could fall in this realm of scepticism. A via media has to be struck which could be an organisation that is jointly managed by the Centre and the states. An excellent example in this regard is the Joint Terrorism Task Force (JTTF) established by the US after 9/11.[10] The JTTF, located in various cities across the US, includes representatives from the federal state and municipal enforcement agencies, and performs several important roles, including the clearing of all terrorism related information.

Over time, functioning through joint institutions will enable the states to gain a well informed, trans-boundary perspective about the complex and sensitive issues concerning national security management and, in the process, also defuse their prennial complaint about the central government's interference with the powers of the states in the arena of internal security management. The aforesaid aspect assumes paramount importance, given the trans-boundary activities and reach of insurgents and terrorists.

Notwithstanding the stated cruciality of efforts at the macro levels, the internal security management will not take off, in the absence of capacity building and local ownership of policing and administration. Given the inadequacies, capacity generation for policing and intelligence at an unprecedented – indeed, hitherto unimagined – scale is required to recover the vast regions of India that have been given over to a vacuum of security and governance, especially in the LWE affected regions of the central-eastern tribal belt of our nation.

There has, in the recent past, been an overwhelming emphasis on raising special forces' capacities to deal with terrorism and insurgency. Unfortunately, within a degraded general policing and law and order environment, small contingents of special forces can have very limited utility. The greatest decentralisation of response capabilities is required to deal with contemporary internal security challenges, and this can only be secured through a comprehensive revitalisation of policing structures and a restoration of the integrity of the thana. Prime Minister Manmohan Singh had rightly noted,

"Unless the 'beat constable' is brought into the vortex of our counter-terrorist strategy, our capacity to preempt future attacks would be severely limited".[11]

Unfortunately, despite the Prime Minister's observations, the emphasis on the military-intelligence aspects of responses to terrorism persists. There are two underlying reasons for this: one, such an emphasis also defines the contours of the international discourse on the subject, with most Western theorists looking at campaigns such as Iraq and Afghanistan, or, earlier, Vietnam, Ireland or Malaysia, where the military-intelligence dyad was the principal response mechanism. The second factor is our own model of central response, what is often called the 'battalion approach', which relies heavily on the allocation of central paramilitary or military forces to deal with rising movements of political violence. This 'emergency response' then gets bogged down into a permanent paradigm. In many cases, such allocation of central forces contributes directly to the further emasculation of state police forces, and neglect by state leaderships of the need to maintain or expand the capacities of the security apparatus of the states themselves.[12]

Concluding Concerns: Security Management

As brought out earlier, the absence of a non-partisan approach has led to several states questioning the central government's role in national security management. Also, as a general practice, instead of progressively improving the capability of their police and security maintenance apparatus for effectively dealing with arising disturbances, the states have been perenially seeking assisstance from the MHA. The states are seldom questioned on the reasons for their failure to maintain internal security, nor about their failures to deal with the root causes of the recurring disturbances in their territories.

The Constitution of India prescribes that the states shall be responsible for maintenance of public order and that the union government has the duty to protect the states against internal disturbances. A holistic national security policy and the mechanisms for its administration must be urgently finalised in consultation with the states. The Centre must not lose any more time in evolving the required Centre–states synergy for the same.

Apart from finalising the national security policy, the central government needs to take time-bound steps to establish appropriate institutions / agencies for effective security management across the country. It must enact laws and establish all the required processes and procedures for prompt investigation and trials of federal offences; and it has to establish a National Security Administrative Service for maintaining and operating the security management apparatus in the entire country.

Meanwhile, the existing gaps in the capacities of the governmental machinery need to be bridged. The security apparatus alone is not relevant to Counter-Insurgency-Counter-Terrorism (CI-CT) objectives. While temporal priority must be given to security objectives, the reality remains that, without the delivery of a modicum of civil governance and across the country, no enduring gains can be recorded. Security responses, moreover, are themselves enormously dependent on the general efficiency of governance and of the policy establishment, as most critical decisions remain vested in authorities outside the security establishment. Wider societal capabilities also have critical implications for security and stability.

Only clear political perspectives and mandates can create the necessary foundations for the development of institutional mechanisms for the coordinated execution of security efforts, initiatives and policies. The institutional apparatus of governance must be equipped to engage in the continuous assessment and analysis of existing and emerging threats; to coordinate flows and maximise utilisation of available intelligence and resources from a multiplicity of agencies; to continuously define policies and protocols for the response to each new area or pattern of terrorist activity; and to ensure that these are translated into action by the appropriate agency and department of the government .

Notes

1. Law and order challenges are linked to the issues of insurgency and terror. The same networks service both petty crime and major crime, including terrorism. For instance, while there is much talk of the necessity of 'ending terrorist finance', the reality is that this can never be separated from other organised criminal financial operations, from the ugly underbelly of otherwise legitimate commercial activities, and from the flourishing black economy at large, which could very well fall into the domain of law and order. The overwhelming proportion of illegal financial operations are collusive – based on a continuing and symbiotic relationship of acquiescence between criminal enterprises, on the one hand and, on the other, government agencies and officials, as well as enterprises whose primary businesses lie within the ambit of the law. It is the vast black economy in India that provides the context of the movement of funds by terrorists as well. *Hawala* networks are not only used by terrorists, drug-traffickers, arms smugglers and other criminals, but also by corrupt businessmen, bureaucrats and politicians.
2. http://www.satp.org/satporgtp/ajaisahni/09AS-35USI-NSP.htm#32
3. Ibid.
4. DO No. 21011/78/2014-PM.I, dated September 09, 2014, available on MHA website.
5. Ajai Sahni, "Global Terrorism in an Age of Uncertainty", in Col. S.K. Sharma, ed., *War Against Global Terror* (Centre for Joint Warfare Studies, 2009), pp. 15-28.
6. The remarks were made by Mr. Prakash Singh, former DG BSF who had filed a PIL in 1996 on the urgency to implement police reforms and based upon which, the Supreme Court had directed the state governments to implement the same, in the year 2006. He was speaking as a panelist as part of discussion on NN Vohra's book, *Safeguarding India – Essays on Governance and Security*, on July 23, 2016, at the IIC, New Delhi.
7. NN Vohra, "Management of National Security – Some Concerns," First Air Commodore Jasjit Singh Memorial Lecture, Centre for Air Power Studies, New Delhi, July 18, 2014.
8. Ibid.
9. http://www.idsa.in/idsacomments/inter-state-council-and-internal-security_sranjan_250716
10. https://www.fbi.gov/about-us/investigate/terrorism/terrorism_jttfs
11. Prime Minister Manmohan Singh, "Remarks on Internal Security at Chief Ministers' Conference", September 05, 2006.
12. http://www.satp.org/satporgtp/ajaisahni/10AS-usi.htm#59

14. CRIMINAL JUSTICE SYSTEM, UNDERTRIALS AND ALIENATION

On paper, India's commitment to the rule of law distinguishes it from many of its peers and neighbours. According to the 2012 World Justice Project data, India fares well on openness of government and democratic controls. In the category of limited government powers, which evaluates the checks on the government, India ranks 37th of the 97 countries surveyed around the world, is first among five in its region, and comes in second out of 23 lower middle income countries.[1]

Yet the rule of law that exists on paper does not always exist in practice. When it comes to procedural effectiveness, India fares poorly. In the categories of absence of corruption and order and security, India ranks 83rd and 96th globally. Every element of India's rule of law supply chain—including the legislators who draft the laws and the police, prosecutors and courts who enforce them—is problematic. Indeed, the supply chain, never strong to begin with, has become deeply broken—threatening not only the rule of law but a belief in the value of law itself.

The country's legal undergirding is badly outmoded and constrained by a tendency to pass new laws rather than modify or eliminate old ones, like the colonial era Police Act. Weak laws yoked to an even weaker enforcement system virtually guarantee that the powerful will transgress with abandon. India's investigative agencies have become politicised and starved of resources, infrastructure and leadership. While the judiciary has many bright spots—including the Supreme Court—the courts on the whole face challenges ranging from vacancies and backlogs to flawed efforts at self-regulation.

This chapter briefly reviews the work related to the undertrials' life in LWE affected areas in particular and the country in general. While doing this, it also attempts to situate the issue in the broader context of extremism, deprivation of the Adivasis and the state-system in India, and their interrelatedness.

Life of Undertrials in Indian Prisons

"India has very few documents about life in its horrific jails"[2]. The limited numbers of available documents provide a rather grim picture of undertrials in India's jails. A recent study of the criminal justice system in India has shown that prisoners languish behind bars for several years, sometimes decades, awaiting their day in court. This situation prevails despite the Supreme Court ruling in 1979 that defendants have a fundamental right to speedy trial[3]. This means that there is a huge gap in encouraging judicial pronouncements and how they play out in reality[4]. Moreover, many Indian prisons accommodate 100 to 200 per cent over their capacity, amidst squalid conditions[5].

About 70 per cent of the total population in India's prisons consists of undertrials and first-time offenders. Although the Supreme Court had outlawed many malpractices rampant in the jails, they keep happening. Not only do the prisoners remain unaware of their rights, most lawyers too remain ill-informed about the provisions of the legal aid at hand. A majority of India's prisoners comprise economically the poorer rural people.

Undertrials and their families from economically backward sections have little means of meeting the expenses of a bail. They also undergo severe persecution as torture of prisoners begins from the time one is admitted into a jail[6]. All these further impoverish them physically and socio-economically[7].

An analysis of the court and prison statistics of Bastar reveals a complete breakdown of the criminal justice system. The jails are severely overcrowded. While the average occupancy in jails across the country is 112 percent, the corresponding figures ranged from 255 percent at the Jagdalpur Central Jail to an astounding 428 percent at the Kanker District Jail. Most of the prisoners were illiterate Adivasi men between the ages of 18 and 30 and an overwhelming majority were undertrials[8]. Similarly, Jharkhand has a total prison capacity of 14,243 persons; however, the total occupancy was 18,220, which is 128 per cent of the actual prison capacity (as in December 2013)[9].

Fig 14.1

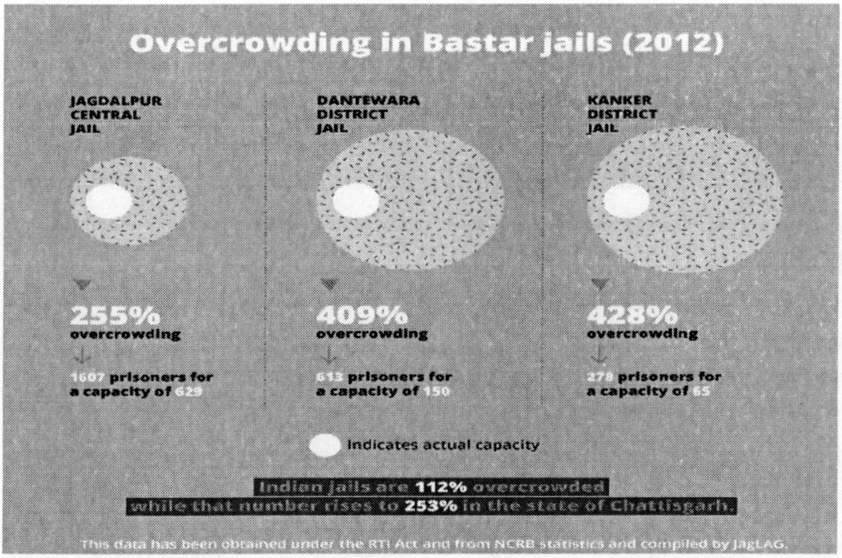

An analysis of the case disposal statistics between 2005 and 2012 revealed that two-thirds of undertrials in Jagdalpur had to spend between two and five years in prison before receiving bail, while, on an average, across the country, 75 per cent of undertrials spend less than a year in prison before receiving bail. An astounding 96 per cent of the cases between 2005 and 2012 ended in acquittal, indicating that in most cases, the police had arrested the people unnecessarily; with the apprehended Adivasis having no links with the Maoists[10].

Out of a total of 382,000 prisoners in India, about 254,000 are undertrials. Out of these, only one-third, i.e. only 127,000 are convicted and serving their sentence. Two-thirds of 382,000 (i.e. 255,000) prisoners in India's jails are not proved guilty[11]. The enormous gravity of the situation is evident from the fact that there are more people under trial in India than there are people in the Netherlands or Kazakhstan. In 2013, the cases of as many as 85 percent of people put on trial were pending, according to the National Crime Records Bureau (NCRB).[12]

Prison Statistics India 2013 shows that the percentage of the total number of prisoners who belong to historically marginalised social groups such as Dalits, Adivasis and Muslims, is much higher than the proportion of their share in the total population. For example, Dalits (SCs) constitute about 16.2 percent of India's total population; however, they constitute 22.5 per cent of convicts and 21.3 per cent of undertrials. Adivasis constitute 8.6 per cent of the population; however, 11.7 per cent Adivasis are convicts and 11.3 per cent are undertrials.[13]

The prison staffing is also quite discouraging. Jharkhand has only one prison staff for 19 jail inmates compared to one prison staff attending to eight prisoners as per the national level data[14]. Given the sample of revealing and scandalous information about India's jails and those incarcerated inside them,they point towards the need to take a closer look at India's legal system.

Indian Legal System (ILS)

By allowing incarceration which deprives persons of their right to liberty by unnecessary detention, the existing system violates the basic principle of criminal jurisprudence –every person shall be presumed innocent till proven guilty. From this, it follows that the present legal system, including all its implementing agencies – the police, the judiciary, the prosecutors, the defence lawyers and the prison department –often fail to follow the Criminal Procedure Code and other related rules that have been laid down[15]. The police allegedly arrest the "suspects" under the Unlawful Activities

(Prevention) Act, 2004, brand them as terrorists, keep them in unofficial detention, and scare them by physical torture. Moreover, it is reported that the allegations of the police are sufficient evidence for the jail authorities to punish those awaiting trials[16].

A report of the National Mission for Delivery of Justice and Legal Reform published in 2012 says, "Justice—Social, Economic and Political'—is the spirit and vision of our Constitution. It is the duty of the State to secure a social order in which the legal system of the nation promotes justice on a basis of equal opportunity and, in particular, ensures that opportunities for securing justice are not denied to any citizen by reason of economic or other disabilities." However, in actual practice, the ILS has mostly been made dysfunctional so that it serves purposes that are contrary to the lofty ideals being stated. A scholar has made the crisis of the ILS clearer in these lines:

> Observe how many of these fellows [the powerful and the rich] get bail. Observe, once the cases start, the innumerable clauses and sub-clauses these fellows are able to invoke in their favour. And contrast all this with the helplessness of the simple tribal who is dispossessed of his land by the sahukar from the plains, who retreats in the forest and clears some land to keep himself from starving, and who is then arrested for violating the Forest Act. Contrast the clauses that come to their aid with the helplessness of those who have been languishing in jail for seven years as under-trial prisoners. ...
>
> And while you are at it, count the number of landlords in our vast country who have been sentenced for not paying minimum wages or for exacting a higher-than-legal share of the crop from their tenants. ...
>
> What does all this tell us about the judiciary, about the legal system? Is he not right then who tells us that the "Law is nothing but the convenience of the powerful."(And, incidentally, the one who said this was not Mao nor some Naxalite, but Gandhi).[17]

It is clear that the legal system in India remains seriously flawed and malfunctioning, producing contrary outcomes for India's economically poor citizens. With this awareness, we proceed to examine and understand the issues and situations related to Adivasi, Dalit and other "backward" caste undertrials who have been accused of being "Naxalites."

One of the most important reasons why Naxalism or extremism in India continues is the refusal to accept any serious analysis of the phenomenon to disclose its deeper causes. Most reports and working papers, presented by the Law Commission of India and other such state-sponsored committees to study LWE, continue to remain mere inventories of crimes related to terrorism.[18] As was brought out earlier, "Most Indian states have tended to ignore potentials of PESA to their peril. Realizing the potential of the PESA Act would enable STs in LWE districts to realize their potentials as citizens, and help the state to realize its objective of utilizing the resources of the Scheduled Areas, where tribals live."[19]

Adivasis being Hunted as Naxalites

The real issue is of justice. In the prevalent system where justice is not available to the people, they get alienated, are led to revolt, and move toward extreme paths. Hence, the Maoists get the support of the most marginalised people[20]. While LWE acquires a favourable niche, conducive for strategic guerrilla warfare and forging some support-base among dispossessed and marginalised Adivasis in inaccessible areas, the state has not been able to win over the local population, making these territories into conflict zones. The situation was further complicated by several vigilante militias like Salwa Judum, Santi Senas and breakaway factions of LWE forming themselves into armed criminal gangs[21]. The Adivasis do not have an opening or an alternative to look up to, in crises—a fact that is exploited by the Maoists. They see the police as oppressors and the courts do not give them a hearing. The situation becomes all the more troublesome for the Adivasis as they are being sanwiched between the state and the Maoists.

At the age of 17, Kawasi Himde was arrested for "being involved in the killing of 23 policemen" in Dantewada district of south Chhattisgarh. A young girl, full of energy, at the time of her arrest in 2008, a tired Kawasi Hidme walked out of jail in 2015, when a Dantewada court found her not guilty. "I was never involved in any Maoist activity. Yet, I have lost seven years of my life. I am exhausted now with a number of health issues caused by police torture. What was my fault?" she asks[22].

The disturbing Jangampal incident is a typical example of how, every time Maoist activity intensifies in Chhattisgarh's Bastar division, Adivasis are picked up and framed as Maoists or sympathisers. While some of these villagers are released after preliminary enquiries, most waste away in prisons for years, unaware even of the charges against them—the flimsy charges, forced confessions and shoddy investigation. The police intensify search operations after every round of heightened Maoist activity or a strike[23]. There are numerous similar stories of how Adivasis, mostly the assertive among them, have been accused, arrested, tortured and imprisoned, and later acquitted, being found not guilty.

Alpa Shah's *In the Shadows of the State: Indigenous Politics, Environmentalism, and Insurgency in Jharkhand* eloquently delineates several complex linkages among the LWE, rural Adivasis and the Jharkhand state. The book explicates how the Adivasis get caught up between the state's repressive forces and armed criminal gangs. She says that armed terror groups in Jharkhand sell both terror and protection. Often, their customers are elite politicians, industrialists and other such agents of the state in Jharkhand, which finds little legitimacy with the Adivasis.[24] There exists a clear nexus among Maoists, politicians, mafias of various kinds, industrialists, contractors and bureaucrats who constitute the state in Jharkhand.

While the state supported corporates have been successfully prevented from grabbing Adivasi land by the stiff opposition for the very reasons that such instances of land-grab have often been unjust, unconstitutional and have progressively impoverished Adivasis, the state has not, or has very minimally, made any meaningful investment in the rural agrarian infrastructure to provide alternate livelihood opportunities to the marginalised rural populace[25]. Moreover, in Jharkhand, the Adivasi land, in principle, has been protected by the Chotanagpur and the Santhal Pargana Tenancy Acts (CNTA 1908 and SPTA 1949). An Adivasi villager in these territories could clear the uncultivated 'wasteland' to make it cultivable with the permission of the concerned village headmen before the 1963-65 settlement took place. However, the Bihar government declared such wastelands as state property during the last settlement. Presently, about 40 per cent of the total land in Jharkhand's scheduled areas belongs to the state[26]. In short, the poor Adivasi is being singled out to suffer by all the players in the arena, including the Maoists. This has resulted in victimisation of these voiceless people at the hands of laws enforcers; by becoming alibis for all 'ills'.

While Adivasi men are being tortured and languish in jails, their family members face great trouble trying to get them out on bail besides their struggles to earn a living in the absence of the family's main bread-winner[27]. A story that appeared in *India Today* described how young Adivasi men were lured by the police department in Jharkhand through a crafty "surrender policy" for supposed Naxalites. This was the story of 514 hapless Jharkhand men, most of them poor tribals, with no history of breaking the law, who begged, borrowed or pledged their family resources to raise the money to pay the middleman, risk the tag of a Naxalite and spend close to two years in the old Ranchi jail campus, all in the hope of getting a low-paying job of a constable in the CRPF, of donning a uniform and escaping the drudgery of life in some of Jharkhand's most backward regions[28].

A PIL filed by Jitendra Jain on behalf of "Fight for Human Rights" (FHR) alleged that there were thousands of "tribals" languishing in various central jails, without any trial, in Naxal-affected states like Chhattisgarh, Madhya Pradesh, Odisha, Jharkhand and West Bengal. Advocate K.R. Chitra, who argued on behalf of the FHR, stated that Adivasi undertrials were languishing in various jails for very long periods without any trial and as a result, unrest and hostilities were prevailing in the tribal areas of the country[29].

The PIL also said that often Adivasi undertrials were not informed about the grounds of their arrests; they were not even duly represented by lawyers of their choice as there are very few interpreters available in the courts who could speak the Adivasi languages; and, hence, they are deprived of their fundamental right of a fair trial as they are unable to explain the real facts and circumstances to the judicial officers. Furthermore, the PIL stated that most of those arrested in cases related to Naxal violence, were lodged in distant central jails, and, hence, they and their relatives' rights to meet each other have also been denied[30].

The kind of accusations the police make while they randomly pick up villagers under the UA (P) Act are basically of two types: firstly, helpers of Maoists; and secondly, for possessing "Naxalite literature," although the term "Naxalite literature" is not even defined. Persons accused of being "helpers of Naxalites," are assumed to be "guilty by association." This practice of such detentions under vague assumptions and imposition of criminal codes by the police on the Adivasis is rampant despite the Supreme Court ruling that a person's ideological association with any banned organisation does not make him/her a criminal unless he/she is found engaging in any criminal activity or making others indulge in such activities[31].

State Response to the Plight of Undertrials

Towards the plight of prisoners in general and that of undertrials in particular, much of the positive contribution has come through judicial intervention. The country's higher judiciary has often sought to improve the welfare of India's prisoners, especially the undertrials[32]. The serious judicial intervention on the issues of undertrials began as early as 1979 when the plight of undertrial prisoners was written about by *The Indian Express.* The paper carried a series of reports on the horrendous conditions of thousands of prisoners spending years in prison without even being brought to trial. As a direct result, the issue received some serious judicial consideration. The report led to the filing of a writ petition through a lawyer activist in the Supreme Court,[33] that subsequently admitted the petition and in 1979, the Supreme Court delivered an important verdict: "speedy trial was a fundamental, constitutional right for criminal defendants"[34].

Around the same time, the plight of undertrials was taken up by the executive branch. In 1977, the government asked the 78th Law Commission to study the issue in depth and suggest reform measures. Subsequently, the issue concerning the undertrials was picked up by the AN Mulla Committee, which was constituted by the government in 1980 on prison reforms. Taking cognisance, the committee observed that "most prison inmates belong to economically backward classes which could be attributed to their inability to arrange for bail bond[35]. It said that legal aid workers were needed to help such persons in getting them released either on bail or on personal recognisance. However, the recommendations of the committee were not taken seriously by successive governments.

Some of the most influential interventions to improve the condition of undertrials emerged in the 2000s. The Supreme Court (SC) in 2000 directed the union government and all state governments to constitute Fast Track Courts (FTCs) to speed up the resolution of cases involving undertrial prisoners, especially those whose trials have been pending for over two years. Accordingly, from April 01, 2001, all undertrial cases from the district and subordinate courts were transferred to the FTCs. The real momentum came in 2005, when the government passed an amendment to the Criminal Procedure Code by inserting Section 436A. The new provision read: "The maximum period for which an undertrial prisoner can be detained: where a person has, during the period of investigation under any law undergone detention for a period extending up to one-half of the maximum period of imprisonment specified for that offence under that law, he shall be released by the court on his personal bond with or without sureties"[36].

In the last few years, the executive has taken some positive steps concerning undertrial prisoners. The executive branch in 2010 made a forceful intervention on the issues of high pendency of undertrial cases and the Ministry of Law and Justice launched "The Mission Mode Programme for Delivery of Justice and Legal Reforms–Undertrial Programme". The programme aimed to resolve two-thirds of all undertrial cases and ease congestion in jails by July 31, 2010. The programme sought to work with state governments and the Legal Service Authority[37].

It was in 2014, seeing no visible progress on its past directives, that the Supreme Court Bench, on September 05, issued a series of strictures to various institutions managing the country's criminal justice system. In a major departure from its earlier directives, the court directed judicial officers across states to accelerate the pending trial process and release those prisoners who have spent "half of the maximum sentence prescribed for the offences under the Criminal Code". The Supreme Court termed the issue of undertrials languishing in jails as "serious" and reminded the Centre not to remain a "mute spectator" and rather act as a "nodal agency"[38].

Mounting Numbers of Undertrials: Fuelling Alienation – Leading to Conflicts

Crisis in Justice System

The slow march to justice for thousands of undertrial prisoners has to be seen in the larger context of a criminal justice system afflicted by serious structural and procedural bottlenecks. Countless undertrials are paying the price for India's centralised justice system which has a very low ratio of judges, a dysfunctional prison system, and an alarmingly low police-population ratio. Little priority is given to investigation and prosecution and there is a lack of strong commitment to use emergent information and communication tools in carrying out justice delivery functions.

The foremost challenge is the low population-judge ratio[39]. The scenario is even worse in the lower courts, with more than 3,300 posts remaining vacant against a sanctioned strength of 17,715 judges[40]. All this has a clear bearing on the languishing of undertrials for want of bail. With a backlog of litigations stretching over three crore, pre-trial detention is being used a punitive measure, resulting in denial of bail.[41]

Delayed Investigations

However, the low bench strength seems pale in comparison to the role played by police and prosecution functionaries in delaying the investigation and trial processes. It is well known that a great majority of undertrials languish in prisons because the police do not finish investigations and file the chargesheets in time[42]. There are also issues of "unjustified or unnecessary" arrests that police officials often resort to, to demonstrate the progress of the investigation in high-profile cases. According to one reliable estimate, a mammoth 60 percent of all arrests are unnecessary[43].

Dysfunctional Prisons

Among all the institutions in charge of the criminal justice system, the prison administration plays the most critical role in addressing issues concerning the undertrials. For instance, as per the Prisons Act, 1894, the Jail Superintendent has to maintain a register of all prisoners admitted and one showing when each prisoner is to be released. In every sense, the prison authorities are custodians of the undertrials' rights and their timely release. In reality, this is rarely the case. There are only a few prisons in the country that maintain a proper record of undertrials, let alone informing them about their rights under Section 436A[44]. The key reason for such a sorry state of affairs is continued low attention paid to administrative requirements, including staffing and modernisation. For instance, on an average, only 66 percent of sanctioned posts are met nationally and, in some cases like Jharkhand, this proportion is as low as 21 percent.[45]

Inadequate Funding

Behind the inadequate infrastructure, poorly qualified prosecutors, lower police-population ratio, and understaffed prisons with appalling facilities, there lies a grossly underfunded criminal justice system. As an example, the judiciary was allocated less than one percent (Rs. 1,100 crore) of India's total budget outlay in 2014-15. The resource commitment on policing, a critical aspect impacting the state of undertrials, is even more worrisome. State governments spend a minuscule share of their allocation (3-5 percent) on policing. After meeting salary requirements, a meagre percentage is spent on upgradation of investigators' knowledge about forensic techniques and new *modus operandi*[46].

Slow Penetration of Information and Communication Technologies (ICTs)

Another challenge is the absence of a basic judicial infrastructure that affects the presence or absence of opportunity in leveraging the use of ICTs to speed up trials. Both the prosecution and trial systems have not kept pace with the technological progress. For instance, the digitisation of jail records should spell a significant difference in prison system management. Similarly, setting up video conferencing facilities at district prisons can facilitate the trial process at little additional cost. But the criminal justice administration is several decades away from embracing ICTs as most justice delivery functions are carried out in the manual mode[47].

The Way Ahead

The solutions involve active and time-bound cooperation from various stakeholders such as courts, police, prosecutors, prison administration, legal aid and the undertrials themselves. The pathway to ease the situation facing the undertrials has to be comprehensive rather than kneejerk such as fast-track courts. Besides judicial reforms, the resolution of challenges can happen through a combination of infrastructure funding, police training, and modernisation of the prison system. To be sure, these are tall orders that need time and resource commitment. For immediate results, a few ideas may be worth considering.

First, should be to target the low hanging fruit: one of them is making the district judicial committee deliver. State authorities need to revamp and streamline Undertrial Review Committees (URCs) at their level. This was something envisioned by the Mulla Committee as far back as 1979 and has since been reiterated by numerous Law Commission reports. The URC can turn into an excellent inter-agency coordinating body that allows for all relevant persons to join together to assist the courts in the speedy trial and release of undertrials. An important step that the URC can take is to discourage policemen from hasty/unnecessary arrests. In this regard, there is a clear guideline from the National Police Commission (1977) for the police to avoid hasty arrests and the same has been reiterated by the Supreme Court in numerous cases[48]. However, this would be a non-starter without serious police reforms.

Second, the country's ailing legal aid system needs an urgent overhaul. Such useful state instruments which can prove vital for thousands of illiterate and poor undertrials need the strong endorsement of the union government and states. In this regard, the Law Commission's proposal for new lawyers to do a two-year compulsory stint with the legal aid system is still hanging fire and needs to be enforced immediately. Further, the country needs a public defender system as well. In India, the state public defenders receive a meagre compensation to defend the accused whereas in the United States, the funding comes from both the state and the federal government. In fact, India can learn a lot from the Latin American countries, especially Colombia and Bolivia, which have impressive legal aid systems that help address their alarmingly high rates of incarceration[49].

Third, the justice delivery establishment needs to embrace innovative alternative dispute resolution tools to reduce unnecessary pendency, especially in cases of petty crimes. In this regard, globally acclaimed plea bargaining tools can come in handy. To illustrate, a plea bargain is an agreement in a criminal case whereby the prosecutor offers the defendant the opportunity to plead guilty, usually to a lesser charge or to the original criminal charge with a recommendation of a lighter than the maximum sentence. Thus, most criminal defendants are offered the plea bargain. A plea bargain gives criminal defendants the opportunity to avoid sitting through a trial, risking conviction on the original, more serious charge.[50] Although India had introduced plea bargaining in its criminal justice system in 2006 (via Criminal Law Amendment Act, 2005), any serious traction on this has yet to be seen.

Fourth, there is an urgent need to begin the process of re-engineering the criminal justice system which is rusty and appears to belong to an earlier century. For immediate results, Lok Adalats, mediation, plea bargaining, and negotiated settlements can be pursued. Further, employing innovative tactics such as clubbing of similar kinds of cases, leaving administrative functions to court managers, introducing modern management tools and systems for docket and case management, can all help improve the plight of undertrials. In this regard, the decision of the National Human Rights Commission (NHRC) to establish human rights cells in the state police headquarters is a move in the right direction.[51]

Fifth, ICT offers plenty of hope for undertrials. E-courts, which are increasing in number across many parts of the world, should be taken in right earnest. These can seamlessly bring together diverse criminal justice functionaries. This reiterates what was said long ago in the report of the "Justice V.S. Malimath Committee on Reforms of the Criminal Justice System" (2003), which emphasised the use of modern science and technology in harnessing criminal investigation and training to improve the basic process which would benefit the undertrials.[52] For instance, through the Integrated Services Digital Network (ISDN) technology, courts and prisons can be connected through video linkage. If a video camera and a television set is provided in a separate room, all the prisoners can be assembled easily. Simultaneously, another video set is put up in the chamber of the presiding magistrate. This will provide the jail authorities another mode of communication, so that they do not need to transport the prisoners to the courts which, in turn, brings down financial and manpower costs. While the present Union Law and Justice Ministry's initiative of the monitoring and tracking system to oversee implementation of the Supreme Court's verdicts is commendable in this regard, it needs to do much more on ICT[53].

Finally, the emphasis should be placed on ensuring the implementation of existing provisions, such as regularising the functioning of the Undertrial and Periodic Review Committees. Ensuring that poor undertrials do not languish in jails for long periods, the establishment of full-fledged e-courts in taluks and higher courts, and the use of technology in analysing and grouping cases pending in courts, are equally urgent needs. The highest court's ultimatum and plan of action should be rigorously followed at the district level to put an end to the inhumanity of punishing those who, according to universally accepted principles, ought to be presumed innocent until proven guilty[54].

This chapter has briefly reviewed the state of undertrials in India, certain striking issues highlighted from jail statistics, India's malfunctioning legal system, Naxalism, and its spread in predominantly Adivasi regions. Several other lacunae related to the law like outdated statutes, delays, judicial reforms, etc. have not been touched upon, being beyond the scope in the context of LWE challenges.

It has also highlighted how Adivasis are being hunted as Naxalites in their own homeland. The vested interests, mainly the rural elites, section of politicians, criminals and corporates have further worsened the state of affairs, which, if not curbed, would elude any conflict resolution in the long run. In such a context, the state apparatus needs to look for a holistic solution in which the Adivasis are made the prime stakeholders[55].

Maoist violence is the consequence of violent neglect of the Scheduled Castes and Scheduled Tribes (especially in the central tribal belt) and widespread tribal unrest due to the commercialisation of forest resources. The problem should be handled politically and administratively, implementing the constitutional provisions for the Dalits and Adivasis that have so far been ignored.[56]

An insensitive and high-handed approach shall only aggravate the troubles of the Adivasis in the rural areas, and they shall continue to be picked up from their homes and villages on false charges of being Naxalites or being involved in LWE often based on misinformation and bias against the Adivasis. Consequently, the impoverished Adivasis to bear multiple burdens of being falsely implicated.

Notes

1. World Justice Report, "Rule of Law Index : India Profile", 2012.
2. N. Fernandes, Forward to A. Ferreira, *Colours of the Cage: A Prison Memoir* (New Delhi: ALEF Book Company, 2014).
3. H Khatoon and Others (I) vs. Home Secretary, State of Bihar (1980). Supreme Court Cases 81, Decided on 12.02.1979 in Writ Petition No. 57 of 1979.
4. J.K. Krishnan, and C.R. Kumar, "Delay in Process, Denial of Justice: the Jurisprudence and Empirics of Speedy Trial in Comparative Perspective," *Georgeton Journal of International Law*, Vol. 4, pp. 747-784.
5. M.S. Malik, "Preventive Detention and Human Rights," *SVP National Policy Academy Journal,* November 08, 2013, p. 17.
6. "Humanising the Prison Walls," *Combat Law*, July 22, 2010.
7. R. Garg, and S. Ritwik, "The Problems of Under-trials," http://www.legalservicesindia.com/article/print.php?art_id=1280.
8. http://blog.mylaw.net/four-women-lawyers-help-bastars-imprisoned-adivasis-access-justice-in-a-broken-system/
9. Prison Statistics India (2013) National Crime Records Bureau, Ministry of Home Affairs, Government of India.
10. Ibid.
11. P. Thakur, "Same Day Bail for Salman Khan, but Over 2.5 Lakh Undertrials Languish in Jails," *The Times of India*, May 08, 2015.
12. "Indians Under Trial Exceed Dutch Population," *India Spend,* May 07, 2015.
13. "Prison Statistics 2013: Higher Proportion of Muslims, Scheduled Caste and Scheduled Tribe Convicts and Undertrials in India's Jails," October 30, 2014, on www.counterview.org
14. Ibid.

15. n. 6.
16. Fernandes, n. 2.
17. U. Baxi, "The Crises of Indian Legal System, Alternatives in Development: Law", *Stranger Journalism*, 1982, pp. 4-5.
18. "Law Commission's View of Terrorism," *Combat Law*, February 12, 2010, p. 2.
19. B.D. Sharma, "Panchayats (Extension to the Scheduled Areas) Act: Realizing Its Potential," in S. Mehrotra, ed., *Countering Naxalism with Development: Challenges of Social Justice and State Security* (New Delhi: Sage Publications, 2014), pp. 129-147.
20. S. Ranjan, "Maovad: muddhavikasnahin, nyay" (Maoism: the issue is not development, but justice) *PrabhatKhabar*, October10, 2009.
21. For instance, Jharkhand presently has more than 17 fractions of what the media and the administration term under the generic label "Left Wing Extremism (LWE)."
22. P. Dahat, "Acquitted after 7 Years, Tribal Woman says she was Tortured," *The Hindu*, March 03, 2015.
23. D. Raza, "The Curse of Bastar: Tribals Caught in the War Against Red Terror," *Hindustan Times*, April 26, 2015.
24. A. Shah, "The Markets of Protection "Terrorist" Maoist Movement and the State in Jharkhand, India," *Critique of Anthropology* 26(3), 2006, pp. 297-314; A. Shah, "Alcoholics Anonymous: The Maoist Movement in Jharkhand, India," *Modern Asian Studies*, 45(05), 2011, pp. 1095-1117; and G. J. Kunnath, "Under the Shadow of Guns: Negotiating the Flaming Fields of Caste/Class War in Bihar, India," *Anthropology Matters*, 2004.
25. D. Stuligross, "Resources, Representation, and Authority in Jharkhand, India," *Asia Pacific Viewpoint* 49(1), 2008, pp. 83–97; A. Prakash, *Jharkhand: Politics of Development and Identity* (New Delhi: Hyderabad: Orient Longman, 2001); S. Jewitt, "Political Ecology of Jharkhand Conflicts", *Asia Pacific Viewpoint* 49(1), 2008, pp. 68-82.
26. C. Upadhya, "Law, custom and Adivasi Identity: Politics of Land Rights in Chotabagpur," in Sunder, eds., *Legal Grounds: Natutral Resources, Identity*, and the *Land in Jharkhand* (New Delhi: Oxford University Press, 2009), pp. 30-55.
27. Raza, n. 23.
28. S. Amitabh, "The Story of 514 Hapless Jharkhand Men who were Lured into Surrendering as Naxals," April 23, 2015.
29. "Plight of Jailed Tribal Undertrials 'Serious': SC" *Decan Herald*, July 07, 2013.
30. Ibid.
31. S. Swamy, "How Long Will the 6,000 Jharkhandi Adivasis Languish in Jail?," *Jharkhand Khabar*, March 14, 2012.
32. The judiciary took up the issues of undertrials on numerous occasions such as the Bhagalpur blindings, Hussainara Khatoon, Mantoo Mazumdar, etc.
33. A lawyer, Kapila Higorani, was so shocked to read the report, that she appealed before the Apex Court for a Writ of Habeas Corpus in 1979.

34. Hussainara Khatoon v State of Bihar, (1980) 1 SCC 98.
35. Mulla Committee Report on Prison Reforms, 1980-83.
36. Shailes Gandhi, "Caged Ordeal", *Deccan Herald*, September 07, 2014.
37. Department of Justice, Ministry of Law and Justice, Government of India, http://doj.gov.in/?Q=node/209.
38. For details see Bhim Singh v. Union of India, Ibid.
39. India has 15 judges per million population, making it one of the lowest in the world. The Supreme Court, in the All India Judges Association case in 2002, had ordered an increase the number of judges to 50 per million, but there has not been any positive movement on this. See Bibek Debroy, "Justice Delivery in India: A Snapshot of Problems and Reforms", *ISAS Working Paper*, No. 47, July 2008.
40. Damayanti Datta, "Sleepless in Supreme Court", *India Today*, June 27, 2014, http://indiatoday.intoday.in/story/ supreme- court-cji-rm-lodha-bar-council-of-india-cbi/1/368783.html.
41. Vrinda Bhandari 2014, Ibid.
42. Madhurima, "Undertrial Prisoners and the Criminal Justice System", *Journal of Human Rights Initiative*, 2010, http://www.humanrightsinitiative.org/new/2010/undertrial_prisoners_&_criminal_justice_system.pdf.
43. The 120th Report of the Law Commission of India (1987), http://lawcommissionofindia.nic.in/reports/ 177rptp2.pdf.
44. Madhurima, n.42.
45. Bhandari, n.41.
46. Ajay Shah, "Reinventing Criminal Justice System", March 11, 2015, http://ajayshahblog.blogspot.in/2015/03/ reinventing-criminal-justice-system.html.
47. Address by former Chief Justice KG Balakrishnan, at the Joint Conference of Chief Ministers and Chief Justices, at Vigyan Bhawan on April 08, 2007, http://supremecourtofindia.nic.in/speeches/speeches_2007/8.4.2007.pdf
48. See Ministry of Home Affairs, Government of India, National Police Commission, 1977, Third Report.
49. Richard M. Aborn and Ashley D. Cannon, "Prisons: In Jail, but not Sentenced", *American Quarterly, Winter 2013.* http://www.americasquarterly.org/aborn-prisons.
50. Parvez Alam Khan, "Unique Remedy to Reduce Backlog in Indian Courts", *Manuputra*, http://www.manupatrafast.com/articles/PopOpenArticle.aspx?ID=68b01806-8cbc-4ddc-a3df- 8e1fb2abdc70&txtsearch=Subject:%20Criminal.
51. The National Human Rights Commission Report, Government of India, http://nhrc.nic.in/Documents/ Publications/nhrcindia.pdf.
52. Committee on Reforms of Criminal Justice System Government of India, Ministry of Home Affairs Report, Vol I, http://www.mha.nic.in/hindi/sites/upload_files/mhahindi/files/pdf/criminal_justice_system.pdf.
53. The Ministry of Law and Justice has set up the Mission Mode Programme for Undertrials to coordinate with various prisons and track the developments in real time basis. See the details, http://doj.gov.in/?q=node/209.

54. Yogesh Vajpeyi, "The Undertrials in Jail: The idea of Injustice", *The New Indian Express*, April 23, 2013, http://www.newindianexpress.com/columns/Undertrials-in-jails-The-idea-of-injustice/2013/04/28/ article1564581.ece.
55. K.B. Saxena, "The Naxalite Movement and State Policy" in Merothra, ed., n.19, pp. 71-83.
56. K.S. Subramanian, "State Response to Maoist Violence in India: A Critical Assessment," *Economic & Political Weekly*, 45(32), pp.23-26.

15 MODERNISING AND REFORMING THE POLICE

As per the Phillipines model (and the same could be applicable to us), there are five pillars of the criminal justice system, which are: the community, law enforcement or policing, prosecution service, courts and correctional institutions. These five pillars are used during the investigation and prosecution of suspected offenders and villains. This is to check that all parts of the judicial system are working as they should be. If any one of these is found not to be, the Filipinos would refer to it as *"Wala tayong maasahan na hustisya"* meaning it has become dysfunctional[1]. The aspects concerning the third, fourth and fifth pillars have been discussed in the previous chapter. In this chapter, facets concerning our law enforcement or policing are discussed, in relation to the challenge posed by LWE in India.

As part of its multi-pronged strategy to deal with the LWE menace, the MHA has taken special steps on the security front. Due to the socio-economic roots of Naxalism, emphasis is being laid on employing the local State Police Forces (SPFs) with assistance from the Central Armed Police Forces (CAPFs) for ensuring appropriate security.

The Centre has been implementing the presently ongoing Modernisation of Police Forces (MPFs) scheme since 2000-01, with an annual budgetary allocation of Rs.1,000 crore for ten years, with the assistance of the states. The MHA claims that this scheme provides the much needed assistance and impetus to the police organisation in the states. However, as far as deliverables are concerned, there exist several gaps.

Evolution of the Ongoing MPF Scheme

As per the VIIth Schedule to the Constitution of India, "Police" and "Law and Order" are "State Subjects" and, as such, it is the responsibility of the state governments to modernise and adequately equip their police forces for meeting the challenges to law and order and internal security. The concerned state governments take the necessary action to deal with law and order problems, terrorism, Naxal insurgency and other related issues, etc. The central government supplements their efforts and resources by various measures, which include deployment of CAPFs to assist the SPFs, sanctioning the India Reserve Battalions (IRBs) to the states, assistance for strengthening the state police and intelligence agencies through modernisation schemes, reimbursement of Security Related Expenditures (SREs) under the said scheme, assistance in training the SPFs through the Army, Central Para-Military Forces (CPMFs) and Bureau of Police Research and Development (BPR&D), sharing of intelligence, bringing about inter-state coordination and assistance in development works through a myriad schemes of different ministries.

As was briefly touched upon in the previous chapter, traditionally, policing has been a neglected area in most of the states. The state governments have overlooked the requirement and need of developing basic policing infrastructure, as policing is a service function and not a revenue earning department. The police budget has been traditionally limited to mere payment of pay and allowances in most of the states and no effort has been made to build even basic minimum facilities for policing duties.[2]

Like any other governmental adminstrative machinery in the country, the Indian Police too have inherited a colonial legacy in the present system. The British gave adequate powers to police personnel in India, with little administrative facilities. They deliberately left the police personnel on their own for managing their basic amenities and administrative requirements. Hence, police personnel misused the immense power vested in them and exploited the public. The police during the British period was to serve the political masters and not the people. The basic needs of police personnel, including administrative, infrastructural and welfare measures remained neglected in the post colonial period also. Increased public awareness, political interference, media watch, the Right to Information (RTI) Act, etc, have now made the police more accountable, and policing has earned a negative image in the society.

The total police budget in India has been a meagre one percent of the GDP.[3] The general trend has been that the budget of the police in all the states put together is always less than the union police budget, whereas, the size of the CAPFs is less than half of the strength of the central forces.

To supplement the efforts of the state governments in modernising their police forces, the MHA has been implementing a Non-Plan Scheme for Modernisation of State Police Forces since 1969-70 on a Centre-state cost sharing (50:50) basis. Initially, Rs. 50 lakh was allocated annually for the scheme. In 1978-79, the allocation was raised from Rs. 50 lakh to Rs. 7 crore per annum. Further, from 1999-2000, the allocation was further enhanced to Rs.100 crore. During the period 1969-70 to 1999-2000, a total amount of Rs.536.74 crore was released to various state governments on account of this scheme, which, in real terms, is a meagre sum for such a vast project. The MPF scheme, therefore, could not have the desired impact on policing in the states, thus,S far.

BPR&D conducted the base survey in the year 2000 to assess the deficiency in various areas of police administration in the states. The survey indicated that a minimum sum of Rs. 25,000 crore would be required to meet the current deficiencies in the SPFs in the country. Consequently, in January 2001, the Cabinet Committee on Security (CCS) decided to enhance the annual central allocation under the MPF scheme to Rs.1,000 crore from 2000-01 for 10 years[4]. The focus of the MPF scheme is on strengthening the police infrastructure at the cutting edge level through constructing secure police stations, equipping police stations with the required mobility, modern weaponry, communication equipment, forensic set-up and housing, etc.

Brief History

When the scheme was introduced in 1969-70, the pattern of assistance given by the Centre was 75 percent loan and 25 percent grant. In 1973-74, this was changed to 50 percent grant-in-aid and 50 percent loan on the recommendations of the Sixth Finance Commission. In the first phase of the scheme, Rs. 43.84 crore were released to the state governments from 1969-70 to 1977-78[5]. Subsequently, the Police Commission recommended that the scheme be extended for another ten-year period from 1978-79, with a substantial increase in allotment of funds[6]. The government of India extended the scheme up to 1989-90 with an outlay of Rs. 100 crore. During this phase, an amount of Rs. 89.29 crore was released to the states.

The scheme was further extended to a third phase, which lasted from 1991 to 2000. The outlay was increased and an amount of Rs.120 crore was sanctioned for release during the five-year period 1991-95. The amount was increased to Rs.50 crore in1996-97 and during 1999-2000, further enhanced to Rs.100 crore.

In 2001, the government enhanced the annual allocation to Rs. 1,000 crore, with effect from 2000-01. In the review of the scheme undertaken in 2005, the states were categorised into two groups: 'A' and 'B.' Jammu & Kashmir and all eight northeastern states were included in category 'A' entitling them to 100 percent central assistance and the remaining 19 states were put in category 'B', which allowed them 75 percent assistance. A special component to strengthen the police infrastructure in the 76 Naxal-affected districts of nine states at the rate of Rs. 2 crore per affected district annually for five years was introduced. The total funds released from 2000-01 to 2009-10 to various states under the scheme came to Rs. 10,086.83 crore.[7] The Government of India has continued the scheme for a further period of five years i.e. from 2012-13 to 2016-17. An amount of Rs.8628.43 crore has been allocated under the 'Non-Plan' and Rs.3750.87 crore under the 'Plan' items[8].

The states continue to be divided into the same two groups: 'A' and 'B', but the funding pattern sees a change. While group A states receive 90 percent (earlier 100 percent) central assistance, with 10 percent to be contributed by them, group B states share the expenditure in the ratio of 60:40 (earlier 75:25) (Centre: state). There has been another change recently. According to the 2014-15 revised budget estimate, the Centre granted around Rs. 1,433 crore to the states for the scheme. Another Rs. 537.50 crore was given as non-plan expenditure under this head[9].

Review and Implementation Mechanism

The scheme was last reviewed in 2005 and in view of the changed security scenario, the states were recategorised into two groups, namely 'A' and 'B' involving central assistance at 100 percent and 75 percent, respectively w.e.f. 2005-06.[10] The Naxal-affected states fall in category B; generally, these states are considered to be economically and infrastructurally backward, ill-developed and lacking in basic policing facilities and should have been given 100 percent assistance.

Fund Allocation Formula

The central allocation to the states under the MPF scheme was determined in the year 2001 on the basis of population (35 percent weightage), sanctioned strength of police force (25 percent weightage), number of police stations (15 percent weightage), incidence of crime per lakh of population (25 percent weightage). No weightage was given to economic backwardness, lack of basic policing infrastructure, etc. Hence, the states which are traditionally capacity deficient, with least policing resources and infrastructure did not get any special attention. Poor performing states have less crime registration due to lack of public awareness and poor police credibility. Hence, the fund allocation formula went against the Naxal-affected states.

Special Provisions for Naxal-Affected States Through MPF

Strengthening of Special Branches

A well-equipped intelligence set-up plays a crucial role in ensuring internal security and the success of counter-insurgency operations. To begin with, 5 percent of MPF allocation has been earmarked for strengthening of Special Branches (SB) and equipping them with modern security and communication gadgetry in four Naxalite affected states, viz., Bihar, Chhattisgarh, Jharkhand and Odisha. The states have been requested to enhance SB manpower from their own resources. All the states have been advised to earmark 5 percent of MPF allocation for strengthening their intelligence set-ups. Rs.40.00 crore was sanctioned in 2008-09 for this purpose.[11]

Strengthening of the Police Infrastructure in 76 Severely Naxal Affected Districts

The MPF scheme has a special component for strengthening the police infrastructure in 76 highly Naxal affected districts at the rate of Rs. 2.00 crore per district per year, initially for a period of five years[12]. Naxal-affected districts are provided 100 percent central funds. On the advice of the Naxalite Management Division in the MHA, special allocations were given to 32 affected districts in FY 2010-11 for fortification of police stations.[13]

Other Measures for Improving Police Capability in Naxal-Affected States

Improving Police Training Capability

With a view to building the capacity of police personnel in jungle warfare and counter-insurgency operations, 20 special Counter-Insurgency and Anti-Terrorism (CIAT) training centres were planned in Assam, Bihar, Chhattisgarh, Jharkhand and Odisha (4 centres in each state) with an outlay of Rs.52 crore during the 11th Five-Year Plan. Also, under the aegis of BPR&D, the Central Academy for Police Training was set up to induct and train trainers across the country and to direct recruit Deputy Superintendents of Police (Dy SPs), as well as for in-service and specialised training to Dy SPs/Addl SPs of these states.

Security Related Expenditure (SRE) Scheme

A non-plan scheme, namely the Security Related Expenditure (SRE) scheme has been under implementation since April 01, 1996, to supplement the efforts of the states in dealing with the Naxalite problem effectively. The scheme was revised comprehensively in February 2005, thereby, increasing the rate of reimbursement from 50 to 100 percent and also covering more districts and more items for reimbursement. The revised scheme also permits advance release of funds to the states. In order to provide additional support to the states, the ceiling on reimbursement of infrastructure cost has been enhanced from Rs.8 crore to Rs.15 crore.

Under the revised scheme, 76 districts in nine states (Andhra Pradesh, Madhya Pradesh, Bihar, Maharashtra, Chhattisgarh, Jharkhand, Odisha, Uttar Pradesh and West Bengal) are covered and the MHA reimburses 100 percent expenditure incurred on security related items such as *ex-gratia* paid to families of victims of Naxalite violence, providing logistic and camp facilities to the CPMFs, the amount spent on special training given to the state police personnel, provision of insurance for state police personnel involved in Anti-Naxalite Operations (ANOs), a lump sum grant to Village Defence Committees (VDCs)/Nagrik Surakasha Samitis (NSSs) for SRE, lump sum amount per surrendered Naxalite, expenditure incurred on publicity material, advance releases under the SRE scheme, hiring of vehicles, including helicopters, weapons or communication equipment not covered under the MPF scheme, etc.

Pilot Project for Development of Infrastructure in Naxal-Affected States

A new scheme named "Special Infrastructure Scheme in LWE Affected States" was launched with an outlay of Rs 500 crore in the Eleventh Plan, with a view to filling the gaps in infrastructure not covered under any other government scheme to provide accessibility to the Security Forces (SFs) in such areas[14]. Based upon a detailed analysis of the spread and trends of Naxalite violence, 33 affected districts in 8 states were taken up for special attention on planning, implementation and monitoring of development schemes. Several schemes of 20 development ministries/departments have been identified for support.

However, in the budget of FY 2016-17, there have been feelers with regard to scrapping of the Special Infrastructure Scheme (SIS) fund, since the 14th Financial Commission had enhanced the devolution of the tax share of 42 percent (from 32 percert) from the Centre to the state. The key security scheme was meant for four states – Chhattisgarh, Jharkhand, Odisha and Bihar—to help them create Special Anti-Naxal Forces (SANFs) based on the highly successful model of Andhra Pradesh's elite Greyhounds crack commando force.

As per experts, the decision will definitely weaken the anti-Maoist strategy as the SANF was meant to be the lead force to tackle the Maoists. All its personnel were inducted from the tribal region of the states from where the Maoists also get the cadre for their PLGA. The states are unlikely to continue the SIS scheme with the same vigour and zest as the Centre will lose control over it after it is handed over to the states[15].

The Parliamentary Standing Committee on Home Affairs has opposed the move and has backed the ministry's proposal to bring SIS and SRE under the centrally-sponsored umbrella scheme, "National Scheme for Modernisation of Police and Other Forces". "The committee is not ready to buy the argument that merely by enhancing the share of the states in the net proceeds of union taxes to 42 percent, the central government can justify delinking SIS from central assistance," the panel stated in its 197th report[16]. The committee, comprising 10 members from the Rajya Sabha and 21 from the Lok Sabha, raised the question of how state governments can put in money into schemes like MNREGA, PM Rural Road, Indira Awaas Yojana, and, at the same time modernise the police forces to fight terrorists and lawless elements when the actual increase in their pool is very small and, in many cases, even works out to be less.[17] Directors General of Police (DsGP) from several states have warned the Home Minister that the government's decision to slash central funding for the SPFs could hit their combat capability in the insurgency and terrorism-hit states.[18]

Evaluation of Ongoing MPF Scheme

The MPF scheme faced teething problems in the initial stage of implementation. The central government has been regularly reminding the states at the Chief Ministers' Conferences and through letters to Chief Secretaries, to send the perspective action plans for the modernisation of their police forces.[19] However, the states have been found wanting in utilising the allotted funds. The lack of initiative on the part of a majority of states in the early stage of the MPF scheme was apparently due to their inability to spare the requisite matching funds. This had led to a situation where the union government was keen to modernise the SPFs but the states were unable to implement the scheme owing to paucity of financial resources at their disposal.

This peculiar situation emanates, to a large extent, from the federal structure of our polity. As mentioned earlier, according to our constitutional framework, the subjects of 'police' and 'public order' fall within the jurisdiction of state governments, whereas the overall responsibility for the maintenance of internal security has been vested in the union government under Article 355. The Parliamentary Standing Committee on Home Affairs in its report in 2003-04 had this to say:[20]

> When it comes to the control and superintendence of police forces, the states do not want to yield even an inch of their jurisdiction. But, at the same time, when it comes to improve and strengthen their police forces, they simply raise their hands expressing their inability to do so because of financial constraints.

In order to overcome this problem, the committee recommended that the union government must make earnest efforts to ensure the active participation of state governments in modernising their police forces.[21] However, the committee, while analysing the demands for grants for 2003-04, remarked that the union government should not have a feeling of helplessness in convincing the state governments to focus their attention on this issue as Article 355 places the responsibility of protecting the states from internal disturbances on the shoulders of the union government . Therefore, the union government is well within its right to issue the necessary instructions to the state governments to come forward and join it in modernising their police forces in the larger interest of maintaining internal security.

The committee, keeping in view the poor financial position of the states, had also proposed a new funding pattern based on the 75:25 ratio and recommended that the Centre may further consider stopping the release of funds in respect of states that are found wanting vis-à-vis the implementation of the scheme. The committee recommended that a specialised central agency to be entrusted with the task of overseeing the implementation of this scheme[22].

Delay in Release of Fund to the States

There has been undue delay in the allocation and release of funds to the states by the MHA. After receiving the funds from the MHA, the states have to release a matching share as per the plan, but the states' Home and Finance Departments take considerable time in issuing the allocation to the Police Department. This is due to the states' inability to provide a matching state share. Consequently, the fund is generally released at the end of the financial year. Hence, the tender formalities cannot be completed in time and the budget is not utilised in the same financial year. The revalidation sanction is sought from the respective state Home Department, which, once again, takes considerable time.[23] A new system has been adopted for release of funds from 2008-09. A high power committee of the MHA considered the Action Plan in February-

March 2008, and the first instalment of funds for 2008-09 was released to the states in April 2008[24].

Complement of Training, Leadership and Ethos

Impact on Police Training

In June 1995, a survey of 100 out of 145 police training institutions in the country conducted by the BPR&D had revealed that police training is highly neglected[25]. The study had further found that only 1,105 head constables and 9,861 constables were given refresher training out of 13 lakh police personnel in the country. The sanctioned police strength has gradually increased as more forces are being raised and the strength of the police is being augmented. The study had projected that it was feasible to give training to police personnel once in 20 years with the existing training infrastructure in the states. Not much has changed since then, except for more recruitment and increase in police strength by a further three lakhs. Police strength is expected to increase rapidly in the near future due to the ever increasing internal security requirements of the country.

The MHA has recognised that lack of specialised training to state police personnel was severely affecting their anti-Naxal operations. As per the abovementioned study, and subsequent projection on modernisation and upgradation of police infrastructure, training of the police was the single area which needed to be supported in a big way. A research study on this issue undertaken by Om Shankar Jha, a serving Border Security Force (BSF) officer in November–December 2008, observed that there is a huge deficiency in the police training infrastructure, resources and personal commitment in the Naxalism-affected states.

Presently, there are 162 police training institutions in the country, 105 belonging to the states and 57 to the Centre, which are inadequate for police training, especially in combat training. The MHA had released adequate funds for commissioning at least one CIAT centre in each state in FY 2008-09. However, things are quite different on the ground. Such schools were still in the conceptual stage and had not been commissioned, even after a lapse of five years, i.e. till 2013.

Assessment of Overall Impact/Additional Lacunae

Police officers in general are of the opinion that the MPF scheme is providing quality equipment, gadgets, computers, GPS, etc which is commendable. But, the real problem lies in the quality of manpower recruited. The end-users of these gadgets i.e., the police constabulary should be capable of using them. For example, the Remote Sensing (RS) satellite data, even if provided to a police station, cannot be of any use to an almost illiterate constable. In Bihar and Jharkhand Police, constables are recruited with VII class education level. Despite the BPR&D's suggestive guideline (which is not a compulsion to the states), no corrective measure have been taken, thus far. Even the Jharkhand High Court has directed the state government to recruit matriculate constabulary, but the state's political leadership overruled the court's directive by passing legislation in the state assembly. This has been subsequently challenged in the court but the status quo remains. The police authorities have still not been able to convince the legislature on this issue. Therefore, it will take many years of persistent effort to build real police capability. Strong political resolve, and an unambiguous anti-Naxal policy with no political interference are required for police capacity building and achieving a realistic anti-Naxal capability by the SPFs.[26]

A positive training culture has to be developed in the state police which is acutely lacking. Very few police personnel are willing to undergo strenuous physical training, which is inescapable for professional competence in an insurgency environment. Also, the men need to be tech-savvy to use the electronic gadgets procured for them. The district police personnel are reluctant to work in the STF despite the 50 percent extra allowance. Sophisticated weapons are, therefore, of little use to them.

Police leadership with a strong operational orientation is required to be deputed to fight the Naxals, alongside unwavering modernisation efforts. The police at the grassroots level needs to be adequately motivated and sensitised. Unless they are operationally oriented, they will continue to suffer casualties. Mine Protected Vehicles (MPVs) and Bullet Proof (BP) vehicles are secure only when used tactically; else, these are sitting ducks. The police suffer large numbers of casualties due to IED blasts and ambushes owing to tactical ignorance, a careless approach, and not strictly adhering to Standard Operational Procedures (SOPs). Operations are generally planned and executed at the police station level in association with CPMF companies. More professional planning and execution by an effective higher-level leadership is required. Hence, an adequately trained and motivated leadership is required to lead the anti-Naxal operations. The MPF can bring in visible changes in resources, but the 'police work culture' continues to be traditional and unchanged. The police leadership training needs to be relooked at, as also the overall policing needs a transformation to derive the real benefit of the modernisation process.

Modernisation of the police forces initially had a different direction and it was meant for a general uplifting of police capacity in overall policing aspects. However, gradually some specific elements suited to the Naxalism affected states were added to this, which is apparently inadequate. The government should consider bringing in a separate and specific modernisation scheme, especially for the Naxalism-affected states. These states cannot compete with other states in implementation because of inherent disadvantages. Their requirements are altogether different and unique. The Naxalism-affected states need 100 percent central assistance in MPF allocation. If J&K and the northeast states can be given 100 percent central assistance, then why not the Naxalism-affected states also?

As per Maj Gen (Retd), GD Bakshi, the police organisations are not structured and trained to fight insurgency. The officer-to-men ratio is not conducive to dedicated anti-Naxal operations. At the most, they are expected to tackle the maximum violence level of terrorism besides the routine law and order duties. Hence, the the MPF should not aim to paramilitarise the SPF. Otherwise, in the future, the police work culture will also be militarised, and the very much desired community policing concept will be defeated. Hence, he advises that, only a limited element of SPFs in each state, should be trained like a special anti-Naxal force, so that it can conduct team-based operations on receipt of specific intelligence. Anything beyond this capability, should be tackled by the CAPF.

In order to achieve a better impact of schemes like the MPF, the policing system in India needs to be given greater autonomy, with due accountability. The government should implement the much awaited and much required 'police reforms' and new 'Model Police Act'. The modern-day police has to be community-oriented, rather than being a tool in the hands of the administration.

CAG Audit

Five years after the launch of the MPF scheme, i.e. in 2006, the Comptroller and Auditor General (CAG) evaluated its working and selectively commissioned performance audit reviews covering 11 general category states and five special category states.[27] The findings and recommendations are enumerated in the following paragraphs.[28]

As a major funding agency and guardian of internal security, the MHA is the principal stakeholder in the police reform programme. In practice, however, the CAG's audit found that there was a perceptible gap in the standards and expectations between the Centre and the states.

The functioning of the apex body – the State-Level Empowered Committees (SLECs) – was a case in point. There was hardly any policy direction emanating from the business transacted by the SLECs. The SLECs had, by and large, reduced themselves to discharging the role of purchase committees, the audit report observed.

The scheme requires every state to draw up a long-term Perspective Plan (PP) and align it with the annual spending programme through its Annual Action Plan (AAP). While the PP was to be proposed by every state in 2000-01, the AAP has to be submitted to the ministry by May 15 every year. The AAPs are to be first cleared by the SLECs before they are forwarded to the Home Ministry. The CAG noted that there was considerable delay in approving the AAPs owing to their delayed submission to the ministry as well as the time taken by the ministry to clear the same. As a result, there was little time left to use the approved outlay in the same year. As the PPs were tentative, deviations from them were rampant.

The experience of the states in the utilisation of funds was not very promising as there were significant shortfalls in relative cost-sharing and wide gaps in actual expenditure against the plan outlays. The states were caught in a vicious circle of delay in the finalisation of the AAPs, causing delayed release of funds and ultimately failure in utilising them. Some states had adopted a short-cut method of locking up the funds in personal deposit accounts to show them as expenditure, which did not benefit the state concerned or the programme, the CAG pointed out. This has often been flagged in various meetings and correspondence from the MHA to the states.[29]

There could not have been a better mechanism to monitor the fund flow or to measure the effectiveness of the scheme than the AAP. Far from having it in place, the states have adopted an ad hoc approach and defaulted in timely submission of the plan to the ministry, which has, in turn, affected the release of funds.

Some states had even gone to the extent of showing their non-plan expenditure on salaries as the states' share of the scheme. Such an approach may have helped the release of the Centre's share in the short-run, but, in effect, it reduced the total outlay and hindered their modernisation programme.

The scheme's emphasis on the mobility of the police forces had been diluted as a large number of vehicles were seen to have replaced old ones, while some vehicles were diverted for VIP escorts. A few vehicles remained in parking lots for want of drivers. As a result, the net addition to mobility was little. The police's response time was too long in some states, while, in others, there was no record to show any improvement.

The scale of weapons to be procured by each state is guided by the norms laid down by the BPR&D. Weapons procurement data on each state reviewed in the audit revealed that procurement of sophisticated weapons such as AK-47s, 7.62 mm SLRs (Self Loading Rifles) and 5.56 mm INSAS (Indian Small Arms System) rifles, was far below the states' requirements.

As a result, the CAG found that police stations continued to depend on outdated and unserviceable weapons. Instances of issue of expired ammunition also figured in the report. In some cases, the weapons were supplied to the bodyguards of SPs, in violation of the ministry's guidelines.

Retention of sophisticated weapons in the armoury of the police reserve has been another regular feature. Delay in training was often cited as the main reason for the stockpiling. There was also a dearth of weapons as acquisition of weapons from ordnance factories was delayed.

In most cases, residential and non-residential buildings meant for the families of police personnel were far short of the provisions in the BPR&D norms, owing to delays in construction. Thus, the security of the police force was not ensured and the level of satisfaction of housing was very low.

A dependable police telecommunication network, or POLNET, is vital for effective law and order maintenance. POLNET is a satellite-based integrated network providing direct communication links from the national capital to the state capital and the district headquarters on voice, data, fax and computer, and extending the connectivity up to the police stations on voice. The Centre directly procured and delivered the equipment to the states but its installation and the selection of sites for that was left to the states. A large part of the equipment in some cases was found inoperable either owing to the hardware-software mismatch or owing to a wrong selection of sites. In a number of cases, even the earmarked communication equipment supplied to the district police headquarters lay idle in the stores.

sSome states such as Andhra Pradesh felt that the POLNET equipment supplied to them was inferior to their own versions (for example, the Andhra Pradesh statewide area network) that had demonstrated better connectivity and robustness. The network for use in crime investigation and transmission of crime-related data was not successfully set up in some states. In some others, it was functional only up to the district level. The network was handled by untrained personnel, and there was a shortage of some communication equipment.

The CAG found specific instances of mismatch between the goals of modernisation and the practice in some states. Some of the aspects are as given below.

Andhra Pradesh, which is considered a model policing state by many experts because of the success of the Greyhounds (the special anti-terrorist squad of the state) in tackling LWE, came out as a rogue state in the CAG audit. Owing to delays in the approval of the AAP, implementation of the scheme was delayed in the state and only 13 to 82 per cent of the funds were used in the same year. The state government spent Rs.31.37 crore on works not covered under the AAP and not approved by the SLEC.

In the period under audit (2002-07), the state government was deprived of central assistance to the tune of Rs.136.49 crore owing to underutilisation of funds. Funds worth Rs.79.55 crore were parked in banks by the Police Housing Corporation, and the interest earned (Rs.2.56 crore) on the amount was appropriated for other purposes. The corporation submitted the utilisation certificates even for the unspent amounts.

Bihar spent only Rs.251 crore between 2001 and 2006 against the total approved plan of Rs.435 crore. The slow pace of spending deprived the state of the central share of Rs.121 crore.

In Jharkhand (2000-04), the MPF funds advanced to construction agencies (Rs.61.76 crore) and retained in civil deposit (Rs.8.65 crore) were reported to the Centre as utilised.

Madhya Pradesh was deprived of central assistance amounting to Rs.77.93 crore owing to slow progress in the implementation of the scheme between 2000 and 2006. An inflated expenditure of Rs.159.42 crore helped the construction agency pocket the interest earned on the amount. The agency did not refund the unspent balance to the state, the CAG audit revealed.

Odisha, too, came in for criticism for treating an advance of Rs.38.28 crore in 2000-04 to the construction agency as expenditure and for inflating the utilisation certificates furnished to the Centre for this purpose. Significant underutilisation of funds under the major components, namely, arms (70 per cent), computer (100 per cent), traffic control equipment (85 per cent) and upgrading of the fingerprint bureau (100 per cent), was also reported in the state.

CAG Recommendations

Following its performance audit of the 16 states, the CAG made the following four recommendations:

- The SLECs should reorient themselves from playing the role of purchase committees and actively get involved in designing PPs and AAPs, besides taking up the responsibility to monitor the scheme.
- The Ministry of Home Affairs should establish a system to monitor the timely and appropriate use of funds sanctioned and released.
- All states must ensure its immediate installation after the procurement of the police telecommunication network and the forensic science laboratory/fingerprint bureau equipment. Weapons procured should be distributed immediately among the targeted police stations.
- All vacant posts in the states must be filled up in a time-bound manner so that the benefit of the scheme is derived optimally.

These recommendations can be optimised only if the Centre and the states display the requisite will. But the bottom line, as revealed by the CAG report, is that the battle against LWE could, in practice, be marred by wastage of money, corruption, inefficiency, and lack of communication between the Centre and the states.

Concluding Recommendations

- The Naxalism-affected states should have overall priority for allocation (as per their need) over the other states.

- Economically and infrastructurally backward Naxalism-affected states need to be given 100 percent central assistance.
- The MPF in Naxalism-affected areas may be separated from the routine modernisation process covering all the states in general and a separate MPF scheme, need-specific to such states, may be initiated, with simplified implementation procedures like in command area schemes.
- Improvement of police training facilities needs to be given more priority in all the states in general and the Naxalism-affected states in particular.
- The present practice of giving sanction by the high powered committees of the states is time consuming and needs to be relooked at.
- MPF funds should be directly given to the Police Department with adequate financial sanction power to the Directors General of Police (DsGP) of the states.
- Each state should be asked to form a central purchase committee under the financial competence of the DsGP for smooth implementation of the MPF scheme.
- The MHA should release money in time in the beginning of the financial year and a time-bound monitoring mechanism needs to be introduced.
- The state police should be given adequate scope and liberty to set its own priority as per local need basis.
- Since the MPF allocation is limited, it needs to be prioritised as per specific need. Resources needed most urgently may be procured on priority basis.
- The MHA should take a relook at its allocation formula. The backward and relatively less developed states need more allocation in comparison to the economically developed states, as they are acutely deficient and lagging behind.
- The police reform commissions set up by successive governments have articulated steps for reforming the police. Any future reform must be guided by the following five principles:

- **Subsidiarity:** The police is highly centralised at the state level, yet it needs both greater centralisation (empowering federal investigative agencies for issues like insurgency and terrorism) as well as decentralisation (at the local government level).
- **Autonomy:** The police requires greater autonomy from the pernicious political control.
- **Accountability:** Greater autonomy needs to be complemented by investments towards accountability, such as creation of an independent supervisory board, as an oversight body.
- **Personnel:** The gap between the small very selective IPS and a large, ill-trained constabulary reflects the deep social stratification of our society. This requires changes in organisational structures and promotion pathways and much greater efforts at training lower level personnel.
- **Resources:** Ultimately, as brought out ealier, change will be hard to come by without sharply increasing resources available for the police, especially at the thana level.

The "police" and "law and order" are state subjects as per the VIIth Schedule to the Constitution of India and it is the prime responsibility of the state governments to improve the functioning of their police forces and to equip them adequately with the latest technology for meeting the emerging challenges to public order and internal security. The central government is supplementing the efforts of the states/union territories in this regard. The MPF scheme is a significant initiative towards capacity building of the SPFs which has been widely welcomed by police officers and men in all the states in general and in the Naxal-affected states in particular. Especially as it is proving to be resuscitation to the deficient policing machinery in the economically backward Naxal-affected states, where the regular police budget has been insufficient due to the fiscal crunch.

The MPF scheme has been able to bring some positive impact on policing, but still much needs to be done. Its implementation needs to be more user oriented, rather than thrust upon the states. Besides materialistic modernisation, improvement of manpower for quality handling of resources needs to be given due emphasis. The overall policing machinery needs to be transformed in a holistic manner. Proper recruitment, followed by realistic training, equipping, incentives, leadership and clear-cut directives will lead to motivation for work and transform the policing system in a holistic manner.

One of the major concerns is the limited societal pressure to reform the police. The middle class and the rich have exited the public services across a broad spectrum, including relying on the police. And the centrality of identity politics for India's socio-political class has further weakened a common societal interest – by making social representations in the police their prime focus, rather than enhancing police effectiveness[30].

Notes

1. https://www.scribd.com/document/139707366/5-Pillars-of-the-Criminal-Justice-System
2. Police budgets in most states, as per the MHA documents, are committed to the extent of over 90 percent on salaries alone.
3. 98th Report of the Parliamentary Standing Committee on Home Affairs, Demands for Grants, 2003-04 (New Delhi: Rajya Sabha Secretariat, 2004), evidence of the Union Home Secretary to the Standing Committee.
4. Ibid.
5. National Police Commission, Third Report, January 1980, p. 40.
6. Ibid., p. 41.
7. MPF Scheme, Modernisation Division, MHA.
8. Money spent on vehicles, weaponry and equiment for training, forensic laboratories and policing are components of 'non-plan' expenditure, while 'plan' expenditure covers construction of police stations and outposts, police lines, housing, infrastucturals for training and laboratories.
9. http://indianexpress.com/article/india/india-others/police-chiefs-sound-alarm-in-wake-of-cuts-to-modernisation-budget/
10. The state of J&K and all 8 northeast states, namely, Arunachal Pradesh, Assam, Manipur, Meghalaya, Mizoram, Nagaland, Tripura and Sikkim (2007-08 onwards) have been classified as 'A' category states. The remaining 19 states fall in category 'B'.
11. Annual Report 2007-08, Ministry of Home Affairs.

12. Annual Report 2013-14, Ministry of Home Affairs.
13. "Year End Review on Internal Security", a press release of the Ministry of Home Affairs, December 31, 2013.
14. Status Paper on Naxal Activities as on September 01, 2008 (New Delhi: Ministry of Home Affairs, September 30, 2008), p. 24.
15. http://www.dnaindia.com/india/report-curtains-for-another-key-anti-maoist-scheme-2073909
16. http://indianexpress.com/article/india/india-news-india/security-infrastructure-panel-backs-mha-bid-to-bring-two-schemes-under-central-plan-2783221/
17. http://www.dnaindia.com/india/report-police-modernisation-is-your-obligation-panel-to-tell-centre-2072218
18. Praveen Swami, "Police Chiefs Sound Alarm in Wake of Cuts to Modernisation Budget", *The Indian Express*, March 30, 2015.
19. 98th Report of the Parliamentary Standing Committee on Home Affairs, Demands for Grants, 2003-04 (New Delhi: Rajya Sabha Secretariat, 2004).
20. Ibid.
21. Ibid.
22. Ibid.
23. Om Shankar Jha, "Impact of Modernisation of Police Forces Scheme on Combat Capability of the Police Forces in Naxal-Affected States: A Critical Evaluation", *IDSA Occasional Paper No.7,* December 2009.
24. n.13..
25. "Police Organisation in India", Commonwealth Human Rights Initiative, 2008.
26. Ibid.
27. "The Compendium of Performance Audit Reviews on Modernisation of Police Force", by CAG, available at http://www.cag.gov.in/html/Compendium_MPF/MPF.pdf
28. V. Venkatesan, "Reluctant Reform", *Frontline*, Vol 27, Issue 9 April 24–May 07, 2010.
29. http://mha.nic.in/sites/upload_files/mha/files/MPF2014-15.pdf
30. Devesh Kapur and Milan Vaishnav, "Strengthening the Rule of Law", in Vivek Debroy, Ashley Tellis and Trevor Reece, eds., *Getting India Back on Track – An Action Agenda for Reform* (Random House India, 2014).

16. CIVIL SOCIETY, NGOs AND CONFLICT RESOLUTION

Political participation in India has evolved continuously, within the overall dynamic socio-political milieu. New social groups have entered the political arena and begun to use their political resources to shape the political process. The Scheduled Castes and Scheduled Tribes, previously excluded from politics because of their position at the bottom of India's social hierarchy, have begun to take full advantage of the opportunities presented by India's democracy. Women and environmentalists constitute new political categories that transcend traditional distinctions. The spread of social movements and voluntary organisations has shown that despite the difficulties of India's political parties and state institutions, India's democratic tendency continues to thrive.

Civil society activists are "those that occupy the organisational space between the family and the state". The phrase 'civil society' in India has gained general currency since the beginning of the 1990s. The wide range of formations that may possibly constitute the mosaic of civil society in India are: Community-Based Organisations (CBOs), Mass Organisations, Religious Organisations, Voluntary Development Organisations (VDOs), Social Movements, Corporate Philanthropy, Consumer Groups, Cultural Associations, Professional Associations, Economic Associations and others, which include the media and academia[1].

In India's context, civil society has had diverse relationships with the state ranging from the adversarial anti-dam movement of the Narmada Bachao Andolan to the relationship of partnership as demonstrated by non-profit organisations focussed on development that provide service delivery functions in areas like health and education in rural areas, often working closely with local administrations. Since the idea of civil society is so ubiquitous, it is as good a place as any to begin the discussion of the role of NGOs in Indian politics. This chapter discusses the role that a civil society and NGOs can play in mitigating and resolving the LWE related conflicts.

Civil Society in India: The Gandhian Foundation

India has a vast and rich experience as far as people's mobilisation is concerned. Our long history of the freedom movement is full of such local, regional and nationwide movements which combined both political protest and social reforms. A society which has witnessed such a high degree of moral and social commitment of our reformers and political leaders is bound to look up to such representations, towards the betterment of society.

Mahatma Gandhi was perhaps the one and only leader who gave equal importance to both political protest and social reforms. He believed that no political reform could be sustained without the required social transformation. Not only did he have the courage to challenge the British empire but also spoke up against his own people, the ills inherent in their social customs and their moral degeneration. He strongly believed that temptation towards any kind of violence was the root cause of all social problems manifested in different forms. He was rather disappointed at the fast erosion of moral values and continuation of violent tendencies deeply rooted in our society. Moral erosion resulted in corruption, and the roots of violence in our society resulted in phenomena like communalism and Naxalism (a post Gandhi phenomenon).

The post-Gandhian era has further seen such decay that has obviously resulted in loss of the social bond or social capital. In general terms, it could be said that social capital is the fruit of social relations within the society. This is something close to the enlightened society of the Gandhian connotation. This state of enlightenment comes only when individuals and groups work in harmony for the overall progress of society.

Can a sincere review of the Gandhian movement suggest something to address both corruption and violence, especially the Naxal violence, which is also linked to the agrarian land disputes? In this context, it is important to acknowledge that the genesis of the current Naxal violence has gone beyond the inequitable distribution of land and lies at the bottom of ambitions to capture political power through undemocratic means under a fake ideological commitment of its cadres.

Gandhi was perhaps unique in terms of identifying and utilising positively such available resources of social capital for the collective growth of a society that could create an imagined ashram community despite caste and class differences. That community experience helped him to have a better insight into the Indian realities. His touch with rural India made his thinking more complex, yet closer to the Indian reality. From the experiments he made in Champaran and Kheda, he learnt that without the active participation of the poor and socially backward, no popular movement would yield results.

Gandhi devised an intelligent programme of social reconstruction based on the abolition of untouchability and promotion of khadi. This programme resulted in the involvement of the upper castes which, in turn, exposed them to the multi-layered social structure resulting in their exposure to the issues and problems of the poor. Once they became conscious of the plight of the poor, they immediately joined hands to elevate their conditions. Moreover, Gandhi was sure of the fact that without the active cooperation of the elite, no plan of social engineering would succeed. In the present context, vis-à-vis the Naxal conflict, the civil society, to include the national and regional elite and the media has demonstrated glaring indifference.

Gandhi had experimented with his constructive programme at the time of the non-cooperation movement in 1921. It was, in fact, the first mass movement organised on an all-India level. Participation in the mass movement became an educative experience for a worker who remained within the fold of the movement, through social reconstruction programmes. It was followed by the civil disobedience movement, the second mass movement on an all-India plane by combining social and economic issues. Gandhi's movements helped increase the social capital which he wisely invested in India's struggle for freedom. Perhaps that is why Indian society can still claim to have some social capital left with it in comparison to other societies of the world.

Given the perspective of the present condition of Indian society, the space of social capital has shrunk considerably. The state machinery is unable to stop corruption while, on the other hand, rural and tribal India suffers from Naxal violence and counter-violence emanating out of it. If civil society in India wishes to root out the menace of corruption in the political class, it also should act against the menace of Naxal violence without which the reforms would be incomplete.

Gandhi always viewed state power with suspicion yet he never disputed its inevitability. Despite his dislike for electoral politics, he never tried to draw a line of separation between civil society and the political class. Instead, he believed in realising an essentially non-violent self-reliant, self-regulating civil society in phases, which may replace the state at the end in something of a utopian draw. After his death, the general optimism about the state, that it could play an important role in the regeneration of a constructive society, shattered quickly. The government had a rather different vision of modern India and had no faith in the Gandhian model of development.

While Gandhi believed in village oriented development, the government was pushing for infrastructural development in order to pave the way for the industrial growth and environment. Instead of paying attention to the civil society viewpoint, largely represented by Gandhian constructive workers, the government close the alternative model of development.

Within the society itself, the interaction, networking and sharing for the required social transformation gradually became stagnant in the absence of a nationwide civil society mobilisation. After winning political freedom, obtaining socio-economic freedom was supposed to be the shared goal for free India, but here civil society and the democratic government came into conflict. After Gandhi's death, his followers his who preferred constructive programmes as their future vocation, automatically assumed the responsibility of representing civil society in India, especially in matters where they thought it necessary to appraise the government .

The socio-political and economic milieu in India after independence, was dominated by growing agrarian unrest, as the long-awaited land reforms were ignored due to the aggressive opposition from landlords, the dominating political class. This provided fuel to the fire of radicalism propagated by the radical Communists, who waited for a peasant upsurge. With no sign of the government taking notice of these developments, Vinoba Bhave, launched the 'Bhoodan movement'.

The joining by Jayaprakash Narain (JP) of the Bhoodan movement gave it a momentum. JP, was a hero of the 1942 movement, had an all-India image because he was the leader of the Socialist Party. The Bhoodan movement touched the most sensitive institution of private property and the need for its redistribution. Property in the form of land got questioned by the movement. Those who were associated with various constructive-work organisations, inspired and initiated by Gandhi, formed an organisation known as the Sarva Seva Sangh, which was an institution of experts for planning and executing programmes. The Bhoodan movement affected the interests of the landed elite. They opposed the movement and owing to the support that they obtained from a section of the political class, the movement was sabotaged.

The Bhoodan movement was a novel experiment that created a new awareness among the people. It aimed at creating an egalitarian society. It was realised by one and all that socio-economic issues such as land distribution could not be tackled by the laws of the state alone. It is unfortunate that the idealism so generated could not be sustained for a long period.

JP was rather more experimental and wanted to address social issues in the changing political scenario. Naxalism emerged as a new phenomenon during his time. He tried to address it in his own way. JP took up the challenge thrown by the Naxals as he could realise the magnitude and extent of the problem and its possible social repercussions.

After making an intensive socio-economic survey of the area he selected (Musahari bloc in Muzzafarpur, Bihar), he started working with the local people in coordination with the local authorities, and could manage to channelise the righteous forces of the district through hundreds in the Gram Swaraj Sabhas, which, in some manner, are still intact. He tried to strengthen the Gram Sabhas which played a crucial role in the affairs of villages in the Gandhian model of development, wherein the village Panchayats were viewed as the nucleus of the Indian democracy. He not only succeeded in restricting Naxal violence from spreading in the district on the ground level but also countered it on the ideological level. This could be taken as a precursor to the Panchayati Raj Institutions and the related Act that the government enacted in 1992. The model, if implemented optimally, holds the key to empowerment of the tribal population in the LWE affected areas.

Though the present challenge is from Naxalism, the problem is much wider in the form of poverty, unemployment and a myriad socio-economic injustices. The government's failure to implement laws pertaining to land reforms had inevitably led to the growth of rural violence. It was not that the so-called Naxalites had fathered all such violence but those who had persistently defied and defeated the reform laws for the past so many years – be they politicians, administrators, landlords and corporate houses—were also responsible.

The civil society intervention could play a very crucial role in not only providing an alternative mode of holding the state accountable but also mediating negotiations with the rebels. Putting all the responsibility on the state, will not can provide any solution to the problem of Naxal violence. A sustained mass mobilisation against this menace can address the challenge effectively. And this will be possible only when civil society involves itself in tackling this problem. The people's sufferings have to be channelised through a widespread democratic movement, with no place for violence.

Social unrest provides the grounds of the internal dynamism of change, an opportunity that needs to be utilised by civil society. Social unrest tends to grow out of the socio-economic compulsions of the weaker sections of society and if such inherent tendencies of society are let loose, these are bound to turn violent, as we see in the case of Naxal violence.

The Bhoodan movement, based on the socialist principle, was started with the objective of egalitarianism. Today, when we have stepped out of the socialistic mode of thinking, such persuasions have become meaningless and non-effective; calling for modifications in the mode of mass mobilisation on the part of civil society. The Naxal problem is no longer linked to the land issue, instead, it survives on the crisis of identity and the government's deliberate surrender of the natural resources of the country into the hands of big corporate houses in the name of development.

Leaders like Gandhi, Vinoba and JP had learnt the importance of civil society's involvement in the process of social transformation from their hard experiences. But it is unfortunate that they failed to prepare the second and third generation leadership who could intelligently find ways to extend their work. Today, India needs a situation wherein all components of civil society function with its optimum capacity. Such initiatives on the part of civil society are bound to churn out leaders who can take on the mantle.

Encouragingly, the popularity of the Anna Hazare movement (2011) indicated that a new kind of resurgence of mass awakening is inevitable when protest and reform become unavoidable. In recent years, there have been enough examples at the international level that also indicate such trends. The abundance of available human capital and the tool in the form of information technology make conditions congenial towards accelerating social reforms. The younger generation which is more congenial and sensitive towards social issues, requires sensitising and moulding by civil society towards resolution of conflicts emanating from the Naxal violence. Also, a well prepared civil society could play a crucial role in the rehabilitation of the former insurgents to facilitate their absorption into the societal fold.

Negotiations with Rebels and Civil Society

Dialogue is a fundamental component of resolving conflicts and civil society has often demonstrated resilience and ingenuity by facilitating such initiatives in the past. India has a long tradition of engaging in dialogue with insurgent groups. The motives for engaging in dialogue may vary and the eventual outcome, with a few exceptions such as in Mizoram, has rarely resulted in durable peace. Nevertheless, it is crucial to highlight that consistent efforts towards negotiating with the insurgents should be recognised as the state policy, and civil society should be persuaded and supported to participate as the reliable non-governmental component in the process.

A review of Indian peace-making efforts since independence in 1947 suggests that the Indian state has generally not shied away from eventually talking to those who oppose it. Of equal importance is the fact that a dialogue process can often have positive effects such as a reduction of violence, even if the eventual solution remains elusive. The Government of India's dialogue with the National Socialist Council of Nagaland (Isak–Muivah), is an example of this situation.

The dialogue process with the Naxalites in Andhra Pradesh (late 1990s) assumes immense importance in the light of the contemporary debate on how to deal with a leftist inspired insurgency[2]. When the talks between the Maoists and the Hyderabad government took place in October 2004, two things were clear. One was the acknowledgement by the state that the Naxalite movement was not just a law and order problem, but had socio-economic roots that could be discussed on the road to reducing violence. Second, it was brought home to the Maoists that the realm of the present Indian state did provide some space for socio-economic change, and that if the space indeed opened up, the need for resort to armed struggle may be reviewed. The prospect of dialogue between the PWG and the government kindled hopes of finding a way out of the problem. And such initiatives by the government , in conjunction with civil society are crucial in view of the spinoffs that accrue.

A similar initiative on the part of civil society was spearheaded by Swami Agnivesh in the year 2010, to negotiate with the Maoists. Exchanges between the government and the rebels had commenced in spite of differing perceptions over several issues. The process eventually was aborted with the killing of the Maoist leader Azad, alias Cherukuri Rajkumar, in August 2010. Nevertheless, in the last few years, there have been calls to engage in dialogue with the Maoists. However, any such dialogue process will require an immense amount of planning, the close involvement of civil society and the media, and careful framing of the agenda.

Efforts will have to be made by the government to somehow break the barriers that are coming in the way of holding a dialogue with the Naxal leadership. The Punchi Commission on Centre-State relations had remarked that if the open talks offer was not being accepted by the Naxal leadership on account of the resistance to the 'abjure violence first' principle, then an alternative appropriate initiative should be taken. Indeed, it would be ideal if the Naxal leadership accepts the Government of India's offer and starts the dialogue, but going by their declared strategy of violence, acceptance of such an option appears to be somewhat remote for the present. In such a situation, a Track II, involving the civil society initiative may be one of the alternatives that could be thought of.

Such initiatives have been tried successfully in several other situations where direct dialogue was not forthcoming. The commission further added that if this recommendation was accepted by the government, then the Track II effort should be headed not by a single interlocutor but by an 'interlocution team' of three to four persons, who, besides having a component of known internal security and intelligence experts, should also have one or two eminent persons who are not only perceived to be sympathisers of the tribal grievances pertaining to social justice and economic development issues but, at the same time, also understand that absence of peace, and particularly where such a large area of the country is concerned, will play a detrimental role in the overall economic development of not only the affected areas but the nation as a whole.

The inclusion of knowledgeable and well meaning outside persons will indicate both seriousness and concern on the part of the government and also help build public opinion further against the violence being perpetrated by the Naxals, even if their leadership does not respond to the Track II initiative. As per the commission, the main objective of the interlocutory team has to be to sensitise the Naxal leadership (and the cadres, if possible), without being defensive of the several initiatives taken by the government . The goal has to be that the team, by using its skills and knowledge, makes the Naxal leadership understand that the state will not be cowed down by such acts of violence, and the best option lies in having a dialogue so that a beginning can be made towards a peaceful resolution of all issues. In other words, the main task of such an interlocution team should be to persuade the Naxal leadership to abjure violence for, say, a fixed period of time, initiate a formal dialogue, and then see the outcome.[3] Indeed, full support of the state governments will be a prerequisite for any success to be achieved.

NGOs and Empowerment of the Marginalised

Some NGOs cooperate with the central government in a manner that augments its capacity to implement public policy, such as poverty alleviation, for example, in a decentralised manner. Several NGOs have also served as watchdogs, attempting to pressure government agencies to uphold the spirit of the state's laws and implement policies in accord with their stated objectives. These organisations also endeavour to raise the political consciousness of various social groups, encouraging them to demand their rights and challenge social inequities. Finally, some social groups serve as innovators, experimenting with new approaches to solving social problems.

Analysing the relationship between NGOs and Indian politics is a task fraught with difficulties. Considerable terminological confusion afflicts the sizeable literature on India's NGOs. There is also a long history to be considered: India's 'modern' voluntary sector, broadly conceived, goes back to at least the late 19th century. Disagreements over its relationship to political activity were present from the start. And to complicate matters, discussions on NGOs are often subsumed within the larger discourse of 'civil society'.

NGOs are not political parties; they are not social movements; they are not labour unions; they are not even, according to some critics, agents of popular struggle at all. Indeed, apart from their status as entities distinct from the government , existing within a realm of associational freedom, the Indian NGOs' defining characteristic is their constitutional inability to engage in politics[4]. A key World Bank operational document—1995's Working with NGOs—defined NGOs as "private organizations that pursue activities to relieve suffering, promote the interests of the poor, protect the environment, provide basic social services or undertake community development".[5]

In India, NGOs can be defined as organisations that are generally formed by professionals or quasi-professionals from the middle or lower middle class, either to serve or work with the poor, or to channel financial support to community-based or grassroots organisations[6]. In short, these are the public interest groups that are not 'people's movements'.

The origins of what might, thus, be called 'movement populism'—the idea that more formal organisational forms are alienated from the ordinary people's concerns and perpetuate elite biases—lay in the widespread discrediting of NGOs that has taken place in India since the early 1980s. Given the extent of their recent demonisation, paradoxically, NGOs once enjoyed a golden era, before their fall from grace.[7] The reputation of NGOs, in India has been through a roller-coaster ride. Their denigration and defamation has been at the hands of all the political parties, across the spectrum, starting from the mid-1970s. The criticisms have been based on political and ideological grounds and often the foreign funding aspect of the NGOs has come under the scanner.

Statistics compiled by the Home Ministry indicate that in 2000–01, nearly 20,000 organisations were registered under the Foreign Contribution Regulation Act (FCRA)1976, though only 13,800 submitted their accounts to the government, as required. The total foreign funds received by these groups increased by more than 25 per cent between 1998–99 and 2000–01, from Rs 34 billion to Rs 45 billion[8]. Similarly, in the year 2015, out of 22,702 NGOs registered under FCRA, 13,193 actually received grants[9]. About 9,000 NGOs have rightly got their FCRA permissions cancelled for not submitting accounts or responding to repeated reminders[10]. Critiques of the government maintain that the political parties and even the government itself, receive tremendous amounts of foreign funding but escape accountability. It is beyond doubt that some of the NGOs may be involved in undesirable practices that are detrimental to the national interest but to impose a blanket ban is unwarranted.

Without going further into the controversy surrounding the NGOs, it would be worthwhile to look into certain NGOs' activities wherein these organisations have stood with the government for the betterment of the society and in the national interest. Such NGOs hold tremendous potential, if appropriately coopted, to provide an alternative form of expression to the alienated population in a conflict ridden society.

Many NGOs in the past have engaged in both struggle-oriented and constructive work. During the 1990s, the Rajasthan-based Mazdoor Kisan Shakti Sangathan (MKSS) operated a small number of 'fair price' shops. Notwithstanding the controversial initiative, the main motivation for running the ration shops was to counter the neo-liberal orthodoxy that food subsidy bureaucracies – in India's case, the PDS—inevitably produce unacceptable levels of corruption, including diversion of foodgrains to the non-needy. By operating shops in a transparent fashion, the MKSS hoped to demonstrate that it was possible to treat customers fairly and provide a livelihood for the shops' proprietors without resorting to corruption[11].

Often, several NGO activities have overlapped with civil society movements. NGOs are, in fact, often eager to support such movements. The local people often fail to distinguish in practice between certain NGOs and their associated movement groups. These can be seen as dual-purpose associations. The movement-like activities of social activist Anna Hazare in Maharashtra are difficult to disentangle from the Hind Swaraj Trust, an NGO that he also helps to run[12]. In Mumbai, the Rationing Kruti Samiti, a formidable movement for accountability in the PDS during the 1990s, was closely interwoven with the activities of an NGO called Apnalaya, but remained organisationally separate.

The trend since the mid-1990s has been towards the creation of hybrid organisational forms, in which the tactics and structural features of both movement-style groups and NGOs have been incorporated pragmatically. The Bharat Gyan Vigyan Samithi (BGVS), founded in late 1989 to promote literacy, is a good example of organisational cross-breeding[13]. It is a classic NGO in many respects, undertaking programmes, channelling funds to Community-Based Organisations (CBOs), and focussing on conventional good works. Formed in association with a government initiative—the Total Literacy Mission—the BGVS sees itself as a "broad democratic movement", one "in which even the state participates". The BGVS particularly aims to encourage women's "participation in a process of social mobilisation" and sees itself as part of struggle politics[14]. Its approach has stressed the need to "link literacy with many basic livelihood problems and even with the questions of the exploitation, oppression, and discrimination against women". It is an NGO that sees itself as capable of spawning movements. Movements, thus, created can, in turn, catalyse the formation of additional NGOs. By tapping into local women's movements of various kinds—such as the anti-liquor campaigns in Andhra Pradesh in the 1990s—

BGVS programmes have assisted "the conversion of the literacy movement into a women's employment generation programme". In its "Samata campaign", the BGVS' "aim was to consciously develop and transform the literacy campaign into a cultural and economic movement for women".[15]

The blurring of the boundaries between the NGOs and social movement groups, and, as we have seen, between the NGOs and the state, is just one of many factors that have allowed the NGOs to enter, gradually and often indirectly, the domain of electoral politics. Thanks to India's constitutionally mandated system of democratic decentralisation—which created new tiers of elected local government , including one for every village—there is now an almost 'natural' point of entry for NGOs into a sphere once reserved for political parties. The parties have a much greater incentive to court NGOs, particularly those with strong grassroots networks.[16] With effective implementation of PESA in the tribal belt, the participation of such NGOs could be a game changer by supporting governmental initiatives.

A good example of an *indirect* means through which NGOs impinge upon electoral politics is to be found in a study on '*naya netas*' (new politicians).[17] These are the members of the non-elite castes who have emerged as important 'political fixers', more so in the tribal regions. People increasingly turn to *naya netas*, rather than established figures from the dominant landowning castes, to assist in brokering transactions with officials at the block or district headquarters. However, *naya netas* have also been instrumental as 'political entrepreneurs' who, on behalf of a village or hamlet, negotiate with party leaders at election time for the price to be paid for the locality's votes.

Interestingly, in some cases, it is through NGO-led projects that *naya netas* obtain the skills and necessary contacts. NGOs draw on the local people for their operations. For many rural development NGOs, just to take one category, outreach to remote locations (where dialects may be spoken) requires a large number of field operatives. The biggest NGOs involve thousands of young people as outreach workers, survey enumerators, health education assistants, and so forth. This exposes them to the world of officialdom and often involves training in technical skills. The NGO-implemented government programmes are a training ground for *naya netas*, often bringing them into contact with party leaders[18].

Another organisation that at one time edged close to party politics was the Ekta Parishad (EP), a group based mainly in Madhya Pradesh. The EP, like the BGVS, defies classification. It calls itself "a mass movement based on Gandhian principles", but is in essence a coalition of NGOs whose common agenda is to place livelihood resources in the hands of ordinary people. It "patterns itself after a trade union"—though the workers involved are in the informal sector: agricultural labourers, small-scale peasant proprietors, forest dwellers, and so forth. The EP's literature even recounts the familiar explanation for its existence: "there is a vacuum left by political parties and people are looking for other channels for representation".[19] Its leaders want to broaden the 'public space' within which people can demand rights.

The EP's focus has been on pressuring the state government to implement laws that prevent the alienation of tribal land. The EP counts among its successes the creation of a statewide task force on land alienation and restitution, the distribution of over 150,000 plots of land, and having pressured the state to withdraw spurious criminal cases against tribal people. It claims a membership of 150,000 dues-paying members, but says its wider following constitutes a 'formation' of more than 500,000. The EP sees struggle as peacefully coexisting alongside "the promotion of constructive work". It has assisted organisations to establish 'grain banks' designed to help the tribals to evade the grasp of moneylenders[20].

Many NGOs, such as the Karnataka-based SEARCH, train some of the hundreds of thousands of people elected to Panchayati Raj Institutions. Because one-third of Panchayat seats are reserved for women, some NGOs specialise in training women representatives or women's groups seeking to engage with the participatory structures—beneficiary groups, vigilance committees—established under local government regulations. NGOs that implement watershed development and other such grassroots projects become intimately involved in the workings of Panchayats.

India is not the only country where democratic decentralisation has provided an opportunity for NGOs and movement groups to enter the electoral domain. As in India, this has been especially evident among groups that straddle the NGO-movement divide. Chilean NGOs "played an important role in helping Popular Economic Organisations (*Organizaciones Econimicas Populares*) and Self-Help Organisations (*Organizaciones de Auto-Ayuda*) to contest the 1992 local elections and to subsequently participate in local government structures". NGOs in the Philippines "sit alongside political parties in local government structures created under the 1991 Local Government Code and have actively participated in election campaigns, including the 1992 Presidential and the 1995 local and Congressional elections".[21]

Historically, Indian civil society has been known for its innovative experiments which were then scaled-up as national government policies and programmes, and even taken to other countries by the donors and the UN agencies. For decades after the painful Bihar famines the in late 1960s, the Indian voluntary sector continued to evolve in diverse ways, specially focussing on conscientisation and mobilisation of the poor and the marginalised. It brought into the public sphere issues related to the tribals and Dalits, women and children, workers and the disabled. Its grassroots work highlighted concerns which had been hidden from the public discourse – violence against women, environmental degradation, occupational health and pollution, child and bonded labour, displacement and urban poverty.

It is obvious that the state and civil society have to jointly meet the challenge. Building consensus between the two has to be the first step. Civil society has the liberty to question the state, while the state has a responsibility to listen to the voices of dissent. Of the three main components of a rebellion—people, guerrillas and the state—

logic dictates that the centre of gravity is the people. The Maoists have the ear of the people and it does not at this juncture matter whether it is through coercion or attraction. The state will have to win back the confidence of the masses. Strategic communication has to be effectively used to establish the link at the earliest. Civil society can act as a medium of exchange, particularly when the state has lost touch with the grassroots through acts of omission and commission. The need is to reengage with the liberals rather than to reject them. This has perhaps been the biggest failure of the state—castigating those who spoke for engagement; and the message to the tribals, deftly coloured by the Maoists, has been that the government is their "enemy". Gaining the confidence of the people in the affected areas will take time, but has to be addressed. Once this is achieved, it would provide cover for the security operations and for denying the Naxals space in which to operate with impunity.

Notes

1. R. Tandon, *Voluntary Action, Civil Society and the State (*New Delhi: Mosaic Books, 2002).
2. By the late 1990s, violence between the Naxalites and the Government of Andhra Pradesh had reached a stage where many in civil society felt that the suffering of a large section of rural society was a serious concern which merited civil society intervention. In 1997, a group of civil liberties activists, former bureaucrats, journalists and lawyers formed the Committee of Concerned Citizens (CCC) to mobilise public opinion in favour of a peace process.After five years of patient effort, the CCC succeeded in building a public constituency, and in 2002 and 2004, it brought the revolutionaries and the state government to the table for negotiations.
3. "Report of the Commission on Centre-State Relations, Volume V", "Internal Security, Criminal Justice System and Centre State Relations", March 2010 (http://interstatecouncil.nic.in/downloads/volume5.pdf)
4. Stephen N. Ndegwa, *The Two Faces of Civil Society: NGOs and Politics in Africa* (West Hartford, CT: Kumarian Press, 1996).
5. World Bank, (Operations Policy Department), *Working with NGOs: A Practical Guide to Operational Collaboration between the World Bank and NGOs* (Washington DC: The World Bank, 1995), p. 7.
6. Siddhartha Sen, "Some Aspects of State-NGO Relationships in India in the Post-Independence Era", *Development and Change*, Vol. 30, pp. 332–333, 327–355.

7. Rob Jenkins, "The Oxford Companion to Politics in India", Niraja Gopal Jayal and Pratap Bhanu Mehta, eds., *Non-Governmental Organisations* (Oxford: Oxford University Press), pp. 423–440.
8. The *Economic Times*, September 04, 2003.
9. The acceptance and utilisation of foreign contributions is regulated under the Foreign Contribution (Regulation) Act, 2010 (FCRA) and Foreign Contribution (Regulation) Rules, 2011 (FCRR) framed thereunder. They provide for procedures to grant registration and prior permission for receipt of a foreign contribution and its utilisation, maintenance of accounts, inspection of accounts of the associations, etc. They also prescribe various offences and penalties that may be imposed, including suspension and cancellation of registration in case of violation of the provisions of FCRA and FCRR. The government receives inputs from various security agencies, including the Intelligence Bureau, from time to time, about the violations of FCRA.
10. Trilochan Sastry, "NGOs' Foreign Funds and a Trust Deficit", *The Hindu*, June 29, 2015.
11. Rob Jenkins and Anne Marie Goetz, "Civil Society Engagement and India's Public Distribution System: Lessons from the Rationing Kruti Samiti in Mumbai", Consultation Paper for the World Bank, *World Development Report 2004: Making Services Work for Poor People* (Washington DC).
12. Rob Jenkins, "In Varying States of Decay: Anti-Corruption Politics in Maharashtra and Rajasthan", in Rob Jenkins, ed., *Regional Reactions: Comparing Politics Across India's States* (New Delhi: Oxford University Press, 2004).
13. http://www.bgvs.org/html/literacy_campaign.htm
14. Report of the Committee of the National Literacy Mission, December 14, 1990.
15. Ibid.
16. Ibid.
17. Anirudh Krishna, *Active Social Capital: Tracing the Roots of Development and Democracy* (New York: Columbia University Press, 2002).
18. Ibid.
19. www.ektaparishad.org
20. Ibid.
21. Gerald Clark, "Non-Governmental Organizations and Politics", *Papers in International Development,* No. 20 (Swansea, UK: University of Swansea, 1996).

17. ENABLING THE GRASSROOTS

Slump in Maoists' War: An Opportunity to Reap

On September 20, 2014, *The Indian Express* carried a report, captioned, "Ahead of Global Meet, Maoists Admit to Setbacks". The report mentions a letter uploaded on the CPI (Maoist) website[1]. Maoist organisations across the world met in Milan, on September 27-28, and the CPI (Maoist), addressing the global meet, admitted that it has been facing several setbacks since the Indian security forces launched Operation Green Hunt. Several issues of concern have been flagged in the letter, like conceding ground to the Indian state in several areas, harm to party structures in villages, dwindling mass support base, surrender by party cadres, etc. As resurrection measures, mentioned in the said letter, the CPI(Maoist) attempts were the strengthening of people's government at the district level and encouraging a community-based economic model of 'self-reliance' in Dandakaranya. Also, it is being reported in the media that the Maoists are losing ground in their stronghold, Bastar, in the face of waning support from the tribals.[2]

The aforesaid is not a recent development and the CPI (Maoist) leadership has been harping upon the same since beginning of 2013, if not earlier. In a searing self-assessment in April-May 2013, the Central Committee admitted to the said facets as also to increasing arrests, surrenders and killings of cadre, to include the betrayal by Sabhyasachi Panda and the slaying of Kishenji, damage to the weapon manufacturing and supply chain,[3] difficulty in carrying out activities in north Telangana and along the Andhra-Odisha border.[4]

The state could not have asked for a more opportune time to further invigorate its counter Maoist strategies. The same should, in tandem, cover the realms of development, security and legislation. However, there has been no distinct indication on the part of the government to give feelers of the '*seizure of initiative*' and efforts to fill in the voids, so created. A strategy, in the short, medium and long terms, needs to be devised and implemented without further loss of time. Some of the priority issues are highlighted in the ensuing paragraphs.

To begin with, the constitutional aspects need to be addressed on a war-footing. Sensitivity and action towards them has caught on, but execution is still at the 'drawing board' stage. These measures have the longest gestation period, given our politico-executive set-up, and have a direct bearing on the majority of the affected population, the Adivasis of central India. These Adivasis form the rank and file of the Maoist movement, not because of ideology but primarily for the extreme impoverishment and challenges faced by them.

The Vth and VIth Schedules under Article 244 of the Indian Constitution provided for self-governance in specified tribal majority regions. In 1999, the Government of India issued a Draft National Policy on Tribals to address the developmental needs of the tribal people. Special emphasis was laid on education, forestry, healthcare, languages, resettlement and land rights. The government even established a Ministry of Tribal Affairs. The draft was meant to be circulated among the MPs, MLAs and civil society groups. A Cabinet Committee on Tribal Affairs was to constantly review the policy. But little has happened since. The draft policy is still a draft, which means there is no policy.[4] Continuing with the inertia by the state is not desirable, since the Maoists shall use this breather for consolidation.

A time-bound implementation of PESA warrants the attention of our policy-makers. Enacted in December 1996, it has so far achieved very little in terms of implementation. Most of the affected states have not even fully accomplished the initial stages of implementation which commenced with legislative measures, to formulate the respective State Acts.[5] This has to be done, keeping the essence of PESA in mind, which has 'face-to-face' community governance at its tenet. The Act was to enable Gram Sabhas (GS) to self-govern their natural resources. Since, historically, the Adivasis have been functioning as a community, vis-à-vis individually, PESA in its essence aligned with their aspirations. This is why the CPI (Maoist), in its latest statement, has stressed upon the community-based economic model of 'self-reliance' in Dandakaranya. The Maoists are known to have adapted in a much better manner to local needs, in contrast to the state agencies; as also, their decision and implementation loop does not metamorphose for so long.

In tandem, it is imperative that various players like Adivasi activists, NGOs, journalists, grassroots political cadres, etc work towards enhancing the awareness of the Adivasis and give them a medium to raise their concerns. Dedicated journalists like Shubhranshu Choudhary, through their innovative ways, have been taking the voices of the tribals to the world outside and also providing them an accessible medium in cellular phones, to communicate with each other on local issues and concerns. His voice portal, CG-Net Swara,[6] enables ordinary citizens to report and discuss issues of local interest. Such methods, in the middle and long terms, have the potential of weaning away the Maoists' support base amongst the tribals. The government, at the local and national levels should encourage such innovations to occupy more space. This shall help in bridging the communication gap and ward off the 'keep the state away', syndrome of the Adivasis.

With regards to development, it is pertinent to mention that implementation of various welfare programme should be focussed upon. The government just cannot afford to announce scheme after scheme, given the inadequate set-up to implement these. Also, clarity on the Forest and Land Acquisition Act needs to be arrived at, in the earliest timeframe, to allay the speculations that are doing the rounds in the Maoist inclined media that behind the cover of revisiting the Acts, the government is attempting to safeguard corporate interests. This propaganda needs to be scuttled by fast tracking revisions, in case the same are intended, lest it boosts the Maoists' mobilisation.

Complemented by focussed implementation of welfare programmes, the opportunity has to be wrested by the security apparatus to bring about tangibles in the speediest manner, thus, instilling confidence in the environment against the Maoists. Also, our information campaign needs to show and project what is being done, to manage favourable perceptions for the state. The perception is gaining ground amongst the Adivasis that eventually it would be the 'state' and not the 'Maoists' that shall bring in genuine and long-term development – and in the process, also preserve their identity and safeguard their aspirations.[7]

Unfortunately, weaknesses in the security mechanism, manifesting in lack of synergy between the state and central security forces, have led to 'turf wars'. And, ironically, such cracks are showing—coinciding with the weakening of the Maoists movement. A case in point has been the rift that surfaced recently between the CRPF and Chhatisgarh Police, in the immediate aftermath of the Tahakwada attack, in which 11 CRPF and four police personnel were killed. The IG CRPF in Chhattisgarh, blamed the state police leadership for blocking a "massive operation" by the CRPF, across the Maoist "base zones" in Bastar, which, he asserted, could have prevented the March 11, 2015 attack. The last leg of the proposed operation was intended to target the Darbha and Tongpal zones, around March 10, and, which, as pointed out, would have sanitised the entire area, thus, averting the fateful incident. Senior Chhattisgarh Police leaders subsequently criticised the CRPF brass for "raising confidential issues of national security through the media". The merits or otherwise of the CRPF proposal notwithstanding, the spat exposed the continuing discord between the central and state forces on the issues of strategic and tactical responses to the Maoist challenge.[8]

Further, the CRPF, in the first week of September 2015, shared the findings of the probe into the incident. The enquiry inferred that most of the survivors who followed the first section that was ambushed, instead of helping their trapped colleagues, stayed behind and later deserted them. The probe has found 23 of the 28 survivors, *prima facie* guilty of "inaction and lack of satisfactory counter-action". The paramilitary force has already suspended 17 of its personnel and suggested that the state police act against six of its men for dereliction of duty. The inquiry also noted that "there was delay in sending reinforcements". The Tongpal police camp was only a four to five-minute drive from the spot, but the reinforcement party did not arrive in time. The state police, however, has remained non-committal on it so far.[9]

Rather than pointing fingers at each other, the need of the hour is to analyse the lessons learnt, implement measures to overcome the weaknesses and, most importantly, to train together under a hands down leadership at the execution level. The several agencies in the fray, in general, have to develop affiliation towards the common intended goal. The period of relative calm should be utilised to further weaken the insurgent organisation, and the reverse cannot be afforded. The system will do well to realise the same and the faster it is, the better it would be for our fight against the Maoists who thrive on the Adivasi cadre, and the front organisations led propaganda machine, an aligned intelligentsia and revenue generation from extortion and protection, in cohort with the industrialist-politicians-bureaucracy nexus. Incidentally, this may be the last opportunity that the state may have to retrieve the overall situation. The alternative, later, could be too horrific even to contemplate.

For any insurgent organisation, surviving is the essence of winning. The Maoists have been emphasising a focussed approach to preserve their subjective forces. The efficient harnessing of diminished resources and concentrated attacks on the state's weak links are an integral part of this effort and the Maoists have always been able to make headway towards the same, whenever they have desired. Despite defections, losses and a visible degree of demoralisation; the core leadership remains committed to its cause.[10]

Tapping New Rural Elite for Local Governance

The nation went through general elections in the months of April-May 2014, followed by assembly polls in two states, recently.

Other than anti-incumbency, the predominant shift which was pronounced in the outcomes was the preference of the electorates for developmental issues over the archaic conventional dogmas of caste, religion, etc. This trend was equally prevalent in rural India that holds the key to the development of the nation. Relative enhancements in the standards of education and awareness amongst the rural youth have enabled a new category of 'rural elite' to come into the reckoning, replacing the old guard. This chapter underscores the rise of this class and the tremendous potential that they possess to reinvigorate local governance; thus, actualising the desired inclusive growth and pacifying mutinies that are rampant at the grassroots level.

For rural India, the state has been distant in both physical and cognitive terms. Since the government organisations appear distant and forbidding, a class of intermediaries has been usually involved when individuals need to make contact with the state; a phenomenon dating back to the colonial era. These 'expeditors' do not wield any official power but are familiar with the intricacies of administration. These two themes – a 'distant state' and 'mediated interactions' – provide important insights into the nature of politics at the grassroots level.[11]

People functioning as intermediaries acquire influence and amass political capital. One's standing in local politics is defined by what one does as an intermediary – who is the bridge between the rural man and the state. The said distance has been the biggest impediment to implementation of the government's schemes that originate from superb 'ideation'. The benefits not reaching the intended beneficiaries has led to dissatisfaction that is going to get more widespread with the proliferation of information.

As far as mediation is concerned, the erstwhile upper caste and landed peasantry have been replaced by young and literate intermediaries with widespread representation from the marginalised caste and classes. Political domination in the rural landscape, based on caste affiliations, is becoming uncommon, and socio-economic equations are seeing a change.

As the state expenditure in the rural areas increases and welfare schemes are formulated, villagers as well as government officials are keen to find intermediaries who could help transact on their behalf. These new leaders have immense potential and are looked up to, irrespective of their caste or economic background. The issues related to development have emerged as major criteria for voting, and age-old shibboleths are under demolition. Where the political parties previously relied on caste or patronage–based voting, they are now finding it useful to forge links with this rising leadership. Another factor that has fostered the rise of this particular category of leadership is 'market activity' expanding in rural areas; leadership based on outside connections (with the official set-up and agencies beyond village boundaries) has gained importance, overshadowing, in many instances, other forms of leadership that derived inspiration from ethnic or religious groupings.

The great demand of their services amongst fellow villagers gives the new leaders a position of influence. And unlike the old patrons, the new leaders cannot easily use their special connections with the state for their own benefits at the expense of the community. The spread of education and information has given rise to more widespread capacity for independent actions. Leaders can no longer deceive a significant percentage of the rural population. Instead of dividing the village community on the lines of caste or religion, these new leaders build on wide ranging social networks that bring the villagers together, unified on developmental issues. The villagers too, are increasingly associating themselves with these new political entrepreneurs, outgrowing parochialism of any kind.[12]

Political parties are not distinguishable from each other in terms of the essence of various developmental programmes, as enunciated in their manifestos. With relatively weaker organisations at the grassroots and local levels, these parties are driven to seek alliances with men of influence in the villages. Where these parties previously contacted traditional patrons i.e. the landed and upper castes, with the changing dynamics, officials and politicians are increasingly striking bargains with the evolving new leadership.

The phenomenon of political competition based on development is likely to change for the better. By leveraging the advantages that the new leadership possesses, there exists a unique, better opportunity to decentralise the local governance, than hithertofore.

Notwithstanding the above, building institutions at levels below the districts remains an unfinished task of state building and democracy. Although the emergence of the new leadership is a welcome phenomenon towards democratisation at the grassroots, it can represent a sustainable solution to the challenge of institutional distance only when this leadership is coopted into the fold of governance at the local levels. On the contrary, if the said potential is left untapped, the rural elites would have the entire wherewithal at their disposal, to capture the local economy of the state by blocking others' access to it.[13]

In view of the vacant political space in the villages, until institutions at the local levels are empowered and the state is extended downwards to cover the last mile, the implementation of ideation shall remain a far-fetched dream, infested by non-inclusive growth, breeding dissatisfaction and unrest amongst the 'have-nots'. This is the void that secessionists and extremists exploit for their ulterior motives.

The prospects of making India's growth process more inclusive has not been encouraging and one of the prime factors has been weak and the ineffective local governance, which could be energised by tapping the emerging rural leadership that is forward looking. If rapid growth (on which the government lays optimum emphasis as a measure of economic success and performance) is achieved and sustained, some of this would necessarily 'trickle down' and help the poor.[14] Beyond that, however, the scope of hastening this 'trickle' via deliberate redistribution is limited owing to the absence of vibrant local governance.

The three-tier Panchayati Raj system of India is the largest experiment in grassroots democratisation in the history of humanity. There are around 4 million elected representatives at all levels of the Panchayat system. They represent more than 250,000

Gram Panchayats, 7,500 intermediate tiers (Block Panchayats) and more than 700 District Panchayats. The fact that the Indian system of local governance—the Panchayat system—has its roots in the cultural and historical legacy of India makes it different from many other initiatives of decentralisation of governance.[15]

The government needs to focus on the implementation of welfare schemes through asset redistribution and a basic shift in the growth model which is labour intensive and does not merely chase GDP figures. This shall remain a dream, if not accompanied by effective and participatory local governance, with Panchayats and Gram Sabhas playing the key role, in areas of all hues, scheduled or otherwise. On the whole, so far, the past performance of the Panchayats as agents of redistributive development has been discouraging.[16] One of the major factors that can help explain this poor show has been the indifferent attitude of the rural elites which comprised the traditional vested interests, with a feudal hangover. As these gentry were not adversely affected by the vagaries of backwardness, they could neither comprehend the issues on the ground nor identify with them.

As brought out, the rural landscape has been evolving, with the reins of influence now with the forward looking and aware youth that is beyond any parochial framework and is singularly focussed towards development. This class has emerged as a bridge between the rural poor and the state, and needs to be tapped for participating in local governance which should be one of the Key Result Areas (KRAs), for the government, in order to convert 'ideation' into 'implementation'. The Prime Minister, during his interaction with MPs on October 26, 2014, underlined the facet of implementation of various welfare schemes of the government when he said, "The schemes should reach the grassroots level in a more planned manner so that they have some impact on the lives of the people. The implementation should be more focussed and organised".[17] This focus in an organised manner cannot materialise without local governance, around Panchayat bodies, playing a crucial role.

'Localised Approach' to Counter LWE

In February 2015, the Home Ministry expressed its desire to change its strategy and go for a "more localised approach" to deal with LWE. "The states are now going to be asked to take the lead in counter-Naxal operations, since they are the first responders to deal with the challenge. Central forces will be more for inter-state operations as also to step up operations, led by state police forces", as said by an official from the Home Ministry.[18] It is also appreciated that the extremely disturbed region of south Bastar and regions in south, southeast and southwest Chhattisgarh, astride the inter-state border, are to be the likely focus areas.

This is, indeed, an encouraging development which should not be seen merely as the government's reaction to repeated Naxal strikes, but in the larger perspective vis-à-vis, the new counter LWE strategy of the government . The same is based on elements of security-related measures, development-based approach, rights and entitlement-based measures and public perception management. According to details of the policy, the approach in the worst LWE affected areas will focus on security interventions; in moderately affected areas, it will witness security and development initiatives going hand-in-hand; while in the less affected areas, development interventions will take precedence.[19]

In respect of the abovementioned policy, it is opined that security measures in a '*silo-based*' approach should be watched against, even in the worst affected areas (like south Bastar). Going by the basics of counter-insurgency, tactical operations have to be backed by psychological operations which, in turn, are based on truth and genuineness. The prioritisation and excessive focus on the elimination of violence does not adequately take into account the role of threats in the Naxal conflict. Indeed, it is the violence and credible threat of violence, which permits the unhindered operation of the 'levy economy' and the 'protection market', crippling the prospects for equity in terms of access to the fruits of development.

Over the past decade or so, the government's perception has evolved from a simplistic understanding of Naxalism as a 'security threat' into a relatively more nuanced understanding of the problem as a functional inadequacy of governance at the grassroots level, and in this context, the term 'localisation', indeed, holds the key to conflict resolution, provided the scope of the same is enhanced to rejuvenate the local bodies of governance. The understanding of the 'root cause' phenomenon requires to be taken ahead in all its variants, which include strengthening the local administration, with the facet of 'local policing' forming a part of it.

As a caveat, the government should not address the key issues with an ultimate aim to restore its monopoly over violence. In tandem with local policing, the PRIs as basic units to usher in participatory development should not be lost sight of. At the apex level, representation from Ministries like those of Tribal Affairs, Panchayati Raj, Rural Development and Environment must be ensured by the Home Ministry, during policy formulations.

The Prime Minister chaired the inaugural meet of the newly formed NITI (National Institution for Transforming India) Aayog on February 08, 2015, in which aspects like higher growth rates, infrastructure development, etc. were underscored. He further stressed on planning and execution to be carried out in the realm of "*cooperative and competitive federalism*".[20] In the aforesaid context, empowering PRIs should not be lost sight of. Adopting a balance sheet approach to development and not concentrating on inclusivity of growth shall further compound the challenges of a menace like Naxalism, viciously increasing the friction for development. Mere focus on GDP is futile if the same does not translate into the well-being of the "A*ntim Jan*"[21] much faster than it has so far.

The government's priorities must be actions to, firstly, unclog and repair leaking pipes and fix the apparatus of the state, commencing bottom-up; and, secondly, develop a better scorecard to report progress to the deprived sections in numbers they can relate to their development.[22] Accordingly, the states should be exhorted to give a boost to the local bodies, and 'Team India', as proposed by the PM,[23] should have genuine empowerment of PRIs as one of its agendas. A beginning towards the same had, indeed, been made by various constitutional provisions and numerous plan outlays by the NITI Aayog's predecessor; the progress towards complete implementation, however, has been a tardy affair so far. At the national and state levels, the powers and political settlements are largely known, but when it comes to the local bodies, be they urban or rural, the Centre and the states join in treating them as subservient dependencies.[24]

In the context of 'law and order', the PRIs hold tremendous potential to contribute towards the governmental intent. These institutions were conceived both as a mechanism of local participatory governance and as a tool for a coherent and effective public policy process, to include matters related to law and order. PRIs were seen as having an important bearing for grievance redressal, and socially, a just access to the fruits of development.

The underlying logic of the various policy initiatives that cuts across the three themes of security, development and social justice has to be based on the tenet of 'participation'. This 'governmentality of participation' becomes not just a means of organising institutions of collective decision-making, but also a mechanism for justifying and legitimising them as socially just. The policy initiatives directed towards the Naxal affected areas ought to see a shift toward the logic of participation, with an emphasis on anchoring policies of social justice within the PRIs. The functioning of PRIs holds utmost importance for evaluating the impact of policy initiatives on the conflict processes, and reflects upon the conditions necessary for effective conflict governance.

In the realm of security, the roles of both local police stations and the PRIs – particularly their judicial wings – are crucial for dispute resolution in any stage of a conflict between individuals from different castes and communities over the usage and ownership of resources such as land, etc. However, the decisions of the Panchayats do not always find support from the local police, which undermines their effectiveness. The mutual confidence amongst the local governing agencies, i.e. the PRIs and local police provides a crucial link that holds the desired potential. Cultural orientation should be a key element while revamping our policing in trouble areas and socio-behavioural shades should not be ignored. The police, in these conflict ridden regions is still perceived as a colonial agency, out to enforce the agenda of the 'sarkar'. Resultantly, the efforts so far have not translated into better policing at the grassroots level.

Policing is not about military control of territory but about consensual control of the population. To achieve this, policing has to be embedded within the people's perceptions of insecurity, rather than those of the state, and local governance has a critical role in this context for all pervasive progress. Participatory governance at the grassroots will enhance ownership of policing and is likely to be a major step towards community participation in policing. Given the handicap at hand with the state police in terms of poor-police population ratio, involving locals through the authorised body of PRIs is desirable.

The tendency of amending laws and ministerial directives, either seeking to curtail avenues of public participation or doing away with them altogether shall be a retrograde step leading to exclusivity. Initiatives without, or with limited, popular participation render them disembedded in the local context—equally applicable to the security regime of 'policing'. The PRIs, thus, emerge as a key element for any attempt to ameliorate the issues of under-development, corruption, socio-economic injustice, and law and order. They need to be empowered and involved in decision making on matters affecting their lives. Failure to make any such transfer is likely to become the Achilles' heel of the state apparatus in any attempt to address the Naxal conflict. The government, with its might and determination, needs to bridge the disparity, in favour of the section of population that has witnessed progress and development bypassing them completely.

Notes

1. Vivek Deshpande, "Ahead of Global Meet, Maoists Admit to Setbacks", *The Indian Express,* September 20, 2014, www.bannedthought.net.
2. Pavan Dahat, "Maoists Losing Ground in Bastar", *The Hindu*, September 21, 2014.
3. "Maoists Assessment 2014", www.satp.org
4. Ibid.
5. Ajay Dandekar and Chitrangada Choudhary, *PESA, Left Wing Extremism and Governance: Concerns and Challenges in India's Tribal Districts* (IRMA, Anand), pp. 5-9.
6. http://cgnetswara.org
7. The remarks were given by Shubhranshu Choudhary during his talk on "Weaning Away the Maoists' Support Base" as part of the CLAWS National Workshop on Internal Security on September 12, 2014.
8. Ibid.
9. Ashutosh Bhardwaj, "23 CRPF Men, Cops Left Without a Fight as Naxals Ambushed Colleagues", *The Indian Express,* September 08, 2014.
10. Ibid.
11. Anirudh Krishna, "Local Politics", in Jayal N Gopal and Mehta Bhanu Pratap, eds., *The Oxford Companion to Politics in India* (OUP, 2011).
12. Ibid.
13. Alpa Shah, *Shadowy Practices – Development as Corruption, In the Shadows of the State* (OUP, 2010).
14. Atul Kohli, *Politics and Redistribution, Politics and Governance* (OUP, 2010).
15. John Samuel, "India's Political Structure, an Impediment to Local Governance", Onewordnet, 2012.
16. Ibid.
17. "PM's Message to NDA MPs: Take Ownership of our Key Schemes", http://indianexpress.com/article/india/india-others/modi-message-to-nda-mps-take-ownership-of-our-key-schemes/#sthash.502RaTdk.dpuf, October 26, 2014.
18. VijaitaSingh, "Centre to Tackle Naxal Menace with 'Localised Approach'", *The Indian Express,* February 07, 2015.
19. Bharti Jain, "Rajnath's Counter-Naxal Doctrine Seeks to Fight the Reds Through a Four-Pronged Approach", *The Times of India*, October 17, 2014.
20. Puja Mehra, "Aim for High Growth Rate: PM", *The Hindu*, February 09, 2015.
21. Mahatma Gandhi's advocacy that all progress and welfare is futile if does not affect the 'Antim Jan' (the last person), in a desired manner.
22. Arun Maira, "Macroeconomics and the Common Man", *Live Mint*, February 09, 2015.
23. Ibid.
24. KC Sivaramakrishnan, Bhanu Joshi, "Who Rules the City?', *The Indian Express,* February 10, 2015.